LAMB OF GOD
Saviour Of The World
The Soteriology of Rev. Dr David Martyn Lloyd-Jones

Rev. Dr David Martyn Lloyd-Jones
(1899 – 1981)

J. E. HAZLETT LYNCH

"Verbum Dei manet in aeternum."

Copyright © 2015 J. E. Hazlett Lynch.

All rights reserved. No part of this book may be used or reproduced by any means, graphic, electronic, or mechanical, including photocopying, recording, taping or by any information storage retrieval system without the written permission of the publisher except in the case of brief quotations embodied in critical articles and reviews.

Scripture taken from the New King James Version. Copyright © 1979, 1980, 1982 by Thomas Nelson, Inc. Used by permission. All rights reserved.

WestBow Press books may be ordered through booksellers or by contacting:

WestBow Press
A Division of Thomas Nelson & Zondervan
1663 Liberty Drive
Bloomington, IN 47403
www.westbowpress.com
1 (866) 928-1240

Because of the dynamic nature of the Internet, any web addresses or links contained in this book may have changed since publication and may no longer be valid. The views expressed in this work are solely those of the author and do not necessarily reflect the views of the publisher, and the publisher hereby disclaims any responsibility for them.

Any people depicted in stock imagery provided by Thinkstock are models, and such images are being used for illustrative purposes only.
Certain stock imagery © Thinkstock.

ISBN: 978-1-4908-8190-4 (sc)
ISBN: 978-1-4908-8194-2 (hc)
ISBN: 978-1-4908-8193-5 (e)

Library of Congress Control Number: 2015909269

Print information available on the last page.

WestBow Press rev. date: 06/09/2015

Contents

Summary vii
Dedication ix
Preface and Acknowledgements xi

SECTION ONE 1
Introductory Matters 1

SECTION TWO 35
The Key Players 35

SECTION THREE 67
Review Of What Some Experts Say! 67

SECTION FOUR 103
Theology and Philosophy 103

SECTION FIVE 133
Doctrinal Issues And Controversies 133

SECTION SIX 163
The Soteriology Of Dr D. Martyn Lloyd-Jones 163

SECTION SEVEN 187
Scriptural Exegesis – To the Word and To the Testimony 187

SECTION EIGHT 239
Concluding Comments 239

References and Bibliography 249
Appendix 263
General Index 305

Summary

The biblical, theological and historical understanding of the doctrine of the atonement as held by Rev. Dr David Martyn Lloyd-Jones (1899–1981) was discovered through a critical evaluation of his own published sermons. These sermons were compared and contrasted with the views held by other Reformed divines, and an exegetical exercise on the relevant biblical texts was carried out.

This study sought to discover the theology underpinning his doctrine of the atonement, in the context of the teaching of Scripture and also in the light of various Reformed positions taken by orthodox divines since the Protestant Reformation.

It analysed and interpreted his doctrinal position within its biblical, theological and historical contexts, examined the exegetical approaches used by Lloyd-Jones and compared these with those used by theologians who agreed and disagreed with his theological understanding.

The result is a better understanding of Lloyd-Jones' doctrinal position within the soteriological understanding held by the broad evangelical and Reformed constituency, making an original contribution to a knowledge of this subject. It also facilitates the re-invigorating of the evangelistic thrust of the evangelical reformed churches.

The research demonstrates that Dr D. Martyn Lloyd-Jones' soteriology was closer to that held by John Calvin than it was to that believed and taught by John Owen. It followed Calvin's teaching into the seventeenth century where its greatest exponent was Moïse Amyraut, thus demonstrating that the Doctor's soteriology was clearly Amyraldian and not Owenite.

DEDICATION

To

Margaret, my wife and companion in Christ and also in life of more than 40 years, my pride and joy, my best friend on earth; and to our sons David and Stephen, and daughter-in-law Julie.

All those preachers who preach the same authentic Calvinistic Gospel as did the subject of this book.

Also

To the memory of Rev. Dr David Martyn Lloyd-Jones (1899-1981), the greatest authentic Calvinistic preacher of the twentieth century.

SOLI DEO GLORIA

Preface and Acknowledgements

This study emerges from a lifetime of studying the works of Rev. Dr David Martyn Lloyd-Jones. The journey of exploration commenced in 1971 when I was studying in Leeds, England. His name was new to me, having become a Christian a mere four months earlier. Finding the Christian Union within the Polytechnic was one of my first tasks that October in 1971, which I did.

University and Colleges Christian Fellowship (UCCF) travelling secretary, Brian Maiden, spoke that autumn. In his message, he gave a high recommendation of a book of sermons preached by a Welsh preacher, Dr Martyn Lloyd-Jones, his *Studies in the Sermon on the Mount*. So I set about obtaining my copy of the book. That Christmas, I was given a book of Dr Lloyd-Jones' sermons. It was volume two. I devoured these sermons on *Matthew* chapters six and seven every night before going to sleep. I wasted no time in securing volume one of these studies, which dealt with *Matthew* chapter five. Never before did I have any experience of what the Doctor termed "expository preaching," but what it was soon became obvious to me. It was about opening up and explaining the meaning of the text of Scripture and applying its teaching to life.

Not knowing then why God had led me to Leeds to study Building, I now see that He wanted to introduce me to the sermons of Dr Lloyd-Jones. Through reading his excellent and deeply spiritual books, God called me into the Christian ministry. In early 1972, I bought another of Dr Lloyd-Jones' books - *Preaching and Preachers*. Since 1971, I have read keenly the Lloyd-Jones books and this has brought tremendous blessing to me over those years. His early books contained in the main teaching sermons. My assumption, then, was that Lloyd-Jones was a five-point

Calvinist, as traditionally understood. I never read this in any of his sermons or lectures, mind you, but the idea was impressed upon my mind for one reason only – his major publisher was the Banner of Truth Trust. Its theological position was and still is the five-point Calvinism of John Owen's theology. I concluded, wrongly, that Lloyd-Jones must also have been a 'five-point' Calvinist, and this was my understanding for about twenty years.

The late 1980s saw my struggle with the Bible's universal language coming to a head. As a young gospel preacher, I was bombarded with the idea from commentaries that when the Bible used the word "world," for example, whilst having a range of meanings determined by the context, there were cases when "the world" meant the 'elect world,' a phrase or idea found nowhere in the Scriptures, and not the whole of mankind. When the Bible taught "God so loved the world…" the formative influences on my life and ministry told me that you can't speak like that because God loves only His elect. I had many of Calvin's commentaries, as well as his *Institutes*, in my growing library, but when I read these books, they left me cold. Why was this? Because Calvin presented himself to me as being not very Calvinistic! He too used universalistic language, so I refused to read his commentaries for many years. Rather than helping me, Calvin exacerbated my spiritual and theological struggles with the biblical text.

About the late 1980s, my convictions on matters of basic textual exegesis were beginning to be confirmed. I was finding great difficulty in bringing my exegesis into line with some parts of the Westminster Confession of Faith. As a conviction Presbyterian who, at his ordination, affirmed that "the Scriptures of the Old and New Testaments are the only infallible rule of faith and practice and the supreme standard of the church," I was keen to maintain that supreme position of the Scriptures within the church, and within my own ministry, so proceeded on that sound basis.

After some years of reading Dr Lloyd-Jones' sermons, books of his evangelistic sermons started to appear, but I was not too interested in these, so I concentrated on reading the 'teaching' sermons. The teaching sermons were so deep and challenging and spiritually uplifting that nothing else mattered. So the evangelistic sermons were also neglected for many years. However, when Lloyd-Jones' sermons on *Acts* started to appear, I added these to my collection of unread books. But, in time, I started reading the *Acts* series, published in the UK under the title, *Authentic Christianity*. Then, I discovered that the Doctor used to a great extent universalistic language that was not, to my mind, in keeping with his other works. I had always thought he was Owenite in his soteriology, but now I saw a different aspect of the Doctor's ministry. So I read the *Acts* series afresh and discovered an exegetical approach that was exactly like the approach in all of the Lloyd-Jones sermons – he allowed the text to speak for itself without it being modified to gel with any church confessional position. He let the Scriptures loose in the power of the Holy Spirit, and God used them to bless many souls. The sheer abundance of universalist language he used blew my mind. But the interesting thing is that his exegesis of the Scriptures seemed to make so much sense and seemed to explain the text *as it stood*. He did not resort to theological acrobatics in order to preserve a confessional stance; he just let the Bible speak its God-breathed message to a lost, sinful, guilty and condemned world.

Thus began my theological journey which brought me to a most acceptable place – where the Bible can speak its own message to all men, offering them salvation in the Lord Christ on the sole condition of faith in the Saviour. I had discovered that the authentic Calvinism of Lloyd-Jones was real 'liberation theology.' His soteriology was Amyraldian – a term of abuse of those ministers who embraced and preached the Bible's own universal language; a kind of 'theological swearword.' In later life, I found that Prof. Moïse Amyraut was neither the 'heterodox theologian' nor the 'heretic' that I had believed him to be. In fact, I came to see that he, rather than Theodore Beza, was the faithful expounder of Calvin's theology. I also realised that Lloyd-Jones' soteriological position was being represented, wittingly or unwittingly, as something it was not – as Owenism in modern garb when in fact it was clearly authentically Calvinistic in orientation. The theological dishonesty that undergirded this anomaly was most disappointing and annoying. I determined to put this matter right if at all possible.

This issue lay at the very heart of the Christian gospel. Consequently, the gospel of God's love for humanity and His free provision of salvation for everyone who believes was not being proclaimed in the churches as is required, and as Dr Lloyd-Jones so ably did. The gospel was being submerged under a wrong understanding of the place given to, and the emphasis placed upon, election and predestination in soteriology; and it was also being craftily concealed under a wrong notion and application of covenant theology, notions that rendered evangelism unnecessary. Reformed preaching became dead while remaining 'orthodox.' Modern forms of medieval scholasticism of the kind promoted by Aristotle and expounded by Dr John Owen adulterated the gospel message. My study brought me to a settled opinion on this matter of soteriology, and the ministry of Dr D. Martyn Lloyd-Jones was instrumental in this progression. My findings, I know, will startle some, enrage others, and encourage still others.

I wish to thank my very good friend and colleague, Rev. Dr Alan C. Clifford, Minister of Norwich Reformed Church, for his support and encouragement throughout my journey. He followed a similar pathway, so knew and understood the views I was expounding. I thank him for invitations to present some six papers at the Amyraldian Association annual conferences in Norfolk, England, which focused latterly on the soteriology of Dr D. Martyn Lloyd-Jones. While I have learned much from his gracious scholarship, the views I have arrived at are my own.

I wish to acknowledge the generosity of those who contributed to the costs involved in publishing this book. Modesty forbids them having their names revealed, but I appreciate greatly their donations.

Thanks are also due to Lady Elizabeth Catherwood, Dr Lloyd-Jones' eldest daughter, and to her son, Jonathan Catherwood, for their help with quotations and also with photographs.

My wife, Margaret, is to be thanked for her patience during the writing of this book, especially as she was then recovering from cancer.

Last, and with the deepest gratitude, I thank God my Father and His Son, our Lord and Saviour Jesus Christ, for saving me, and for calling and setting me apart to the gospel ministry. He has been with me during some exceedingly difficult times as a gospel minister, and for bringing me to this settled conviction that God loves all men and Christ died for all men. His abundant grace has brought me safe thus far and will lead me to my home in glory.

SECTION ONE

Introductory Matters

1

Introductory Matters

The design of the atonement is a hotly debated biblical doctrine, and it is one of the most difficult to understand in the whole spectrum of Calvinistic theology.[1] This doctrine is central to the gospel, and preachers must understand it if the authentic gospel is to be declared. Because of our limited grasp of God's ways, we must be careful about being overly confident of our viewpoints on such a controversial doctrine. The debate has provoked much controversy since post-reformation days, and it continues right into the twenty-first century. What God's plan for the world's redemption[2] is, finds no agreement within sections of the church, nor indeed (and sadly) within the Reformed Christian constituency. Even the phrase, the world's redemption, is a contested phrase that was used by John Calvin (1509-1564).

Ongoing discussion within Reformed circles highlights one very important thing: this important doctrine cannot be ignored by any who desire a fuller understanding of the faith. Nor can it be ignored by any who are committed to God's gospel and its world-wide proclamation (*Romans* 1:1). Those concerned for the salvation of lost sinners know that only the death

---

[1] Robert L. Dabney, *Systematic Theology* (Edinburgh: Banner of Truth Trust, 1871/1985), 518.

[2] Cited in Alan C. Clifford, *Calvinus*. (Norfolk: Charenton Reformed Publishing, 2007), 30, 33; *Calvin's Sermons on Christ's Passion*, 95; *Concerning the Eternal Predestination of God*, 102/3. See also, *Calvin's Sermons on Ephesians*, where he preaches, "...Christ is in a general view the redeemer of the world, yet his death and passion are of no advantage to any but such as receive that which St. Paul shows here" 55.

and resurrection of Christ, and a personal faith response to that atoning death, can save their souls from eternal damnation and to eternal bliss.

This study focuses on the preaching ministry of one of British evangelicalism's greatest twentieth-century preachers, the Rev. Dr David Martyn Lloyd-Jones. His commitment to the historic Reformed faith is unquestioned, embracing among other things the doctrines of election and predestination, which some see as the flagship doctrines of Reformed orthodoxy. Most western Christians accept the Doctor's 'reformed' credentials, and as a *bona fide* evangelical and Reformed minister. Indeed, he describes himself as "conservative evangelical."

It also confines its focus to what Christians think they know so well about his theological position but don't, and yet is evident in all his published evangelistic sermons. DML-J self-designates as a man of prayer and an evangelist.[3] Evangelism played a major role in his fifty-four years of preaching ministry. Evangelicals have assumed what his particular theology was – that he was a five-point, limited-atonement Calvinistic preacher – but these assumptions are not well grounded. That DML-J believed and preached the doctrines surrounding the divine sovereignty in all things, especially in salvation, is beyond question. "Salvation is of the Lord," he teaches frequently. He stresses the divine initiative in salvation, and he directs the attention of his hearers to Christ alone for salvation.

Less well known about DML-J's theology is what he believed about salvation, his soteriology. His soteriology is misunderstood and at times misrepresented by those self-proclaimed disciples who claim him as their mentor. This misunderstanding takes a high Calvinist character in which, because he believed in God's sovereignty in salvation, he inevitably believed in "limited atonement." DML-J believed that the saving benefits of the atonement are for those only who believe the gospel, the elect, but that its provisions would not go so far as to cover unbelieving mankind.

---

[3] Throughout this study, the abbreviation, DML-J, will be used for convenience when referring to Dr D. Martyn Lloyd-Jones. Mrs Bethan Lloyd-Jones made public the point about how the Doctor thought of himself.

He believed the atonement has a universal aspect which means all men everywhere must have the gospel preached to them in the assurance that saving blessings are there for all who turn from their sins and trust the Saviour. It is effective for these people because God intends it for all. God's plan was to make salvation available to humanity, a salvation sufficient (in value and design) to save all mankind. It was to make that same salvation effective at the same time in the lives of believers in Christ alone, the elect. God provided for the world's reconciliation, and from that world the elect will infallibly be saved.

The study will focus on answering this question: Was Dr D. Martyn Lloyd-Jones an Amyraldian (that is, authentically Calvinist) in his soteriology or was he an Owenite? It will explore his grasp of (a) the terms in which the New Testament presents the gospel, and (b) what the New Testament actually offers in the gospel message. Some consideration will be given to what happens to those who refuse to believe the gospel when preachers offer it to them.

2

The Problem Stated

The controversy over this doctrine has resulted in confusion[4] among Reformed evangelicals and has frequently generated more religious "heat" than spiritual "light." That "dark and sinister forces" have been working in the church is obvious, and given the doctrine's centrality to the glory of God and the salvation of souls, the devil's fingerprints are evident everywhere. Godly Reformed evangelical theologians have held to opposing views on the extent of the atonement, despite there being agreement on its nature and value.[5] But where disruption exists in God's work, the devil's fingerprints are evident.

This book will not try to resolve a five-hundred-year-old controversy. Rather it will attempt to clarify the teaching of one eminent servant of Christ, Dr D. Martyn Lloyd-Jones,[6] Minister of Westminster Chapel, London (1938-1968), and arguably the greatest British preacher of the twentieth century. His preaching demonstrates that he believed that Christ is the Saviour of the world[7] and that *whoever* believes in Him "should not

---

[4] D. M. Lloyd-Jones, *God the Father, God the Son* (London: Hodder and Stoughton, 1996), 298, 308
[5] Peter Toon, preface to Norman F. Douty, *The Death of Christ* (Pennsylvania: Reiner Publications, 1972), 8.
[6] Dr D. Martyn Lloyd-Jones was ordained into the Christian ministry by the Presbyterian Church of Wales, and he remained a minister within that denomination until his death in 1981.
[7] See, for example, selection #4, 60, 89, 186, 311, 337.

perish but have everlasting life" (*John* 3:16).[8] Other admirers of DML-J regard his soteriological position as being as stated, with the difference that they understand terms like "the world" in Owenite terms. DML-J's major publisher is committed, on paper, to Owenite soteriology. However, it also publishes the works of quite a number of Amyraldian authors, such as, John Davenant's commentary on *Colossians* (though in its edition it omitted his *Dissertation on the Death of Christ* which was appended to Davenant's original work on *Colossians*), some of Richard Baxter's addresses, J. Edwards' works, some of J. C. Ryle's writings, R. M. McCheyne's sermons, R. L. Dabney's writings, and DML-J's sermons and lectures. It published DML-J's *Evangelistic Sermons* preached at Sandfields, his *Evangelistic Sermons on the Old Testament,* and his six-volume series of sermons on *Acts* (chapters 1-8), entitled *Authentic Christianity,* all of which demonstrate a soteriology at variance with Westminster-type theology. This book attempts to provide an accurate understanding of DML-J's soteriological position. Indications are he was firmly Amyraldian and not in the least Owenite in his understanding and proclamation of the atonement. But is this true?

DML-J is heralded by most, if not by all, evangelicals as a great man of God, servant of Christ and as an intellectual. Their reverence for him has at times spilled over into hagiography, as in Murray, Catherwood, and Davies. Others have taken a more critical view of the Doctor, as in Atherstone and Jones, Eaton, Brencher, and Macleod. But however he is viewed, his presence on the British evangelical scene cannot be ignored or dismissed. This study refutes the strict reformed view often linked to the soteriology of DML-J, a view that tries to make universal passages of Scripture conform to a limited atonement interpretation. This approach is called high Calvinism, a viewpoint that departs significantly from Calvin's balanced soteriology, and one that is prevalent in much Calvinistic literature today. Therefore, it is necessary to determine what he believed about one fundamental doctrine of the Christian faith – the cross. Since his death, academics conducted research into aspects of his theology and articles have appeared in scholarly theological journals on aspects of DML-J's

---

[8] See also #32, 256, 331.

beliefs, and this is set to continue. Books have also been written by scholars and theologians; for example, Michael A. Eaton has written on DML-J's understanding of the baptism of the Spirit. But this is the first known study of DML-J's soteriology. It investigates whether or not he believed in "limited atonement" and was Owenite in his soteriology or whether he was authentically Calvinistic (i.e., Amyraldian) in his soteriology. Did he believe in universal redemption or in particular redemption? Was he able to hold in harmonious tension both Scriptural emphases? Both "high orthodox" or "developed" Calvinists and Amyraldians will claim him as theirs, as will branches of Pentecostalism.[9] We can decide the true situation only by reference to his own stated beliefs on this matter as in his published sermons, and not on the basis of what others have said.

---

[9] Cf. Iain H. Murray, *Lloyd-Jones - Messenger of Grace* (Edinburgh: Banner of truth Trust, 2008), 130.

3

The Importance of This Study

That different understandings of the atonement exist is clear. Some of these display only superficial differences that do not seriously affect the understanding and proclamation of the gospel. However, other alternatives influence negatively both the content and preaching of the gospel. Underlying some of these different soteriologies is a particular philosophical understanding and methodology. First among these philosophies is Aristotle's (384–322 BC), a Greek philosopher whose influence was monumental. His works contain the earliest known study of logic and his method of reasoning and logic allowed no loose ends. Aristotle's metaphysics profoundly influenced philosophical and theological thinking in medieval Islamic and Jewish thought. This philosophical thinking continues into "Christian theology," not least the scholastic tradition represented by Roman Catholicism.

Less well recognised is the fact that Aristotelian metaphysics exercises considerable influence on large tracts of Reformed and evangelical Protestantism. This book exposes this influence and tries to rescue Reformed theology from the clogging influences of Aristotelianism. At least, it will throw some light on a doctrine that has been submerged under philosophy and which still causes high orthodox theologians to look askance at those who follow Calvin.

Preachers have contended that DML-J was a high Calvinist in his soteriology. Twentieth and twenty-first century scholars who examined the DML-J corpus have come to a different conclusion. They believe that

DML-J had much more in common with the soteriology of Calvin and Amyraut than with that of Beza and Owen. DML-J's view was a balanced understanding of Scripture that sought to deal fairly with all biblical data without any reliance on philosophical speculation. Like Bunyan, his was the more moderate view of the atonement known as Amyraldianism. Therefore, it can be affirmed with some assurance that, with Bunyan, DML-J combined a real particularism with hypothetical universalism.

This work on DML-J's soteriology will generate more debate within Reformed circles. I urge those who disagree with my conclusions about DML-J's soteriology to check what I say in the original statements found in his published works. I want, in this book, to be a servant of the gospel and a promoter of evangelistic preaching. The plan is to rescue DML-J's soteriology from misunderstandings emanating from high orthodoxy so that future generations will have an accurate and original treatment of his soteriology. Following his understanding of the atonement will invigorate evangelistic preaching, and will bring Christ to lost sinners as an all-sufficient cosmic Saviour. It will serve the interests of the reform of the church, and bring glory to the eternal God, and to His Son Jesus Christ, the Redeemer of the world.

Our understanding of what DML-J did in fact believe and teach *vis-a-vis* the atonement is at times inaccurate. However, the problem is not one of *knowing* what he believed and preached but rather of *believing* what his numerous sermons tell us he believed and preached. This study is, therefore, important because (i) it rescues the gospel from the dumbing-down effect of unhelpful scholastic philosophy; (ii) the Christian church stands in urgent need of a vigorous evangelistic ministry that is biblically-based; (iii) DML-J the evangelist is an excellent mentor for preachers of all ages; (iv) it identifies wrong ideas of what DML-J actually believed about the atonement that must be corrected; (v) it seeks to gain a level of clarification of a critically important issue; and (vi) it makes a humble contribution to knowledge in this field of theology.

The result will be a fresh approach to soteriology *per se,* and to that believed and preached by DML-J. Some believers will begin to question much of what they have believed. This study takes them back to the Scriptures.[10] They will discover that much of published Reformed theology has refused to take the plain teaching of Scripture seriously, preferring rather to fit the Scriptures to confessionalism than allow them to speak with their own clear voice. In this book, DML-J's convictions about the atonement will be presented *in his own words*.

---

[10] Cf. Michael A. Eaton, *A Theology of Encouragement* (Carlisle: Paternoster Press, 1995), 48. Dr Martin Luther also insisted that our understanding of the gospel must be quarried from *sola scriptura*.

4

Positioning the Study

Positioning this study within the historical development of theological thought is both straight-forward and problematic. It is straight-forward because of the volume of evidence that exists from DML-J's published sermons, leaving an audit trail back to the church's great Reformed thinkers that can be followed. It is problematic because most of this evidence is ignored by men who are working to their own theological agenda. That discussions on the extent of the atonement, as it appears in Calvin's theology, are in a sense anachronistic, must also be acknowledged. Some believe it inappropriate to ascribe to Calvin an understanding of the atonement as unlimited, while others place it securely with the "limited atonement" school. Calvin did not address these issues in his day, therefore discussion about them are absent from his works. It was developed, not authentic, Calvinism that created theological controversy over the extent of the atonement. Indeed, it is admitted that Calvin's published works – his sermons, commentaries, treatises, letters and Institutes – all confirm his theology as reflecting the fine balance found in Scripture. This places him very obviously not in the camp of the high orthodox. His theology was faithfully conveyed by Moïse Amyraut (1596–1664) rather than by Theodore Beza (1519–1605).

Beza, Calvin's successor at Geneva, created a form of "developed" Calvinism that was continued by Francis Turretin (1623–1687) in Geneva, and John Owen (1616–1683) in England. This gave rise to Jacobus Arminius' (1560–1609) opposition to Bezan theology which led eventually to the drawing up of the five points of the Remonstrants, published in

1610, the year following Arminius' death. The Council for the National Synod of the Reformed Church summoned by the States-General of the Netherlands,[11] met in the city of Dordrecht, Holland, during 1618–1619 to settle the controversy instigated by Arminius. This Synod was the most representative body of Reformed churches that ever met. The Synod of Dordt examined in great detail the "five points" presented by the Remonstrants and compared that teaching with the testimony of Scripture. The Synod concluded that these "five points" could not be reconciled with the teaching of Scripture, so unanimously rejected them. Mere rejection of these points was deemed unsatisfactory, so the Dordt commissioners set out the true teaching of the Scriptures, of reformation teaching, and of Calvin, regarding those contested matters. This positive exposition of biblical truth, conjoined with negative propositions that exposed and rejected Arminianism, were set out in clear and precise terms. When completed, they arrived at what are called *The Five Points of Calvinism*.[12] These were adopted as the official teaching of the churches represented. The Reformed Churches also adopted the Belgic Confession and Heidelberg Catechism at this time.[13]

These deliberations of the first ecumenical council comprised some of the ablest gospel-focused theologians of the day. This removed the theological uncertainty that had engulfed the churches of the Netherlands and further afield, and threatened the Reformed faith. The level of agreement reached promised a potential absence of controversy around such a central gospel doctrine, but this did not materialise. Had there been less theological polarisation in the preceding years, this controversy might not have developed, and the church spared much hurt, damage and needless division. Interestingly, the resultant five points of clarification arrived

---

[11] Louis Berkhof, *Systematic Theology* (Edinburgh: Banner of Truth Trust, 1969), 151.

[12] The Five Points of Calvinism, which use the ellipsis TULIP are as follows:
   Total Depravity
   Unconditional Election
   Limited Atonement
   Irresistible Grace
   Perseverance of the Saints

[13] These three documents are known collectively as *The Three Forms of Unity*.

at by Dordt embedded within them a universal understanding of the atonement. The relevant section is article three of the second main head of doctrine that declares that the death of Christ is the only perfect sacrifice for sins and is also infinite in value. All can agree thus far. However, the statement goes on to affirm that Christ's sacrifice is inherently able to expiate the sins of the whole world. The authors referenced their statements with *Hebrews* 9:26, 28; 10:14; and 1 *John* 2:2. The high orthodox opponents of general redemption deny this positive universal atonement statement. They believe, in defiance of the clear universal aspect in Dordt, that it recognises *only* the particularistic element of the atonement. If this is true, it leaves the statement of the sufficiency of Christ's death to expiate the sins of the whole world quite redundant.

Prof. John Murray makes the bizarre point that even when Scripture uses universal terms in relation to the biblical doctrine of the atonement, they cannot be appealed to to establish universal atonement.[14] Murray's point is that the context determines what the Scripture's universal texts truly mean. However, using Murray's logic, it is also true to say that the universal texts control the meaning of the particular texts. Such circular argumentation is singularly unprofitable. Just as, in Murray's viewpoint, universalistic texts do not mean universal atonement, so particularistic texts do not mean particular atonement.[15] If there was no universal aspect in the atonement, then the Bible's universal language concerning it, in addition to the phrase in the Canons of Dordt, are quite inexplicable. Dordt's universal aspect can be ignored or denied, but those who do so must explain in what sense Christ's atonement is sufficient to expiate the sins of the whole world.

The truth lies easily with each viewpoint, namely, that Christ in His death made atonement that is sufficient for the sins of the whole world but efficient only for the elect.[16] It is sufficient to save the entire human race, and every repentant sinner who trusts Christ alone will be saved. This

---

[14] John Murray, *Redemption Accomplished and Applied*. (Edinburgh: Banner of Truth Trust, 1961), 75.

[15] *Ibid.*

[16] For further discussion of this paradigm, see later.

Lombardian paradigm, contested by some Reformed theologians, best fits all the Scriptural data. It endorses the position that because the fallen human mind is limited in its ability to understand the divine Mind in all its details, God has made known in Scripture what He wanted men to know. The atonement is limited in its application – it's benefits are applied only to those who believe in Christ; the atonement is unlimited so far as its intention, availability and sufficiency are concerned. This understanding alone does justice to the Scripture data.

The Huguenots promoted the teachings of John Calvin, and the Saumur Academy was instrumental in this movement. Philippe de Plessis-Mornay founded this Protestant Academy and Huguenot University in 1599, and this institution existed until shortly after 1685. Then Catholic King Louis XIV revoked the 1598 Edict of Nantes, thus ending the limited toleration that Protestants enjoyed in France. The Saumur Academy was the most important and influential of Protestant theological schools anywhere in France. It was here that many Huguenots embraced Calvin's understanding of the gospel, a gospel promoted by his faithful 'son,' Moïse Amyraut, through the Saumur Academy. While hypothetical universalism was propounded at Saumur, most, if not all, of its students who entered the Christian ministry taught this understanding of the gospel. The gospel message spread mainly through southern France, and many were ordained to this work. DML-J regarded the work of the ministry as being without equal, because in his view, there was no calling higher, greater or more glorious that any man can receive than the calling to preach this glorious gospel.[17]

This excursus is necessary to position the soteriological controversy within both its historical and theological contexts because DML-J's understanding of the atonement would prove inexplicable without it. DML-J did not initiate this controversy, of course. He preached most of his sermons between the years 1927–1968. These sermons were later published, and they demonstrated his soteriology and attracted no controversy. Therefore

---

[17] D. M. Lloyd-Jones, *Preaching and Preachers*. (London: Hodder and Stoughton, 1971), 9.

an assumption was made by preachers, theologians, and historians that his soteriology was high orthodox. The facts of history blast this wrong conclusion. They demonstrate rather that DML-J followed closely in the steps of Calvin, Amyraut, Dordt, and Heidelberg, and not in the steps of Beza, Owen, Turretin, and Westminster.

Coming to the present day, the importance of this study demonstrates that if its findings are deemed to be trustworthy and accepted as such, then two major things will happen. *First*, the theological contours will have to be re-drawn to accommodate this new knowledge, and *second*, biblical evangelism must become once again the major pre-occupation and focus of the churches. These two things will roll out in a spiritual environment that is suffocating true religion and replacing it with a false religion. This toxic theological and spiritual environment is detrimental to the eternal well-being of the nations and also of the souls of men.

5

Dr D. Martyn Lloyd-Jones' Soteriology

I have used repeatedly the word 'soteriology' and rightly so. The subject of the book, after all, concerns the soteriology of DML-J. Therefore, I will try to define this term a little more precisely. Soteriology (Gk σωτηρία *sōtēria* "salvation" from σωτήρ *sōtēr* "saviour, preserver" and λόγος *logos* "study" or "word") is the study of the doctrine of salvation. This theory occupies a place of central importance in many religions, including Christianity. Theologians use the term "soteriology" increasingly to indicate what was traditionally referred to as "theories of the atonement" or "the work of Christ." Alister McGrath thinks this term brings together two broad theological areas. First, it describes how the salvation of sinners is possible, especially how it correlates with the history of Jesus Christ; and second, how we are to understand the very idea of salvation itself.[18] Hodge broadens the definition to include the plan of salvation, how it was to be accomplished and applied to the matter of human salvation. He thinks soteriology embraces the doctrines known commonly as Christology – Christ's incarnation, His Person, His life, death and resurrection, and including the official work of the Holy Spirit.

The link between Christ and salvation is accepted within Christian theology, irrespective of the position held. The debate highlights the relation between 'the Person of Christ,' and 'the Work of Christ.' This distinction has been largely abandoned in modern times because there

---

[18] Alister E. McGrath, Ed, *Modern Christian Thought*. (Oxford: Blackwell Publishing, 1993), 616.

is growing recognition of the inextricable link between these two areas of theology,[19] being two sides of the same coin. Kant posits that we can only know the essence of a thing by the effects it has on us. So, we can only understand the reality of the Person of Christ by His saving work in our lives. The spiritual and eternal benefits that come to us through faith in Christ is what makes sinners desire Christ. Since the sinner's greatest need is to be reconciled to God, through the forgiveness of his sins, that can only be his when he trusts Christ alone for salvation. The benefits of salvation are available to the world only in Christ as the "Saviour of the world." Thus in New Testament terms Christology and soteriology are inseparably linked.

Since one of Jesus' titles is "the Saviour of the world" (*John* 4:42; 1 *John* 4:14), it follows that the soteriology inextricably connected with this title is intended for the world. Jesus cannot be the "*Saviour* of the world" if He has not come to be the "Saviour *of the world.*" Scholars can give no satisfactory reason as to why He would be called by this title (which He accepts) if He were to be only the Saviour of the elect world.[20] This hermeneutic adds to the Scripture in such a way as to subtract from it, which very practice high Calvinists rightly accuse Romanism for doing. There is no justification whatever for this, at best, dubious procedure, and, at worst, unbiblical approach.

An unexpected source illustrates this point very well. Blanchard in his chapter, "Religion: the root of all evil,"[21] records how Richard Dawkins based his linkage of religion and violence on the findings of the American physician John Hartung. Hartung suggested that Jesus Christ signed up to what he called "in-group morality" and "out-group hostility." He claimed that when Jesus taught His disciples to "love your neighbour," what He meant was this: "Love another Jew." His followers are to love only those neighbours who happened to be Jews. Hence, Dawkins and Hartung were re-writing the Bible and then re-interpreting that re-written text along

---

[19] McGrath, *Christian Thought*, 616, 617
[20] Walter A. Elwell in Elwell (Ed), *Evangelical Dictionary of Theology*. (Basingstoke: Marshall Pickering, 1985), 99.
[21] John Blanchard, *Dealing with Dawkins*. (Darlington: Evangelical Press, 2010), 39.

lines that suggest a form of Aristotelian logic. "Neighbour," according to this approach, does not mean 'anyone to whom one can show oneself a neighbour' – a proper interpretation, but 'the nearest Jew to whom you can be a neighbour.'

This argument demonstrates how Aristotelian-type logic can be used to make a case that is the opposite of what a particular text stated. Despite his high Calvinism, Machen illustrates how this is done with the facts of history.[22] This bizarre idea directly contradicts the clear teaching of Jesus.[23] For Reformed theologians of the Owenite school to co-exist happily with Richard Dawkins in his application of Aristotelian logic is for them to have very strange bed-fellows!

There is the related attempt by liberal theologians to disconnect the 'Jesus of history' from the 'Christ of faith.' Liberal theologians separate the living Christ from the Jesus of history, a procedure associated with Albert Schweitzer and developed by Rudolph Bultmann. Bultmann's reductionism separates Christology from soteriology. It does this in a way that reduces Christology to the recognition *that* a historical figure called Jesus of Nazareth existed, and we can trace the *kerygma* to Him.[24] Theologians use reductionism to shrink the purpose of the atonement to being the means of saving, in intention, only 'part' of the world. They stand against what the New Testament teaches in so many places that Christ died for all,[25] even though believers in Christ alone will eventually experience God's salvation.

Reductionism oversimplifies the divinely revealed data putting them into manageable parts so that they gel with a previously assumed theological system. This process simplifies the understanding of data to the extent that it becomes distorted and falsified. What does not fit comfortably into a theological system that has been accepted as the touchstone of

---

[22] J. Gresham Machen, *God Transcendent*. (Edinburgh: Banner of Truth Trust, 1949), 45–47.
[23] Blanchard, *Dawkins*, 39.
[24] McGrath, *Christian Thought*, 617.
[25] See 2 *Corinthians* 5:14; cf. *John* 3:16.

orthodoxy, namely Westminster-type theology, is consequently minimised. So if soteriological truth is too complex to contain within a particular theological system, it is reduced to fit into that Procrustean bed.

For high orthodox theologians, the fact that "Christ died for all" cannot, by definition, be true. It must then be re-defined to mean "Christ died for all *the elect*." That Christ is the "Saviour of the world" must be reduced to mean that Christ is the "Saviour of the *elect* world" for it to fit happily into the limited atonement position. That Jesus Christ is "the Lamb of God that takes away the sin of the world" (*John* 1:29) is by definition untrue for high orthodox theologians. Therefore, it must be reduced to read that He is "the Lamb of God that takes away the sin of *Jews and Gentiles*," or of "*the elect world.*" Or, to take the best-loved verse in all of Scripture, *John* 3:16, "the world" that God "so loved" must be reduced to mean the "*elect world,*" otherwise the system of limited atonement collapses. If *John* 3:16 is *prima facia* true, then the limited atonement doctrine is, by the same argument, false, because *John* 3:16 refuses to fit into limited atonement philosophy. Dawkins used the same intellectual process to 'prove' the connection between religion and violence.

In his soteriology, DML-J focused not on man but on God. Listening to him preach the gospel, you leave with a deep impression of the power and presence of God in his preaching. His preaching of the cross was the central focus of his ministry at Westminster Chapel. In 1963, he imagined, wrongly, that there was nothing more that he could say about the cross, and this he saw as a Satanic suggestion.[26] But he came to see that as he preached a series of sermons on *Galatians* 6:14 in 1963. The cross is an inexhaustible fountain of truth and its depths are unfathomable. In these sermons, the first sets out his stall very clearly. His biblical balance, reminiscent of John Calvin's approach to gospel preaching, enables him to quote *Hebrews* 2:9 where Christ tasted death "for everyone."[27] He refers to *Mark* 10:45, where Christ Himself said He came to "give His life a ransom for many." For DML-J, "everyone" equates with "many" in contrast to

---

[26] D. M. Lloyd-Jones, *The Cross*, (Eastbourne: Kingsway Publications, 1986/2008), 13.
[27] Lloyd-Jones, *Cross*, 32. See also, Richard Baxter, *Universal Redemption of Mankind*. (Shropshire: Quinta Press, 1694), 3.

a few. In other words, to avoid any misunderstanding, when speaking of "the world," "everyone," and "many," he follows Calvin who in his exposition of *Romans* 5:15 says that "'many' sometimes means 'all.'"[28] DML-J in his exegesis and exposition of this theme is in total agreement with Calvin.

When expounding "the world," he further puts side by side closely related ideas. Speaking about the death of Christ, he preaches, "He came because you and I and all mankind are guilty and under the condemnation of a holy God."[29] He adds in the following sentence, "He came to deliver us from this world." To whom is he referring when he refers to "us"? To "you and I and all mankind." So "us" equates with "all mankind." It is inconceivable that he changes the identity of those to whom he is speaking/referring. Let him continue: "We all belong to the world. We are men of the world, we are born in the world, and we will bear the world's fate unless he can deliver us."[30] He believes that Christ was the Lamb slain from before the foundation of the world (*Revelation* 13:8) for the salvation of us all.

So in DML-J's soteriology, he is not limited or restricted in how he does his exegesis or exposition, thus suggesting that he did not favour John Owen's 'eisegesis.' Owen's tendency is to read into the text of Scripture ideas that patently are not there. For example, see Owen's interpretation of *John* 3:16, which was DML-J's favourite verse of Scripture. He makes "the world" mean "the world of the elect," or "the elect world." For DML-J, "the world" means "every man," "mankind," and "many." The "world" that God so loved was the world understood in its most natural sense – mankind, the human race. Similarly, "every man" cannot mean "every elect man" because this is to do damage, not only to language, but also to the doctrine of the perspicuity of Scripture. In a legal letter sent to a client,[31] a solicitor spoke of how a particular understanding of words used will lodge in the mind of any reasonable reader. When reading Scripture,

---

[28] Calvin's commentary on *Hebrews* 9:28 where *Romans* 5:15 is referred to. Cf. also *Matthew* 20:28.
[29] Lloyd-Jones, *Cross*, 32.
[30] Lloyd-Jones, *Cross*, 23.
[31] Dated 29th May 2013.

a 'reasonable reader' would have no difficulty in understanding what the text was saying.

DML-J did not hold to any 'magisterium,' as Rome and many Reformed men do. While acknowledging the best Reformed opinion and theology, he sat loosely to any theological formulation, however excellent it might otherwise be. These formulations tended to displace Scripture as the final authority in all matters of faith and practice in the minds of those who subscribe them. He drew his theology from Scripture, which to him was the alone inspired and authoritative Word of God. For him, God's thoughts are expressed in the written Word. When considering the theologies of other men and formulations, his practice was to retain them in their subordinate position, giving to Scripture alone the position of supreme authority in all matters of faith and practice.

The cross and our attitude to it is the "acid test" of our profession.[32] For him, the cross is central and indispensable to God's plan of salvation. Therefore, it ought also to be central in our lives, in our faith, and also in all genuine Christian preaching. It is by *believing* that we are saved by trusting what Christ did on the cross for us, the particular soteriological theory being irrelevant. Interestingly, it is neither election nor predestination that is central to gospel preaching, as some ultra-Reformed thinkers would imply.[33] DML-J believes otherwise, as does Calvin.[34]

---

[32] Lloyd-Jones, *Cross*, 45.

[33] Lorraine Boettner in his *Reformed Doctrine of Predestination* (Presbyterian and Reformed Publishing Company, 1932) comes perilously close to teaching this viewpoint. Berkhof (rpnt 1985:219) claims that Calvin was consistent in taking his theological starting-point to be an eternal divine election and also in the mystical union established in the *pactum salutis*, without providing any evidence whatever to substantiate this theory. Clifford's numerous extracts from Calvin's works supplies sufficient evidence that Calvin did not make this his starting point, but rather demanded faith if the benefits of the redemption purchased by Christ was to become the sinner's possession.

[34] David Wenkel, *Scottish Journal of Theology*, Eds David Torrance and Bryan Spinks. (Cambridge: Cambridge University Press, 1973), 270.

The "acid test" of our position is whether or not the cross, the instrument of death by crucifixion, is something we glory in or are offended by (*Galatians* 6:14; 5:11). This test differentiates between the Christian and the non-Christian. To the non-Christian, or the natural man, the man without the Spirit of God (*Romans* 8:9), the cross is an offensive thing. DML-J claims this is as true today as when Paul wrote these words in the first century AD. It is only the true Christian who can "glory" in the cross.

While the Doctor believes passionately in human responsibility,[35] not least when confronted by the claims of Christ, he links this to the preacher as well as to the hearer.[36] He holds the minister responsible for preaching the cross so as to cause offense to the natural man. Indeed, it is this that determines whether or not a preacher is preaching the cross truly.[37] Like Hugh Latimer (d.1555),[38] he preached with great boldness before his hearers the law with its curses and then urged them to flee to the Saviour of the world, Jesus Christ.[39]

Paul never delivered a lecture on the cross. Both Paul and DML-J knew that it was impossible for a Christian to remain untouched by the cross and its saving message. Therefore, it is equally impossible for a Christian scholar or theologian to adopt a clinically detached attitude to this critically important doctrine of the Faith. The Doctor spoke disparagingly about what he called "glorified Bible studies" being passed off as sermons. The message of the cross grips the heart and conscience after enlightening the intellect.

The "we" in his thinking, then, is the "we" of evangelistic theological inclusivity.[40] He says "we are lost" because outside of Christ "all" are lost.

---

[35] See J. E. Adams, *Competent to Counsel*. (Presbyterian and Reformed Publishing Company, 1975), 214 for an intriguing parallel.

[36] Lloyd-Jones, *Cross*, 47.

[37] *Ibid.*

[38] The date of birth of Hugh Latimer is unknown and suggestions include 1470, 1487, 1490, and 1494.

[39] J. H. Merle D'Aubigné, *The Reformation in England*. (London: Banner of Truth Trust, 1853/1971), 207.

[40] Lloyd-Jones, *Cross*, 52. See also *Romans* 3:21, 22.

"We are failures" because outside of Christ "all" are failures. "We are sinners" because apart from Christ "all" are sinners (*Romans* 3:23). DML-J knew his theology because he knew his Bible thoroughly.[41] He argued that the reason Christ did not come into the world sooner was to provide irrefutable proof that man cannot save himself. He wished to demonstrate that all his efforts, even his most noble, were useless and that if ever he was to be saved, he would need Someone to save him. With Dr Francis A Schaeffer (1912–1984), DML-J was convinced of "the lostness of the lost."[42] And also with Schaeffer, DML-J was full of compassion towards the lost.[43] His was the heart of the evangelist. He preached the gospel with power. He pleaded passionately with the lost to come to Christ. He expostulated with his hearers in many, if not all, of the gospel sermons he preached. DML-J had a message for all the lost which, if they believed it, brought them to salvation and brought salvation to them. He knew and preached from early on in his ministry that when Christ died on Calvary, *"the Lord [had] laid on him the iniquity of us all"* (*Isaiah* 53:6). He had a real salvation to offer to *"whosoever"* (*John* 3:16). With Moses and Calvin, he believed *"the secret things belong to the LORD our God, but those things that are revealed belong to us and to our children forever."* (*Deuteronomy* 29:29). He preached Scriptural texts in their most natural sense and meaning without feeling any compulsion either to gratify our curiosity or to fit them to ensure confessional correctness.[44]

---

[41] DML-J followed Robert Murray McCheyne's daily Bible reading system whereby reading four chapters a day, the entire Bible can be read in a year, and the NT and Psalms twice.

[42] Francis A. Schaeffer, *Death in the City*. (Leicester: InterVarsity Press, 1969), 127.

[43] *Ibid.*

[44] D. M. Lloyd-Jones, *Prove All Things*, (Eastbourne: Kingsway Publications, 1985), 88.

6

Amyraut's Soteriology

What was Amyraut's gospel? Alan Clifford asserts "it is undeniable, that Amyraut was Calvin's true disciple," while British theologians such as John Owen followed the theological route set by Theodore Beza.[45] So right at the outset, such a contention, if true, places Amyraut with Calvin rather than Beza with Calvin. What undergirds Amyraut's understanding of the gospel is an idea of the divine will as dual. With Calvin, his starting point was not what God has kept "secret" but what God had revealed His will to be *vis-a-vis* the gospel of salvation. He saw that Christ was the "Saviour of the world" and preachers offered Him in that capacity. Agreeing with Calvin, Amyraut also offered Christ as the Redeemer of the whole world. Conditionality lies at the heart of Amyraut's gospel, meaning, that any sinner will experience salvation on condition of faith.[46] Salvation will not be the possession of anyone if he does not trust Christ. He also believed, with Calvin, that only the elect will receive this freely offered salvation, and this according to God's secret absolute will.

No one will doubt that this is an intellectually challenging paradox, but Calvin and Amyraut held the doctrines of universal atonement and election in harmonious tension. Scriptural data confronted both of these theologians who taught both truths, but they refused to tamper with

---

[45] Alan C. Clifford, *Amyraut Affirmed*. (Norwich: Charenton Reformed Publishing, 2004), 8.

[46] Richard Baxter also believed that salvation was conditional on faith in Christ alone.

the biblical data and looked for a way that enabled them to teach both truths as scripturally revealed. Being highly intelligent and pious men, they kept their logical faculties in check and did not allow logic to dictate exegesis, maintaining the equilibrium of the teaching of the biblical text. For example, in exegeting *Romans* 5:18, Calvin demonstrates his ability in handling the text of Scripture faithfully. Here he contends that Paul presents the gospel of grace in a manner that makes grace common to all mankind primarily because it is offered to all. He bases his argument on the fact that although Christ did indeed suffer for the sins of the world, this same Christ is offered out of the sheer goodness of God to all men without distinction. However, not all men receive Him.[47] To come into possession of the offered salvation, sinners must receive it by faith.[48]

Calvin's successor at Geneva, Theodore Beza, did not accept this exegesis and pursued a more rationalistic line. He, according to Clifford,

> *deleted the universal aspect of Calvin's scheme in favour of limited atonement, which in turn provoked the equally-rationalistic Jakob Arminius to delete the 'particular' aspect of Calvin's scheme in favour of conditional election.*[49]

To understand Amyraut's soteriology, then, one need only study Calvin's. Hence, Amyraut's gospel was the gospel of John Calvin. From his intensive and extensive study of the Scriptures, Calvin concluded that the pages of Scripture reveal God's double-aspect will. His soteriology was essentially and necessarily biblical and depended solely upon what God had revealed in Scripture. This understanding explains why DML-J's soteriology was so close to Calvin's and therefore to Amyraut's. Amyraut's grasp of the gospel meant that he was decidedly unenthusiastic about the views presented by what Clifford calls "the two deviants."[50] Being persuaded by Calvin's

---

[47] Calvin's Comm. on *Romans*, pp.117, 118.
[48] Cf. Brian G. Armstrong, *Calvinism and the Amyraut Heresy - Protestant Scholasticism and Humanism in Seventeenth-Century France*. (Wisconsin: Wisconsin University Press, 1969), 82, 91–93, 100.
[49] Alan C. Clifford, *John Calvin 500 – A Reformation Reaffirmed*. (Norwich: Charenton Reformed Publishing, 2011), 38.
[50] *Ibid*. These two deviants were high Calvinism and Arminianism.

biblicism, he followed a *via media* between the two positions. In this, he was admitting in effect that not everything in Arminianism is wrong, and not everything in Beza's position is wrong either. The truth lay in the middle, and Calvin's view was the only one that owned biblical integrity. His view was the authentic biblical position.

Another strength of Amyraut's soteriology lay in the fact that he maintained a proper balance between heart and mind, an understanding that had "enormous pastoral and evangelistic advantages."[51] His was not a purely intellectual theology – it was one that touched the heart as well.[52] Amyraut wrote nothing that resembled a systematic theology, a fact that held little importance for Brian Armstrong.[53] He did provide treatises that were not beliefs in the sense of Aquinas' *Summa,* or Calvin's *Institutio.* Extant Amyraut treatises demonstrate his uniqueness in that particular century because his approach was at variance with that of seventeenth-century Calvinism, which tended to [over]systematise theology.[54] These theologies had as their starting point the decree of God. They then organised the data by deductively moving from the general principle to the particular conclusion, a general principle that may not necessarily have emerged from Scripture.[55] They also had no regard to historical development[56] and created, not only a new systematic, but a new theological-historical approach to 'doing theology.'[57]

The Salmurian approach to theology differed from the other seventeenth-century European academies in that it adopted an explicitly humanist methodology as opposed to a logical, philosophical and metaphysical

---

[51] *Ibid.*

[52] It is interesting how Clifford cites, in support of his position, scholars such as Richard Muller, Roger Nicole, F. P. van Stam, and P. Benedict. See Clifford, *John Calvin,* 38, 39.

[53] Armstrong, *Amyraut Heresy,* 120.

[54] *Ibid.*

[55] *Ibid*

[56] Clifford seems to have a different view on the significance and interpretation of historical development to that of Armstrong, as explained in his *Amyraut Affirmed,* 25–27.

[57] Jürgen Moltmann as cited in Armstrong, *Amyraut Heresy,* 121.

approach. This approach ensured that biblical data were the primary materials with which to do theology. Believing in the biblical doctrines of predestination and election, Amyraut also recognised a universal element in the atonement, an element that required primary emphasis in theology and evangelism. He believed, with Calvin, that Christ is "the Saviour of the world," and that He died for humanity. With Calvin, he saw the need for a universal offer of salvation through the gospel, with the promise that whoever believes in Christ will be saved. High Calvinists then are faced with the question, "When preachers make a universal gospel offer, what precisely is on offer if not a universally-available redemption?"[58] Amyraut, therefore, uncovered the hypothetical universalism taught at the Saumur Academy by Scottish theologian, John Cameron (c.1579–1625).[59] This understanding undergirded Calvin's gospel preaching and brought this to the fore in his preaching. Amyraut, with Calvin, believed in the biblical doctrines of predestination and election. When it came to preaching the gospel, the free, uninhibited offer of Christ as the all-sufficient "Saviour of the world" was proclaimed, thus preserving the biblical balance. Also with Calvin, Amyraut believed that God's will is single but revealed as dual – His hidden will and His revealed will.

In time, Amyraut's theology was deemed a departure from the authentic reformed faith. The Church courts tried him for heresy and delegates discussed at length four of his contested teachings. These were: (1) the order of the decrees, 17th June, 1637; (2) the sending of Jesus Christ for all universally and Amyraut's doctrine of the conditional decrees, 18th and 19th June; (3) the universality and sufficiency of grace presented to all, 22nd June; and (4) original sin and moral and natural ability, also 22nd June.[60] The National Synod consequently arraigned the Saumur professor to appear before it at Alençon in 1637. However, this Synod was unable to condemn Prof. Amyraut, much to the disgust of the orthodox party.[61] The reason for this failure was the fact that the latter used numerous direct

---

[58] Clifford, *Amyraut Affirmed*, 57.

[59] "John Cameron was the inspiration for, and father of, the distinctive teachings of the Academy at Saumur." Armstrong, *Amyraut Heresy*, 42.

[60] Armstrong, *Amyraut Heresy*, 91.

[61] Armstrong, *Amyraut Heresy*, 103.

quotations from Calvin's works. Therefore, to have condemned Amyraut the Synod would also have condemned Calvin, which very thing they would not and could not do.[62] Therefore, to have condemned Amyraut's soteriology would involve condemning Calvin's.

Detractors of Amyraut brought similar charges against him at the Synod held in Charenton from 16th December 1644 to 26th January 1645. Prior notice had been given concerning this Synod, and the internal politics of ecclesiastical bodies sprang into action. The orthodox viewed Amyraut's theology as having the potential to split the French church, so rather than risk this, Amyraut was again exonerated, and again a third time at Loudun in 1659. So Amyraut's soteriology was found to be based on Calvin's biblical exegesis. Amyraut was not only a faithful disciple of Calvin, but more importantly, he was a careful exegete of the biblical text.

I said that Cameron initiated the idea of hypothetical universalism, which Amyraut also embraced and taught. An explanation is required. Armstrong gives a succinct explanation of this doctrine in which the first divine decree is to redeem the world in Christ, and this decree is universal. Therefore, when Christ died on the cross, God had redeemed all men – hypothetically and potentially. Cameron illustrated the universality of the virtue of Christ's atoning death by the well-worn analogy of the universality of the sunlight. According to this analogy, just as the sun shines on all, yet those who sleep or voluntarily close their eyes or are blind cannot receive its light. The reason for this is not because of any deficiency in the sun, but the fault lies wholly with the man who refuses to use his eyes for his benefit. He concludes then that Christ died for all but His death blesses only those who lay hold of the Saviour by faith.[63] Cameron's theology accords fully with the sufficiency/efficiency formula of the divines. Armstrong concludes that it is hard to see how anyone could regard this teaching as heretical,[64] according as it does with the teaching of the Canons of Dordt.

---

[62] Armstrong, *Amyraut Heresy*, 100.
[63] Armstrong, *Amyraut Heresy*, 59.
[64] *Ibid.*

Historically, and according to Carl R. Trueman, the Calvinism of Amyraut was regarded as being close to that of Calvin by some notable Reformed scholars, a fact that high Calvinists do not admit. Trueman believes that Armstrong in his influential book made a similar case at some length and others have followed in his wake. They argued that there was a fundamental difference between the Reformed orthodoxy of the type represented by Turretin and Owen and that which came from Saumur. Salmurian theology, advocates of this thesis not infrequently argue, was, in fact, more faithful to Calvin. Indeed, Richard Muller disagreed with the title of Armstrong's book, *Calvinism and the Amyraut Heresy*,[65] arguing that Amyraldianism was no time dismissed as a heresy within Reformed theology.

Following this same line of argument, in addition to Armstrong, were three other scholarly studies by Frans Pieter van Stam,[66] Robert T. Kendall[67] and Alan C. Clifford.[68] These scholars have strong leanings in the Amyraldian direction and have argued their respective cases convincingly though their conclusions have been contested by other theologians. Kendall's book focused on faith while Clifford's homed in, among other things, more directly on the soteriological debate of the 150 years between 1640 and 1790. This period commenced some 76 years after the death of Calvin, but it represented a time in English theological history that highlighted the controversies surrounding the soteriological debate.

---

[65] 1969.

[66] Frans Pieter Van Stam, *Controversy over the Theology of Saumur, 1635–1650*. (Amsterdam: Holland University Press, 1969).

[67] Robert T. Kendall, *Calvin and English Calvinism to 1647*, (Carlisle: Paternoster Press, 1979).

[68] Alan C. Clifford, *Atonement and Justification*, (Oxford: Clarendon Press, 1989).

SECTION TWO

The Key Players

7

Introducing Rev. Dr David Martyn Lloyd-Jones (1899–1981):

His Life

David Martyn Lloyd-Jones was born on 20th December 1899 in Cardiff, South Wales. The first ten years of his life were quite ordinary, that is, until January 1910.[69] His father, Henry, had been a fairly successful businessman in Llangeitho, but that cold winter night was to change everything. A fire broke out, nearly costing two of the Lloyd-Jones boys, Martyn and Vincent, their lives as they slept upstairs. Thankfully, the family was saved but Henry and Magdalene lost everything else, a loss from which Henry never seemed to recover financially. Martyn was never to forget that terrible night, an experience that shaped his outlook on life in a permanent way.

Martyn was distracted at school, probably because of his near-death experience. His education proceeded, but the Lloyd-Jones' family faced a new challenge, and one that would change their lives forever. Henry, having been declared bankrupt, gathered the family together and told them they would be leaving Llangeitho forever. As events turned out, they moved to London in 1910,[70] where his father set up a milk delivery business

---

[69] Iain H. Murray, *D. Martyn Lloyd-Jones – The First Forty Years*. (Edinburgh: Banner of Truth Trust, 1982), 16.
[70] The First World War broke out in 1914.

in London with Martyn sharing in the milk rounds. The family attached themselves to Charing Cross Chapel.[71] Martyn attended there throughout his youth and student days in London, continuing his education and training at St Bartholomew's Hospital to become a Doctor. Eventually, he became chief clinical assistant to Sir (later Lord) Thomas Horder, the King's physician[72] and had a lucrative medical career ahead of him. By the age of 26, he had gained his MD degree and the MRCP. Clearly, he was well on his way to ascending the Harley Street career ladder with all that entailed.

Meanwhile, DML-J began feeling the promptings of the Holy Spirit in his life and started to think about spiritual things. At length, he realised he was a lost sinner who needed Christ as his Saviour. His reading and the sermons he heard at times caused him to give serious consideration to his spiritual condition before God. DML-J realised[73] that he was not a Christian, despite the church having admitted him to full communicant membership on profession of faith. While he enjoyed religious debates with other Sunday School scholars, Martyn had this other debate going on which only he knew about, a debate that was raging within his heart. He was becoming concerned about his spiritual condition. He had imagined all along he was a Christian because he was a church member, but he now knew he was not. Only later did he come to see his need of Christ's salvation. He knew that he needed to hear the gospel being preached clearly, and he also knew that his church was not doing this. In fact, his minister preached on the assumption that all were Christians, which was a common reality in many Presbyterian churches of that era, and sadly also of today.

Attending Westminster Chapel to hear Scottish preacher Dr John A. Hutton, he became aware that God had power to change men's lives.[74] Observing the dearth of anything spiritual in the lives of those he treated

---

[71] Now Orange Street Congregational Church located behind Trafalgar Square in central London.
[72] Murray, *First Forty*, 62.
[73] In 1923.
[74] Murray, *First Forty*, 61.

at Bart's, DML-J came to see that Christianity was as relevant to the modern world as it was during the centuries that preceded it. He saw that a man had to become a fool if he was ever to accept Christ as his Saviour. From his reading of Scripture and his experience, he admitted he was dead to God and indeed opposed to Him.[75] He knew he did not love God with his whole being. Therefore, he concluded he was a sinner. Gradually, the truth of God's love for the world dawned upon him. He realised that Christ died for all men, and therefore for him, and he entrusted himself to "the Saviour of the world," whom he was later to preach with great effectiveness. He was unable to put a date to his conversion because the route to coming to a saving knowledge of the truth was a long one. The lead up to his conversion was progressive, but it finally came at some point in or about 1924. This new-found knowledge conflicted with what he saw in his career and realised that the well-being of the soul was much more important than the well-being of the body. Doctors can make sick people well again, but they still have to die and meet God. Only the gospel can benefit sinners for time and eternity, so the logical follow-on of his new thinking was to offer himself for the Christian ministry. The move to the Christian ministry for DML-J did not just mark the end of a promising career, to his mind this move represented something very different. For him, this was but the beginning of the very purpose for which God had created him, spared him, equipped, saved and called him – to preach Christ and Him crucified. This move did not represent in any degree a giving up of something precious to him; it was rather a move in which he lost nothing but gained everything.

So without formal theological training, DML-J was accepted by the Calvinistic Methodist Connexion in Wales and installed as minister of the Bethlehem Forward Movement Mission charge at Sandfields, Aberavon, South Wales. Here, with an outstanding evangelistic ministry that stretched for eleven years, he saw many notable conversions of some of the toughest characters in society. He married Dr Bethan Philips in 1927, just before moving to South Wales; she became a Christian under her husband's faithful gospel preaching in Sandfields. He had preached a

---

[75] Murray, *First Forty*, 63.

few times before sensing that he was being called by God to the Christian ministry and had ministered in Sandfields while working at Bart's hospital. This call was not a sudden matter but lasted for some eighteen months. In a television interview conducted in 1970, Aneirin Taflan Jones asked him whether or not he knew if he could preach. He admitted that he did not know if he could preach, but he did know what needed to be preached and believed that the Lord would help him do that very thing.

His ministry in Sandfields was so different to that of other ministers who came straight out of liberal theological colleges with a corresponding liberal theological education but no message. DML-J knew what he believed, and he declared that message without compromise and with authority. His message amounted to this: he preached Christ and Him crucified, determining with Paul not to know anything else among them (1 *Corinthians* 2:2). Some church members rejected this message and left. But they were replaced gradually with those who were drawn by God's Spirit and gripped by the truth, and these were mainly the working class in South Wales. These sinners repented and turned to Christ under the Doctor's Spirit-anointed preaching. He used no emotionally charged appeals at the end of his sermons, nor did he allow emotionally charged music and hymns to condition his hearers. Rather, he allowed the Lord to do His saving work in their hearts. God used this young man with the clear message of God's love for mankind and His justice and righteousness, bringing one hard case after another to the cross and to saving faith in Christ alone.

On 28th November 1935, he preached in the Royal Albert Hall in London to an assembly of Christians. He addressed the problems he saw with many of the forms of evangelism that were being used in the church, comparing and contrasting them with the biblical model. In the congregation that evening was Rev. Dr G. Campbell Morgan (1863–1945, and then 72 years of age), minister of Westminster Chapel, London. Having heard of DML-J, and having listened to him on that evening, he wanted, in 1938, to have him as his colleague and successor in Westminster Chapel. But at this time, overtures had been made to him to become Principal of Bala Theological College in North Wales. The call to stay in Wales and also to head up the training of future ministers of the Presbyterian Church in Wales was strong. He would not have been unaware that as Principal of a theologically liberal college, he would have faced many problems, given that Christianity and Liberalism are two totally different religious faiths. In 1938, during a time of recuperation, he agreed to assist Dr G. Campbell Morgan in Westminster Chapel, but only for about six months. He commenced his ministry there on the day after the commencement of World War II. The call to the London Chapel prevailed, and the family transferred to London in April 1939. He worked alongside Dr Morgan from September 1938 until Morgan's retirement in 1943, thus providing him with the respite he needed. Dr Morgan died in 1945, and DML-J became sole pastor of that great London congregation within four years of arriving and staying there until health dictated otherwise, retiring in 1968. He then became an itinerant preacher, lecturer, and author for the remaining years of his life, dying peacefully on 1st March 1981, interestingly enough on St David's Day.[76]

His Work:

DML-J's ministry focused on the systematic expository preaching of the gospel, which, to him, was everything. Because it is God's saving power for everyone who believes (*Romans* 1:16), it must have its primary effect on the preacher's heart before he can communicate it to his hearers. God unleashes His power on every congregation where ministers preach it in the power of the Holy Spirit. It is divine dynamite that the preacher handles. Therefore, it must be 'handled with care.' Indeed, this message can only be properly understood and preached by the man who has been broken by it. He must feel its slaying power in his life, and be changed forever by its godly influence.

It was to this work that DML-J gave himself, and no amount of promised worldly success would detract him from it. He had already made up his mind to offer himself for the Christian ministry. He also already knew

---

[76] St David is regarded as the patron saint of Wales.

what the primary task of the church and the minister was – the preaching of the gospel. And in his fifty-four years in the ministry, this is what he did so well. He has come to be known and loved by millions around the world through his published sermons. To some, his *Studies in the Sermon on the Mount* is his classic work,[77] sharing this accolade with *Spiritual Depression – it causes and cure*, and also with his exposition of *Psalm 73*, entitled, *Faith on Trial*. In the early 1950s at Westminster Chapel, he delivered a series of studies on the great doctrines of the Bible, published originally in three volumes. Being unhappy about teaching the message of the Bible in this way, he commenced on Friday evenings in 1955 his mammoth series of expository sermons on Paul's letter to the *Romans*. He reached chapter fourteen, verse seventeen in 1968 when poor health curtailed his ministry in London. The series extended to fourteen volumes. His other major series of studies was his sermons on Paul's letter to the *Ephesians*, running to eight volumes, preached on Sunday mornings and concurrently with his *Romans* series. He published six volumes of sermons setting out what *Acts* understood authentic Christianity to be. On top of these were his numerous shorter series of sermons and addresses given at various conferences – on preaching, the Puritans, those delivered at international student conferences, etc. When he said that preaching was and is the primary task of the church and the minister, he demonstrated this maxim abundantly.

DML-J was responsible for the establishing of various publishing houses that would help to promote the evangelical cause. Observers know of his interest in the work amongst evangelical students and students for the ministry. He set up the International Fellowship of Evangelical Students, the Banner of Truth Trust, The Evangelical Library, London Bible College, and London Theological Seminary. The Puritan Conference, the Westminster Fellowship, Tyndale House, the InterVarsity Fellowship, were also the work of his hands. He promoted research and scholarship that was faithful to the Scriptures.

Great controversy surrounded his stance against the ecumenical movement that was making great strides in the UK in 1966. This controversy involved

---

[77] These sermons were preached from 1950–52, according to John Brechner, 69.

the Anglican evangelical leader, Rev. (later Dr) John R. W. Stott, who was Chairman of an evangelical conference in London. Stott over-stepped the mark when he criticised DML-J's call for the coming together of evangelicals in all the denominations. Some of these denominations had departed from the biblical gospel, and his call was to put the gospel first and create evangelical unity amongst them and their churches. His call had limited success with some men seceding from their compromised denominations, but many remaining within them in the hope of reforming them from inside. On hindsight, it is difficult to agree that those who stayed in had made the right decision, for their churches are probably spiritually worse now than they were in 1966.

His Significance:

Most evangelicals regard DML-J as one of the most influential preachers and evangelical leaders in the twentieth century. His influence for good has been felt worldwide. His preaching gifts were unequalled, and the influence he exerted on preachers across many denominations and none, together with the legacy that he left in his printed and now digitally re-mastered sermons is incalculable. You can find his major books in the Bibliography. Currently, there are at least 1,600 sermons available for download, covering his main sermon and lecturing series. His fifty-four years of ministry have left an indelible mark on British and international evangelicalism.

DML-J was capable of thinking independently without disparaging the contribution of earlier generations of God's servants. He applied his mind to understanding and preaching the gospel, but he was not swayed by everything he read. Instead, his practice was to weigh everything against the clear teaching of Scripture, on the one hand, and by the teaching of the Welsh Calvinistic Methodist Fathers, on the other. These became the touchstones by which he assessed everything else. His practice was to read the entire Bible at least once a year, using Robert Murray McCheyne's Bible reading scheme. His knowledge of Scripture was proverbial, and Scripture was the primary standard he used to assess everything he read.

But he created as much controversy after his life as he did while he was still ministering. His views on Pentecostalism stirred controversy, as did his ecclesiology, and his understanding of the sealing/baptism/filling of the Spirit. However, his grasp of soteriology has not been researched before, specifically his understanding of the universality of the atonement. Since every creature is to have the gospel preached to him, does that mean that what the gospel offers is for all men equally? Has God revealed His will to save all men on condition of faith, or did He send Christ to save only His elect? What DML-J preached, as discovered in his published sermons, stands in clear contrast to what some Reformed theologians and preachers hold to be the authentic Christian message.

In the following three chapters, I introduce three of the most influential theologians/preachers in the life and thinking of DML-J, men described as 'liberal evangelicals.'[78] They were outstanding in their fields, but their importance in the life and ministry of DML-J was in how they helped re-form his thinking on the crucial and central matter of soteriology. A brief encounter with one of the Welsh Calvinistic Methodist preachers who had a profound effect on the development of the subject of this book will follow after that.

---

[78] http://fromdeathtolife.org/chistory/plib.html. Accessed 02/03/2015.

8

Introducing Dr Robert William Dale (1829–1895):

His Life

From nonconformist background and conviction, the Congregational preacher, Dr R. W. Dale, was born on 1st December 1829 in London and trained for the congregational ministry at Spring Hill College, Birmingham, England. In the University of London MA degree, Dale came first in philosophy and was awarded first class honours.[79] He also won the gold medal for his achievements. In 1883, the University of Glasgow conferred on him the degree of LL.D., and about this time Yale University gave him the D.D. degree, a title that he never used. He also refused to use the 'title' "Reverend"[80] and was a strong advocate of disestablishment of the Church of England.

In 1859, Dale became the sole pastor of Carrs Lane Congregational Church in Birmingham, England, succeeding his colleague Rev. Dr John Angell James, a daunting challenge for the 30-year-old minister. This transition was not an easy one for Dale though he remained there for 36 years, dying on 13th March, 1895, aged 66. His successor was Dr John Henry Jowett, who later became minister of Westminster Chapel, London, and was one of Dr Martyn Lloyd-Jones' predecessors.

---

[79] Clark as cited in Douglas, *The New International Dictionary of the Christian Church*. (Exeter: Paternoster Press, 1978), 81.

[80] "Reverend" is not so much a title as a description of the holder's character and job.

Dale was a complex of a preacher, theologian, politician and denominational leader.[81] Wiersbe adds the adjective, perplexing, to describe Dale – perplexing because he gave himself to all of these responsibilities with vigour and great determination. As a preacher who sat under James' ministry for some six years, he discovered that his colleague was a Calvinist who preached the Word of God as it stood. James did not try to mould its message by compliance to a theological system. He admitted that he did not seem to find much about Calvinism in the Bible. He was, in this respect, what we might call an "authentic Calvinist."

During this time, the young Dale began questioning several basic doctrines of the Christian Faith. These included unconditional election, total depravity and limited atonement and represented a development that came as a great annoyance to some of the Christian church members. Had Dr James not intervened privately, and encouraged church leaders and members to be patient with the young assistant, the church would probably have dismissed Dale from his charge. Despite this propitious outcome, Dale felt that Carr's Lane was not the right place for him, and the opportunity of a call to a church in Manchester presented itself to the young man. Dale took the matter to Dr James, asking him to make the decision. James immediately said, "Stay." And he stayed for a further thirty years in that congregation.

His Work

History will remember Dale as a preacher, theologian and author. His doctrinal preaching resulted in a stream of books that included *The Atonement* (1875), *Christian Doctrine*, *The Living Christ and the Four Gospels*, and *Christ and the Future Life*. He also authored books on the *Ten Commandments*, *Ephesians* and *James*.

Dale believed that God was Lord of every aspect of life. This conviction led him into local and national politics, despite Paul's prohibition of

---

[81] Wiersbe, *Walking with the Giants*. (Grand Rapids: Baker Book House, 1976), 44.

preachers becoming entangled in worldly affairs (2 *Timothy* 2:4).[82] The apostle emphasised the total dedication of ministers to their ministry. However, Dale believed that God was as concerned about the government of Birmingham as He was about the government of Carr's Lane Church. A Liberal party member, Dale articulated his views forthrightly. He became embroiled in the controversial Home Rule Bill in Ireland, and for decades exerted a powerful and positive influence upon the religious, educational and social life of the city of Birmingham.[83] God does not confine His sovereignty to personal piety; it embraces all of life's complexities.

As a depression sufferer, Dale often spoke of the bizarre, gruesome sadness and despondency that overwhelmed him and against which he had to battle, sometimes for weeks on end.[84] Wiersbe suggests that while these bouts of depression may have had organic causes, he prefers to think that they may have been brought on by his personal doctrinal struggles and by his sense of civic responsibility. These seasons of depression would often leave as suddenly as they arrived.

What connection, if any, his spiritual and mental conditions had on his theological reasoning, one cannot tell with any degree of certainty. However, he began having great difficulties over the doctrines of man's immortality and eternal punishment. In 1874, he committed himself publicly to the doctrine of annihilation, which taught that only those who possessed eternal life in Christ would live forever,[85] the rest being annihilated or go out of existence.

One year later, Dale threw himself into the Moody and Sankey Crusade in Birmingham. He assessed Moody as the only preacher he heard who preached Hell with tears in his voice. Despite their doctrinal disagreements, both men laboured together to win souls to Christ through the gospel. Carr's Lane received about two hundred new members from

---

[82] See Matthew Henry on this verse. *Matthew Henry's Commentary on the whole BIBLE*. (Marshallton: The National Foundation for Christian Education, 1845 edit).
[83] Clark, as cited in Douglas, *Dictionary*, 281.
[84] Wiersbe, *Giants*, 45.
[85] Wiersbe, *Giants*, 46.

this evangelistic campaign, and he concluded that after many years approximately three-quarters of these new converts 'stood well.'[86]

On Moody's return to Birmingham in 1884, Dale again cooperated fully. However, he thought he noticed a change in emphasis from the earlier campaign that focused on the free grace of God. Now Moody's emphasis seemed to focus on repentance, in the sense of 'doing' a penance.[87] The results from that campaign were inconsiderate and Dale remarked that he did not see the glowing faces this time round that he saw last time. Whether this can be put down to Moody's change in emphasis or Dale's doctrinal change is difficult to ascertain.

His Significance

Whatever we might think of Dale's overall theological position, one thing is clear that he exerted influence far beyond Birmingham. It is also clear that his faith was a living reality to him, and not merely a lifeless idea.[88] He was someone who was prepared to think for himself, and he sought to live by what he thought, despite the personal cost. Fairbairn asserts that he was capable of thinking for himself, issuing in thought that resulted from the hard work of his own brain. His life experiences interpreted his newly formed convictions for him.[89] Dale did not simply "ape" the earlier theologians but through careful, painstaking study, he drew his own conclusions. This practice in itself is most commendable, and the same methodology is traceable in the life and work of DML-J.

Further, Dale was not a confessional or system theologian, but, despite his departures from biblical orthodoxy in places, sought to go with the Bible, and refused to go no further beyond what the Bible clearly taught.[90] He

---

[86] *Ibid.*

[87] *Ibid.*

[88] *Ibid.*

[89] Fairbairn as cited in Dale, 1898/1902:706.

[90] Christopher Catherwood (1984:12) claims that his grandfather, DML-J, insisted that he was never a system Calvinist, but always a 'Bible Calvinist.'

strenuously opposed extreme Calvinism on the one hand, and the High Church movement on the other but cooperated in Moody's Birmingham campaigns.[91] While DML-J did not favour the mass evangelism approach, thus disagreeing with Dale, he did agree with him in his refusal to be bound by confessionalism especially when confessions departed from the clear teaching of Scripture. Both Dale and DML-J were primarily Bible men, or biblicists, despite their different theological emphases.

Dr Dale died while working on an unfinished sermon. The final unfinished sentence focused on the end of life and looked forward to a life of excellence in...'[92] These were his final known words before he left to be with his Saviour forever.

After his death in 1895, his son, Sir A. W. W. Dale, wrote a biography of his father, the most significant part of which is Prin. A. M. Fairbairn's appendix that deals with his work as a theologian.[93] Wiersbe reckons that this is probably the best available analysis of Dale's theology.

What, then, does Fairbairn's conclude? He concurs with Wiersbe that beyond question, Dr Dale held an influential and unique place among the theologians of the latter half of the nineteenth century. He referred to his reputation as a divine and his immense thought.[94] Dale was a theologian by intellectual necessity – he could not have considered himself filling any other role.[95] He applied his keen intellect to his ministry. But his was not a mere intellectual exercise. Dale was a man of faith in Christ, a man who tested everything rationally before it was allowed to shape his thinking.

DML-J's Welsh background would have responded warmly to this approach. Not being a slave to anything but what he believed Scripture

---

[91] Clark, as cited in Douglas, 1978:281.
[92] Wiersbe, 1976:47.
[93] Wiersbe, 1976:48.
[94] Fairbairn as cited in Dale, 1898/1902:705ff.
[95] Fairbairn as cited in Dale, 1898/1902:706.

to teach,[96] he maintained his thought-forms as well as the substance of his beliefs, which were very much his own.

Dale was clearly not a schoolman, limited and restricted by the rules of cold logic. Technical precision was something he eschewed, and when theologians reduced theology to naked scholasticism, he cordially despised it. He never developed his theology in any systematic way, so what he believed has to be gleaned from his published works. Unlike the incomprehensible German theologians, Dale spoke and wrote and was understood. He tested his beliefs by how applicable they were to life. The application of these beliefs was crucial to his ministry and theologising. He wanted, like DML-J, to see lives changed and possessed by what he preached.

Dale grew up in a climate where theological and philosophical liberalism were spreading rapidly. This "advance" had to be either challenged or harnessed for the good of all. Dale opted to challenge it, thus setting a fine example to those to whom he was a mentor.

His greatest theological influences may be traced right back to Puritan theology modified by the effects of the Evangelical Revival.[97] His theological heritage was also defined prior to the Revival by the controversies with the Arminian system and after it by the conflict with the Socinians. Puritan theology was a precise and closely interwoven system of divinity, built on the sovereignty of God in all things, and on the sufficiency of divine grace, especially for salvation, but not limited to salvation. It emphasised the necessity of Christ's atonement in its two-fold application. On the one hand, it was the means by which God could effectually demonstrate His grace, while, on the other, it showed that God's justice was fully satisfied on the cross. Without God's sovereign and gracious will acting on the sinful mass of mankind, no other good could be expected. It was this will that both decided the number of the redeemed and declared the method of redemption. All the doctrines of Puritanism emerged from this basic

---

[96] Lewis in his Foreword to Catherwood, 1984:9.

[97] Fairbairn as cited in Dale, *The Life of R. W. Dale of Birmingham*. (London: Hodder and Stoughton, 1898/1902), 710.

position. Provided this system of divinity emerged from the foundation provided by an absolute divine sovereignty, it had nothing to fear.[98]

Given this basis for Dale's theology, any encroachment of Arminianism with its emphasis on the integrity of human reason and the freedom of the human will, would have been identified and dealt with summarily. Though critical of the legalism of some theologians, Dale saw in the death of our Lord Jesus Christ the sole ground of man's reconciliation with God.[99] He never minimised the seriousness of sin and pressed on his hearers the need for the forgiveness of God.

It was Dale's *The Atonement*[100] (1875) that had had such a crucial effect on DML-J's thinking and preaching. This book brought him to see that nothing but Christ in His death demonstrating the redeeming love of God to mankind can do guilty sinners good. It was a love to all mankind that caught DML-J's interest. This universal aspect of the cross found its way into DML-J's preaching from near the beginning of his ministry and was a main emphasis of his until his death on 1st March 1981.

But this by itself did not deal with mankind's sinful rebellion against a holy and righteous God who revealed His wrath from Heaven against all sin (*Romans* 1:18). Man's sin provokes the divine wrath, and God must address this issue in such a way that the repentant sinner can know God's forgiveness and at the same time maintain God's justice impeccably. God accomplished this through Jesus in His death, the Son Whom God sent for this purpose.

Dale died in 1895 while he was preparing his last sermon for his congregation.

---

[98] Fairbairn as cited in Dale, *Life*, 710.
[99] Clark, as cited in Douglas, *Dictionary*, 281.
[100] Robert W. Dale, *The Atonement*. (London: The Congregational Union of England and Wales, 1875).

9

Introducing Dr Peter Taylor Forsyth (1848–1921):

His Life

Peter Taylor Forsyth was born in Aberdeen in 1848. His father was a postman in the city, and the young Forsyth studied at Aberdeen University before moving on to Göttingen, Germany. Here he studied under Albrecht B. Ritschl, the Protestant theologian who became known as the father of Protestant liberalism. Ordained to the Christian ministry within the Congregational Church, he served pastorates in Bradford, Manchester, Leicester and Cambridge. In 1901, he became Principal of Hackney College in London, a post he retained until his death in 1921. Hackney College later became part of the University of London. His birth was at a juncture in British history when many of the traditionally held beliefs and presuppositions were being questioned, not least by German philosophers and theologians. This increasingly toxic theological atmosphere was hostile to the development of true spirituality amongst Christians. In his later life, Forsyth was increasingly respected in his denomination as a leader, dying in 1921.

His Work

As a theologian, Forsyth was liberal initially[101] and developed a keen interest in historical-critical theology.[102] He addressed the Leicester Conference in 1877 which shared his aims of a church that was better, freer, and larger.[103] As a result, he was suspected of heterodoxy by his ministerial colleagues. However, Forsyth[104] underwent a conversion to evangelical Christianity in his thirties but did so without relinquishing his commitment to modern biblical criticism. He held that, even though God inspired the biblical text, it was not infallible.[105] Forsyth's greatest work was his *The Person and Place of Jesus Christ*, published in 1909. He made a creative contribution to Christology in suggesting that κενωσις (self-emptying) and πληρωσις (fulfilling) are the two movements from God to man and from man to God which savingly occur in Christ.[106] It was, however, his *The Cruciality of the Cross* (1909) that most influenced the thinking and believing of DML-J. His closely aligned book of popular lectures entitled *The Work of Christ* (1910) was a distillation of his earlier work.

Forsyth in his earlier days held to a form of conservative scholastic theology, but in his later times, did not return to this position. Instead, he gave a growing emphasis to the need to embrace and live by the new theological critical freedom that he had discovered. Nor did he relish the evangelical realities attempting to supplant these new discoveries.[107] However he also increasingly came to the conclusion that liberal theology failed to account adequately for the moral problem of the guilty conscience. Searching for a solution to this perennial problem, he found the answer in the doctrine of the atoning death of Jesus Christ. This discovery helped to shape and inform a vigorous interest in, and commitment to, the issues

---

[101] McGrath, *Christian Thought*, 228.
[102] Willmer, as cited in Douglas, *Dictionary*, 382.
[103] *Ibid*. Forsyth seemed to have embarked on missionary endeavour at home through the promotion of church extension work.
[104] McGrath, *Christian Thought*, 228 mistakenly names him as Taylor.
[105] McGrath, *Christian Thought*, 228.
[106] Willmer, as cited in Douglas, *Dictionary*, 383.
[107] *Ibid*.

of holiness and atonement. He rejected many of his earlier liberal leanings but held on to many of the positions expounded by German theologian Adolf von Harnack in his criticisms of Chalcedonian Christology. Bishop Charles Gore and Thomasius also influenced his thought in this regard. That conceded, Forsyth's chief contribution was to the doctrine of the atonement,[108] and especially to the ethical significance of this truth.

Forsyth also opposed strenuously the New Theology associated with the name of R. J. Campbell, thus paving the way for the theological attack Karl Barth made on the liberalism of his day in Germany. His emphases were similar to those of Barth, and some would claim that Forsyth was the forerunner of this neo-orthodox theologian, a 'Barthian before Barth.'[109]

His Significance

Assessing Forsyth's soteriology is not the easiest task to undertake, but I will make an attempt. The fact that he was an intellectual, none, but the most ignorant, will deny. He wrote with learning, passion, and also in his own individual idiosyncratic style. Fiercely critical of Arminianism, Forsyth argued that man must never take the central place that Scripture gives to God alone in theology, thus declaring himself to be a Calvinist in this respect. He believed and taught that God's love, being holy love, was wrathful against sin, a truth that is difficult to explain away. He stressed that there was only one way of reconciliation, and that was by the cross. He viewed reconciliation not as a doctrine but as an act of God in which He reconciled the world unto Himself. In reconciliation, he held that God and man were reconciled to each other at great personal cost to each, thus differing from Denney's construction of this doctrine. Denney claimed that God was always the subject of reconciliation and man the object, but conceded that it is easy to see how both ended up reconciled to each other.

---

[108] McGrath, *Christian Thought*, 228.
[109] The late Rev. Prof. J. Thompson of QUB in a private conversation with the author in c.1978.

Regarding the extent of the atonement, he taught that this was for the whole world, for all men, for all mankind, for humanity. He believed that Christ died once for all, the Lord laying on Him the iniquity of us all (*Isaiah* 53:6). Forsyth was not conditioned in his thinking about the cross by the thoughts of earlier theologians but arrived at this conclusion by way of vigorous thought and pain-staking and disciplined study. For him, what Scripture taught, we must believe and preach. What God had revealed, we too must believe. The universal texts of Scripture must be explained, not explained away, as some did in his day, and in ours. The positive impact of Forsyth's teaching on soteriology on the young Lloyd-Jones is everywhere evident in the latter's preaching and published (and recorded) sermons. DML-J possessed a "largeness" when it came to the atonement, and had a driving desire to reach the world for Christ. He shared his teacher's understanding of the divine design in the atonement, namely, the unwillingness of God that any should perish but that all should come to repentance (2 *Peter* 3:9).

Forsyth believed, in contrast to the liberalism of his day, that sin is nothing short of the deliberate rebellion of mankind against God, especially against His holiness. Correspondingly, man has an obligation to live a life of practical holiness.[110] This solid evangelical emphasis is most commendable and was confirmative of DML-J's developing theological sharpness. His developing of a high doctrine of the Church, the ministry and of the sacraments is also significant. He tended to view preaching in terms of it being a sacrament,[111] though is what sense is not given. He was very critical of what he termed "lay-mindedness" and of individualism that characterised much of Free Church thinking and practice. And he despised what he called a non-doctrinal religion that was also prevalent in the Free Churches.[112] Given the ecclesiology of DML-J in his early days, it seems clear that he did not take his mentor's teaching on the doctrine of the church with any great seriousness. His churchmanship was neither Anglican nor Roman but was the outworking of the biblical principles he

---

[110] McGrath, *Christian Thought*, 228, 229.

[111] Willmer, as cited in Douglas, *Dictionary*, 383.

[112] *Ibid.*

discovered in his study of the Scriptures. Initially this was Presbyterianism but later he came to believe Congregationalism reflects Scripture teaching best of all. DML-J, the Presbyterian, would have had his ecclesiology challenged by his study of Forsyth, thus explaining, partly, why he later became a Congregationalist. Ironically, he remained a minister of the gospel within the Presbyterian Church of Wales.

Despite the theological deviations from strict orthodoxy in some of Forsyth's works, there is an emphasis there that has been largely ignored by many today. For example, he pleaded passionately for the notion of the "justice of God" to be allowed back into the church's preaching. Further, he called implicitly for a decreasing focus on exact theological definition such as Anselm illustrated. He desired a greater concentration on the inextricable link between the cross and the whole moral fabric of the universe and saw the atonement as inseparable from "the rightness of things."[113] The divine action to restore this "rightness of things" was done exclusively through the cross. This restoration necessitated making available a pathway via the cross by which sinful mankind could be morally regenerated. From a human (and theological) perspective this regeneration was an impossibility but from God's perspective He was able to provide it.[114] This idea came from the book, *The Justification of God* (1916), written by Forsyth during the First World War.

---

[113] McGrath, *Christian Thought*, 621.
[114] McGrath, *Christian Thought* 621.

10

Introducing Dr James Denney (1856–1917):

His Life

The birth of James Denney on 5th February 1856 at Paisley, Scotland, marked the nineteenth year of the reign of Queen Victoria. Scotland and the rest of Britain were experiencing new wealth and confidence as the empire was being built, and international trade was beginning to expand to the limits of the imagination. New industrial processes were producing a different world with new problems.

The church scene depicted three major denominations: the Established Church, the Free Church, and the United Presbyterian Church – together with a number of independent bodies, such as the Cameronians. These denominations were numerically small but they held tenaciously to what they held were their important distinctive dogmas. Religious thinking in Scotland was focused largely on the past and displayed a dependence upon the conservative evangelicalism of the sixteenth and seventeenth centuries. At this juncture, the doctrines of grace, vital to true biblical Christianity, were faithfully proclaimed and embraced by the church. This time was a staunchly Calvinistic period of the Scottish Church's history and a resolute reliance on and interpretation of the formularies of Calvinistic doctrine was in evidence. It was a day of theological formality and austere orthodoxy.

James Denney grew up in the sea-port of Greenock, on the Firth of Clyde. His parents were members of the strict Reformed Presbyterian

Church, the small denomination also known as the Cameronians. It had its origin in the courageous controversies which gripped Scotland towards the end of the seventeenth century. In 1876, the Denney family went with the majority of the Reformed Presbyterian Church of Scotland into union with the Free Church of Scotland.[115] Following some experience as a Sunday School teacher and as a clerk, he matriculated as an Arts student at Glasgow University, enrolling in November 1874. Denney was an outstanding student, taking the Moral Philosophy gold medal and the Blackstone Prize in Edward Caird's class in 1879. Denney refused to adopt his master's philosophy. He excelled in Classics under Professor (later Sir) Richard C. Jebb. Jebb wrote a letter to J. P. Struthers, saying, "If there is the faintest whiff of Christianity about the creature, he neutralises it somehow or other with absolute success."[116] Denney took an eminent position at the University from the beginning of his academic career and had the rare distinction of gaining a "double first" honours M.A. degree in Classics and Philosophy in 1879.[117] The most notable influences on the young academic were Edward Caird and Richard Jebb.

Four years of theological training at Trinity College followed these five years at Glasgow University where he acquitted himself well in his studies, graduating with a B.D. degree. Denney confessed that it was Professor A. B. Bruce who let him see Jesus rather than cluttering his lectures with obscure points. He was licenced to preach by the Presbytery of Greenock on 16th May 1883, aged 27. Denney became student assistant minister to John Veitch.[118] Three years later, he was called to be the minister of the East Free Church in Broughty Ferry, Dundee (1886–1897), one of his distinguished predecessors being his friend and mentor Prof. A. B. Bruce.

---

[115] Alan P. F. Sell, *Defending and Declaring the Faith*. (Exeter: Paternoster Press, 1987), 195. Douglas (*Dictionary*, 293) states this 'joining' in different terms, alleging that the Reformed Presbyterians united with the United Presbyterians in 1900 to form the United Free Church.
[116] Sell, *Defending*, 195.
[117] Sell, *Defending*, 196 is incorrect to give the date as 1897, though this is probably a typographical error.
[118] Sell, *Defending*, 196 points out that John Veitch was also a professor of Logic.

Here, Denney was a popular preacher who preached the everlasting gospel to the common people. East Free Church was to be his only pastorate.

On 1st July 1886, he married Amy Carmichael (Mary) Brown, daughter of John Brown of Glasgow. His happy and long marriage to Mary was a witness to Christ in the congregation, community and church at large. She rescued James from the temptation to depart from the Evangelical and Reformed faith of his parents by encouraging him to read the sermons of Charles Haddon Spurgeon. This spiritual exercise, says Nicholl, was responsible for Denney deciding to preach the atoning death of Jesus Christ.[119] The evangelical vigour of this young Baptist preacher changed radically the young Scot's preaching and writing ministries. By training, Denney was disposed to be theologically liberal, but because of his wife's tenderness towards him, he became decidedly more evangelical. This move away from liberalism to evangelicalism is a testimony to a godly wife's life and witness though her husband remained sympathetic to modern biblical criticism.[120]

Mrs Denney contributed considerably to her husband's ministry; whereas he was inclined to be authoritarian, she was a kindly individual and under her warm encouragement, her husband became more compassionate. After a marriage of twenty-one years, she died in 1907 and without children; James was devastated by her death. He found nothing to replace his keen sense of loss. Dr Denney died prematurely in 1917, bringing his illustrious career to an untimely end.

His Work

During an eleven-year parish ministry at Broughty Ferry, Dundee, Denney translated Delitzsch's commentary on *Isaiah* into English in 1891.[121] He was invited, in 1893,[122] to give theological lectures in Chicago, later published

---

[119] Sell, *Defending*, 197.
[120] McGrath, *Christian Thought*, 105.
[121] Sell, *Defending*, 197.
[122] Sell, 1987:197 gives the date as April, 1894.

in 1894 under the title, *Studies in Theology*, two chapters of which deal with the atonement. Some objected to his statements on the nature of Scripture, and on his beliefs about the Person of the Holy Spirit and his eschatology. Despite these, the book was heralded as an important work, and the University of Chicago awarded Denney the honorary degree of Doctor of Divinity.

Also at that time, he was invited to contribute two commentaries to the *Expositor's Bible* series. His stress on the need for expository preaching characterised his ministry, and Denney wrote commentaries on Paul's letters to the *Thessalonians* (1892), and on *Second Corinthians* (1894). These were the basis of his series of sermons on these three Pauline epistles, and demonstrate his desire for a theology that could help men preach the gospel.[123] His commentary on the Greek text of *Romans* in *The Expositor's Greek Testament* series then followed (1900). *The Death of Christ* arrived in 1902, though J. D. Douglas dates it as 1903,[124] which is the date of publication of *The Atonement and the Modern Mind*.[125] *Jesus and the Gospel* appeared in 1908, *The Church and the Kingdom* in 1910, *Factors of Faith in Immortality* in 1911, *War and the Fear of God* in 1916 and *The Christian Doctrine of Reconciliation* materialised posthumously in 1917. He also contributed articles to Hasting's *Encyclopaedia of Religion and Ethics*, *Dictionary of the Bible*, and *Dictionary of Christ and the Gospels*.

The highly regarded *Romans* commentary gave ministers deeper insights into this greatest of Paul's letters, and the one that explained Paul's understanding of the gospel of Christ. For this commentary, Denney used the critical text of Wellhausen, not the *Textus Receptus*. Rev. James Philip (Edinburgh, d.2009) in his IVP commentary on *Romans* leaned heavily on Denney's exposition, which is essentially a restatement of Denney's teaching in the commentary, with appropriate applications.

Denney's *The Death of Christ* was seminal in its extended exposition of the New Testament's teaching on this critically important heart of God's

---

[123] Sell, *Defending*, 197.

[124] Douglas, *Dictionary*, 293.

[125] Sell, *Defending*, 199.

revelation, namely, His way of reconciliation. Here, the professor provides an in-depth study of the heart of the gospel and demonstrates that Christ in His death is the only way of salvation for lost mankind. It was with this work that Denney made his greatest contribution as a theologian, his *The Death of Christ* being rightly esteemed his *magnum opus*.

Dr Lloyd-Jones received great benefit from Denney's book that was to see constant expression throughout his forty-one year pastoral ministry in Sandfields and Westminster Chapel, and also in his remaining thirteen years of preaching ministry. I have not seen any references to Denney in DML-J's sermons, yet they are full of Denney's theology and vocabulary. This book had a life-changing effect on DML-J's future ministry. It was the forerunner of books on the cross by scholars such as Leon L. Morris (*The Cross in the New Testament*, and *The Apostolic Preaching of the Cross*) and John R. W. Stott (*The Cross*). His book of sermons, *The Way Everlasting* (1911), presents his characteristic thoughts with marked simplicity and power and has taught many ministers how to preach the cross of Christ. In 1897, Denney was elected by a massive majority of 456 to John McPherson's 76 votes[126] to succeed Candlish to the Chair of Systematic and Pastoral Theology at his old *alma mater* in the Free Church College, Glasgow.[127] In this Chair, he served for only two years, after which he transferred to the Chair of New Testament Language and Literature (or was it the Chair of New Testament Exegesis and Theology).[128] Following the death of his New Testament professor, Dr A. B. Bruce,[129] he remained in this post until his death in 1917, the last two years of which as Principal of the College. Denney was the first former student of the institution to receive that honour.

Denney's works reveal that his scholarly mind had grappled with the impact of philosophical empiricism and theological liberalism on orthodox

---

[126] Sell, *Defending*, 197.
[127] *Ibid.*
[128] Sell, *Defending*, 197.
[129] McGrath, *Christian Thought*, 105. McGrath is incorrect to state that Denney held the professorship of Systematic and Pastoral Theology from 1897 until his death in 1917.

theology, particularly in the person of Albrecht Benjamin Ritschl, the father of theological liberalism. Some argue he conceded too much to theological liberalism. Undoubtedly, Ritschl himself came under strong philosophical influences, which have left their mark on his theology, and whose theology, in turn, has marked most of the major Protestant denominations in the West.

His Significance

Dr Denney was one of the foremost Scottish Presbyterian theologians whose contribution to biblical theology was considerable. His frequent articles in the now-defunct *British Weekly* were to inspire and help numerous readers. His work on *The Death of Christ*, or as he prefers to term it, "Jesus in His death," was seminal. It influenced succeeding generations of theologians and ministers in Scotland and further afield, including the young Welsh Presbyterian minister, Rev. Dr D. Martyn Lloyd-Jones. DML-J had been influenced by eighteenth-century men like George Whitefield, concentrating on preaching the new birth during his early days of ministry. However, he was encouraged by Congregational minister, Rev. Lewis Edwards, to focus on the cross as the only divine action that "takes away the sin of the world!" (*John* 1:29). Denney emphasised the inextricable link between remission of sins and the cross of Christ, so preachers must declare this aspect of saving truth if sinful men were ever to know God's forgiveness. DML-J read and studied Denney's *The Death of Christ*, and this convinced him that Christ's cross was indispensable to the Christian gospel. If any were to be saved and reconciled to God, it would have to be through this understanding of the gospel. From Denney, he learned that Christ died for all, for humanity, for the world, for mankind, for the human race. He came to see in this atoning death the only way of reconciliation with God. Through this act, God had done for sinners what they could not have done for themselves, and which no other person could do for them. In Christ, He bore their sins and transgressions, making them His very own. Denney's strong experiential emphasis left its mark on the Welsh evangelist, an aspect that found its way into the very 'warp and woof' of DML-J's preaching content.

Gammie explained Denney's conviction about preaching the gospel by saying that the great decision of his life was to preach the atoning death of Jesus Christ. He wanted to do nothing but preach the cross in all its fullness and its double aspect. On the one hand, its power to save, and on the other, its bitter taste and compelling seriousness, its commanding calls to costly discipleship, and to self-denial.[130] His preaching finds a deafening echo in DML-J's conviction about preaching, especially the preaching of the cross as God's only way of reconciliation of the world to Himself. Indeed, DML-J's concern, with Denney, was for theology that helped a man to evangelise, and anything contrary to that was irrelevant.[131] Further like Denney, DML-J coveted one thing only, and that was to be an evangelist.[132] Both preachers emphasised only one great theme – the sin-bearing love of God for mankind demonstrated in Christ's death on Calvary.[133]

Despite Denney's dalliance with modern biblical criticism, he still maintained that the only theology that he was interested in was a theology that ministers could preach, and that helped them to evangelise.[134] As a theological professor, Denney was essentially an evangelist, and the great focus of his preaching and his scholarly endeavours was the cross of Christ. He admitted that though it was his calling to teach, the one thing he coveted was the ability to do the work of an evangelist. He added that that was the work that needed to be done, in his view. There can be little doubt that Denney the evangelist touched the heart of Lloyd-Jones, the evangelist, there being common ground between them, even if he did not agree with everything Denney taught. DML-J was keen to embrace a theology that would make him a better evangelist, given that that was how he self-defined. He sought a message that he could take to the whole world, and found in Denney's understanding of Christ in His death, a message that he could preach to all men. This message offered a salvation that was not only applicable to all men, but that was in the design of God

---

[130] Gammie, A. *Preachers I Have Heard*. (London: Pickering and Inglis, n.d.), 162.
[131] Gammie, *Preachers* 163. Cf. Sell, *Defending*, 195.
[132] Sell, *Defending*, 195.
[133] See Appendix.
[134] McGrath, *Christian Thought*, 105; Douglas, *Dictionary*, 293.

provided to save all mankind. In his *The Death of Christ*, Denney held that the atonement was purely substitutionary and penal in character, and his writings on the atonement defended this general position. However, in his posthumous work, *The Christian Doctrine of Reconciliation*, he modified his position, claiming that the atonement is penal in one sense, and in another sense it is not.

Denney became a leader in the church courts of his denomination after the Reformed Presbyterians united with the United Presbyterians in 1900 to form the United Free Church. He also involved himself as a contributor to the yet distant (1929) union with the national Church of Scotland.[135] Denney saw the responsibility of contributing to the government of the church as an integral part of his work as a Christian minister. Further, his writing and preaching ministries were also demonstrations that he had a care for all the churches. Denney was a strong promoter of temperance and its attendant self-control, and of public righteousness.[136]

---

[135] Douglas, *Dictionary*, 293. Sell, *Defending*, 195, states that in 1876, the Denney family went with the majority of the Reformed Presbyterian Church of Scotland into union with the Free Church of Scotland.

[136] Douglas, *Dictionary*, 293.

SECTION THREE

Review Of What Some Experts Say!

11

Study Dale, Forsyth, and Denney, And Don't Forget Jones.

In his two-volume biography of DML-J, Iain H. Murray[137] reveals that in the early days of his ministry at Sandfields, DML-J appeared to focus on the doctrine of regeneration in his gospel preaching. DML-J was a keen student of B. B. Warfield, John Owen and Richard Baxter, with the latter being the first Puritan he read, and for whom he had a life-long admiration.[138] He was greatly influenced by the Welsh Calvinistic Methodist Fathers, by the Rev. George Whitefield and the Revs John and Charles Wesley. The emphasis of these men, particularly Whitefield, was on regeneration, or the "new birth." DML-J followed this emphasis in his preaching for several years after commencing his public ministry at Sandfields in 1927.

The years after his settlement in Sandfields saw the beginnings of a change that brought about a different emphasis in the Doctor's preaching. This new emphasis did not mean that he forsook his earlier emphasis, for it was thoroughly biblical. What it did mean was that his preaching became more biblically balanced, for up to about that time, he preached little about the cross of our Lord Jesus Christ. Preaching in Bridgend, South Wales, at a Monday evening service, DML-J had an experience that was

---

[137] Murray, *Forty Years*, 191.
[138] Cf. E. Hulse, *The Free Offer*. (Sussex: Carey Publications and Henry E. Walter Ltd, 1986), 152. While DML-J did study Owen's works, the first Puritan he read was Richard Baxter, and it was from Baxter, not Owen, that he learned his soteriology.

to have a profound and lasting effect on his ministry. After the service, the minister of the church spoke to DML-J and said to him that he could not decide what kind of man he was – a hyper-Calvinist or a Quaker? DML-J assured him that he was "no hyper-Calvinist."[139] He was curious as to why the minister should make such a point, so the minister told him that he talked of God's action and God's intervention. His strong focus was on that spiritual change in a man's heart that came from God alone, and that man made no human contribution to his salvation. However, he gave little hope to those who came under conviction of sin. Murray states correctly, with a note of criticism of the Doctor's preaching, that his message lacked biblical balance. He failed to direct his hearers clearly enough to faith in Christ as God's appointed means of relief from the real feelings of guilt and the fear of eternal condemnation in Hell. Murray felt that he stressed human inability inappropriately, without giving the same emphasis to man's responsibility to cast himself upon Christ alone for justification. He believed that the Doctor's preaching emphasis at that time was deficient in that it did not explain sufficiently clearly how trusting Christ alone puts a sinner into a right relationship with God.[140] Murray teaches that faith is God's way for the sinner to receive the benefits of the Christ's purchased redemption.[141] DML-J had largely missed this emphasis at this early juncture of his ministry.

The criticism of DML-J, received at Bridgend, was not unproductive. Rather it provided an incentive to more concentrated thinking on the Doctor's part. He admitted that he was like Whitefield in preaching regeneration and clarifies that he had assumed the atonement without preaching on it or on justification by faith. Having heard, and accepted, the brotherly criticism, he set about renewed theological reading and study and focused on those "absent" doctrines specified by his critic. Not knowing where to go to, he contacted Rev. Vernon Lewis, later principal of the Congregational College at Brecon. Quick to respond to DML-J's

---

[139] Murray, 1982:190. Reference also to J. E. Hazlett Lynch, unpublished address at the Amyraldian Association Conference, Attleborough, NORFOLK, England on 6th April 2006. DML-J warned against the "abomination" of hyper-Calvinism.
[140] Murray, *Forty Years*, 191.
[141] Shorter Catechism, answers to Q.29, 30.

request for help on what to read, Lewis' top recommendations were P. T. Forsyth and R. W. Dale, both English Congregationalists, and James Denney, the Scottish Presbyterian theologian. He studied Forsyth's *The Cruciality of the Cross* (1909), Dale's *The Atonement* (1875) and Denney's *The Death of Christ* (1903). The book that was to prove most helpful to DML-J's thinking was Forsyth's *The Cruciality of the Cross* (1909).[142] Being a wide and discerning reader, DML-J did not dismiss these authors because of any weakness he found in their writings, especially when their understanding of the full inspiration of Scripture was inadequate.[143] Murray explains that this was not the subject of DML-J's study, nor did he have any personal difficulties with accepting the full inspiration of the Scriptures. His focus was on what these men were writing about the atonement. Hence, it is important to review what these highly respected scholars and theologians have written.

Further, DML-J, being proud of his Welshness, used to read the two-volume work on the Welsh Calvinistic Methodist Fathers which he referred to often. When feeling depressed he returned to the eighteenth century and Wales in particular, and would nourish and refresh his soul on the work of God in his homeland. On the fly cover of Owen Thomas' *The Atonement Controversy* (trans. by John Aaron),[144] the publishers stated that in gatherings of ministers DML-J insisted that this classic work was one that gave considerable help to preachers, adding that his evangelistic preaching had been influenced by it.[145]

DML-J demonstrates that what Christian preachers believe about the atonement always affects what and how they preach it. This conviction was undoubtedly the truth about his approach to gospel preaching and its content. Hence, a brief examination of the soteriology of John Jones, Talsarn, will form part of this literature review.

---

[142] Murray, *Forty Years*, 191, 192.
[143] J. E. Hazlett Lynch. Unpublished Doctoral diss., *The Influence of Philosophy on Contemporary Theology with Reference to James Denney's Doctrine of Scripture*. (Indiana: Trinity Theological Seminary, IN, USA, 1990).
[144] Published by Banner of Truth Trust, Edinburgh.
[145] Thomas, *The Controversy*. (Edinburgh: Banner of Truth Trust, 2002).

12

R. W. Dale's Soteriology

Dale's theology opposed Arminianism and any encroachment of this theology. It emphasised the integrity of human reason and the freedom of the human will, and these "deviations" from orthodoxy would have been dealt with instantly. Dale recognised the dangers of Arminianism and believed that it was detrimental to the gospel. He saw in Christ's death the sole ground of man's reconciliation with God.[146] For Dale, the seriousness of sin was not something that could ever become a bit less sombre and pressed on his hearers the need for God's forgiveness.

In his book, *The Atonement*,[147] Dale sets forth what he believed to be the Bible's teaching on the death of Christ. He introduces his overall position when he writes in the preface that Christ's death presents itself as a propitiation for the sins of the world.[148] These words undergird his approach to dealing with the doctrine of the atonement. He views the death of Christ as the objective ground on which forgiveness becomes ours.[149] He illustrates the testimony of Christ and His apostles to the fact of the atonement, and on this foundation constructs a biblical doctrine of that atonement. Dale complains that the premature attempt to formulate such a theory of the atonement has led to the fact of the atonement as the

---

[146] Clark, as cited in Douglas *Dictionary*, 281.
[147] Robert W. Dale, *The Atonement*. (1875).
[148] Dale, *Atonement*, ix.
[149] Dale, *Atonement*, ix.

only basis of pardon being obscured by erroneous theorists – a serious charge.

How does he do this? Dale proceeds in a manner that is common to two of our three influential theologians.[150] After a comprehensive introduction,[151] he analyses the history of our Lord Jesus Christ in relation to the fact of the atonement [152] and then examines the Saviour's testimony to this.[153] Next he looks at the testimony of the apostles – Peter,[154] John and James,[155] and Paul[156] and draws out the salient points from their writings. He then extracts general considerations from the previous that confirm the argument he makes.[157]

Coming to the heart of the gospel, Dale expounds the doctrine of the remission of sins,[158] viewing this experience as entirely locked into what Christ achieved on the cross. Two further illustrations are given, one in Christ's relation to the eternal law of righteousness[159] and the other His relation to the human race.[160] The relevant learning points (which see later) confirm the influence he had on the ministry of DML-J. While Dale seldom refers to Calvin, the doctrine of the atonement that he extracts from the Scriptures follows Calvin's exegesis very closely. Dale exercised a crucial influence on DML-J's thinking and preaching. It helped him to see that nothing but Christ in His death demonstrating the redeeming love of God to mankind can do any good to helpless and rebellious sinners. It was a love to all mankind, to the whole world, which really caught DML-J's interest. Given his upbringing in Wales, the land of revivals, he would

---

[150] Denney and Dale follow this procedure, but Forsyth creates his own (which see later).
[151] Dale, *Atonement*, 1–34.
[152] Dale, *Atonement*, 35–64.
[153] Dale, *Atonement*, 65–96.
[154] Dale, *Atonement*, 97–148.
[155] Dale, *Atonement*, 149–190.
[156] Dale, *Atonement*, 191–264.
[157] Dale, *Atonement*, 265–310.
[158] Dale, *Atonement*, 311–352.
[159] Dale, *Atonement*, 353–398.
[160] Dale, *Atonement*, 399–440.

have known something of what the preachers of a bygone age would have preached, and Dale confirmed much of this teaching. This universal aspect of the cross made its way into DML-J's preaching from near the beginning of his ministry and was a main emphasis of his until prior to his death on 1st March 1981.

Dale corrected a wrong emphasis in the Doctor's preaching, something the Doctor appreciated. Preaching the "new birth" was not wrong in itself, being a truth revealed in Scripture; this "new birth" was needed to bring sinners from a state of spiritual death to spiritual life. Only in this way could a sinner enter the Kingdom of God. In fact, John records Jesus as saying that it is indispensable (δει) if any man is to see or enter God's Kingdom (*John* 3:3, 5).

But this alone did not deal with the sinful rebellion of mankind against the holy God whose wrath, provoked by man's sin, is revealed from Heaven against such (*Romans* 1:18). A remedy was needed to deal with this situation. Two decisive actions were required in the one divine action in Christ. The divine wrath had to be appeased in such a way that the repentant sinner could be forgiven and, at the same time, God's justice maintained unsullied. God sent Jesus to earth for this very purpose, and accomplished this through His sacrificial death.

How does Dale present an atonement designed to deal with mankind's sin? His statements are explicit. Let me give an accurate flavour of Dale's soteriology. He believed that it was the intention of the Saviour to die for men and that His cruel death was an awe-inspiring revelation of divine love for a lost world. He held this view on the understanding that the death of Christ was in some way necessary for the redemption of mankind. Otherwise, there is no explanation for that death if it was nothing more than a demonstration of His love for the world.[161] For Dale, Christ's sacrificial death was much more than a revelation of love. It had something, nay everything, to do with human redemption. Because the apostle John tells us that Christ Himself is the propitiation for (the sins

---

[161] Dale, *Atonement*, lv.

of) the whole world, God has responded to their trust and saved them eternally.[162] For him, Christ's death alone is the objective ground upon which God can remit their sins. Dale's reason is that His death destroyed the eternal consequences of the sin of everyone who trusts Christ to restore them to union with Him.[163]

Again the objective ground of forgiveness is reiterated, and which is received by faith in Christ alone. Faith is the active means by which we take to ourselves God's salvation freely offered to us in the gospel. Faith is the "saving grace" by which we receive and rest upon Christ alone for salvation.[164] Without Jesus in His death, and faith in that sin-bearing death, there is no possibility of sins being forgiven – ever. Forgiveness necessarily involves Calvary. The two are inextricably linked, like conjoined twins. The one reality does not exist without the other. In fact, the one requires the other. We cannot contradict the fact that Dale held robustly to an atonement that was universal in its intent, but limited in its application, namely, to those only who trust in Christ for salvation. The sheer number of universal gospel statements found in his book, *The Atonement*, is impossible to miss. Not only do these revolve around Christ as the Propitiation for the sins of the world; they also rivet attention on what Christ came to do as Saviour of the world. Listen to how he describes the scope of the atonement – the world, all mankind, all men, any man, whoever, for all, the human race, humanity.[165] Indeed, the sheer volume of statements that zoom in on Christ's death being for the "sins of the world" is most impressive.[166]

---

[162] Dale, *Atonement*, ix, 4, 12, 13, 18, 20, 25, 27, 99, 102, 112, 113, 161, 189, 264, 267, 314, 315, 338.

[163] Dale, *Atonement*, lxv.

[164] Shorter Catechism answer to Q.86.

[165] Dale, *Atonement*, 10, 11, 17, 26, 27, 49, 62, 67, 70, 78, 79, 80, 81, 89, 92, 105, 110, 112, 114, 116, 117, 118, 119, 122, 124, 129, 135, 136, 139, 140, 146, 154, 158, 162, 165, 188, 193, 199, 201, 202, 203, 207, 208, 228, 233, 236, 248, 252, 253, 257, 261, 262, 264, 268, 274, 281, 284, 289, 290, 292, 294, 295, 298, 300, 301, 306, 307, 308, 313, 326, 343, 347, 363, 364, 392, 393, 394, 396, 397, 401, 402, 403, 404, 410, 411, 419, 421, 422, 424, 425, 430, 432, 433, 434, 437, 438.

[166] Dale, *Atonement*, 12, 13, 18, 20, 25, 52, 88, 91, 99, 102, 112, 113, 119, 124, 143, 148, 161, 176, 189, 267, 268, 310, 314, 315, 338, 346, 348, 436.

Examining this evidence for Dale's universal atonement, we see an understanding of the gospel, and especially of the atonement, which is tailor-made for the Christian evangelist. Remember DML-J's self-definition as an evangelist and Dale's active involvement in Moody's evangelistic campaigns in Birmingham in 1875 and again in 1884! Because this soteriology is true to God's revealed will in Scripture, it is the message that He honours, and that brings glory to Christ in the salvation of sinners. Dale's message is for all without exception, reveals the loving heart of God, and issues a call from Heaven to all men to repent and believe the gospel. A study of DML-J's published evangelistic sermons will demonstrate a close similarity to Dale's soteriology, and bear eloquent testimony to Dale's positive influence on him as a preacher.

13

P. T. Forsyth's Soteriology

Peter Taylor Forsyth in his book, *The Work of Christ*,[167] takes us right into what he understands as the very heart of the gospel. He forces us to think seriously, soberly, and with understanding about what Calvary actually achieved. For him, the only doctrine that draws so directly on sinful men's personal religion, therefore, is the doctrine of Christ's work on the cross.[168] Looking at things from a different perspective can be a frightening and unsettling thing because we do not know where it will lead us. Even scholars tend to "play safe" and stay within their "comfort zones" because it would be too costly for them to go outside the "received wisdom." So what invariably happens is that the same old thinking tends to be regurgitated over and over again with no new or fresh thinking impacting on or providing clarity to an understanding of the gospel.

This absence of new thinking is particularly noticeable when dealing with the atonement. At bottom, it is not a matter of us dealing with the atonement. It is more about the atonement taking a radical dealing with us. Approaching such a divinely-charged doctrine slays "the old man" and the "old nature" in man, a situation that can cause theological dizziness and spiritual vertigo. So to avoid this some Christian thinkers prefer to "stay safe" and not scale the heights of revealed religion.

---

[167] Peter T. Forsyth, *The Work of Christ*. (London: Hodder and Stoughton, 1909).
[168] Forsyth, *Work*, vi.

Not Forsyth. Only those who have felt the crucifying and redeeming power of the blood of Christ in their lives can approach this mysterious doctrine. He laments a Christianity that is void of dogmatic content, something that he declares does not have apostolic and evangelical substance.[169] He also laments the opposite error where the work of Christ is understood purely in dogmatic terms. Where the revealed doctrine of the cross is squeezed to fit into the Procrustean bed of confessionalism, great damage is done to its saving power. It's divine energy has then been banished from it.

He concludes that religion requires form if it is not to degenerate into a purely subjective thing. But that "dogma" must be drawn from biblical data. Where philosophical formulations become the Procrustean bed into which biblical religion is expected to fit, there is the danger of distortion. Forsyth calls for a holy spirituality, not a barren orthodoxy that profits no one. In order to remove the cross from the realm of sentimentality, Forsyth sees the cross as demonstrating "propitiation" (1 *John* 2:2)[170] and not "affection." It is a robust love that achieves something of eternal significance. Paul would never have written 1 *Corinthians* 13 if it had been against *Romans* 3:25, he argues, because the Scriptural revelation of the Christian Faith centres on the cross. What the cross reveals is no less than the crisis that exists between holy judgement and holy grace.[171] It is holiness acting in judgement against sin and that by the loving God.[172]

From the evidence, DML-J caught Forsyth's vision of the Christian faith and embedded it within his preaching ministry. He did not accept an atonement teaching that was mere sentimentality, nor did he confessionalise the teaching of Scripture. Rather, he, in a sense, opened the gate of Scripture and let the lion (the truth) out. He refused to muzzle the gospel for the sake of confessional tidiness. Forsyth's influence on DML-J is apparent in this respect. In his *The Cruciality of the Cross*,[173] Forsyth does not follow the familiar pattern adopted by other theologians.

---

[169] Forsyth, *Work*, vii.
[170] Cf. Forsyth, *Work*, vii, viii.
[171] Forsyth, *Work,*, viii.
[172] Forsyth, *Work*, viii.
[173] Peter T. Forsyth, *The Cruciality of the Cross*. (Shropshire: Quinta Press, 1909).

They take the key players and parts of the New Testament and expound the teaching given in each section before drawing the threads together. Forsyth, rather, opens up the subject of the *centrality* of the atonement to the New Testament.[174] He sees this as of crucial importance in interpreting the New Testament Scriptures.[175] So central is the cross of Christ to this study that without it the Christian Faith just would not exist or be clear. This argument weighed heavily with DML-J as he re-thought the spectrum of his theology, and the biblical emphases he was labouring to state in his early years at Sandfields. We can trace the paradigm shift in his preaching to the profound influence Forsyth's work had on DML-J's thinking and theology.

Next, Forsyth considers a parallel concern, namely, the *centrality* of the atonement to Christian experience. If the cross is "God's way of reconciliation,"[176] then it must occupy a central position in Christian experience. By the cross, and only by the cross, the "old man" and the "old nature" are slain. It is, therefore, the means of the mortification of the believer's indwelling sin. Moving from the biblical scene, Forsyth explores the *centrality* of the atonement to the leading features of modern thought and concludes his book by studying the moral meaning of the blood of Christ.

By centrality, Forsyth means something much more than that the doctrine of the cross is the hinge of a finely balanced system of biblical thought. It was something much more vital and effective for moral and spiritual life. Forsyth sums this up by saying that centrality means the ultimate end to which human history and destiny are heading. When we meet the cross, we meet finality, the final judgement, the ultimate, the end, ὁ τέλος. There can be no redemption, no salvation, no forgiveness, no justification, no sanctification, no mortification, and no glorification, apart

---

[174] Cf. Stott, 1986:17–46.

[175] Zwingli's interpretative principle was to allow the Scriptures to be their own interpreter, a practice that DML-J adopted in his preaching, and advocated frequently to others. See Jones, *The Great Reformation*, (Leicester: InterVarity Press, 1985), 50.

[176] Incidentally, this was the title given to DML-J's book of sermons on *Ephesians* 2, published initially by Evangelical Press and latterly by Banner of Truth Trust.

from the cross. Jesus died that we might live. He sharpens this by saying that when the Lord Jesus Christ died for our sins, He died once for all,[177] thus emphasising the universal dimension to his thought. In this, he also demonstrates that he was following Calvin's teaching, and, more importantly, that of Scripture.

We can see Forsyth's influence on DML-J at this fundamental level. Neither men viewed the cross in sentimental terms. The cross is crucial and *central* to God's plan of salvation for the world, and ministers must preach this doctrine in their evangelistic endeavours. Obviously, and as an evangelist, DML-J was a preacher who came to preach "Jesus Christ and Him crucified" (1*Corinthians* 2:2). His evangelistic ministry centred on the cross, because, for him, outside of God's atoning work in Christ on Calvary, there is no hope for anyone because there is no gospel. As he developed as a preacher, the atonement became much more prominent in his ministry.

DML-J's departure in 1955 from preaching doctrine and catechisms and confessions *per se* may be put down to the sway of Forsyth, and of Dale, on his thinking. He concluded that mere academic discourses do not lead to edification and mere edifying sermons without doctrinal content become feeble and ineffectual,[178] producing weak and feeble and ineffective Christians. He saw clearly this danger and successfully avoided falling into that trap. Preaching and theology must, therefore, be finely balanced in their God-ordained marriage. DML-J defined preaching in terms of "theology coming through a man who is on fire," and as "logic on fire."

How then did Forsyth understand the atonement? He viewed it in its truly cosmic dimensions in writing about God saving a whole world of human society.[179] Thus he set forth the universal aspect of God's work in the world. He sees cosmic significance in what God accomplished in Christ. Indeed, he attributes the world's existence to the death of

---

[177] Forsyth, *Cruciality*, 5, 23, 54, 74, 86, 117, 136, 169, 172, 182, 211; cf. Forsyth, *Word*, 7, 77, 78, 86, 114, 182.
[178] Forsyth, *Work*, 3.
[179] Forsyth, *Work*, 6.

Christ,[180] without explaining the connection between these two truths and realities. His was a death on behalf of people within whom God had to create the power of responding positively,[181] thus pointing up Forsyth's concentration on grace in his theology. Man is dead in trespasses and sins and until God's Spirit quickens him, enlivens him, regenerates him (*Ephesians* 2:1), he will not make a positive saving response to the overtures of the gospel. There are two reasons for this: he *will* not therefore he *cannot*. He has the natural ability to hear the gospel call of God on his life, but he does not possess the moral ability to follow through in repentance toward God and faith in Christ. Prior to regeneration by the Spirit, man the sinner has power only to resist and oppose God's ways, not to accept them. He has no love for that holiness of life to which the gospel inevitably leads. Christ's death, then, was not a mere display of simple heroism; it was a demonstration of redemption.

He understands atonement as that action of Christ in His death that had primary regard to God's holiness, and man's reconciliation to God. That reconciliation he saw as impossible, unless and until the divine holiness is satisfied once and for all on Calvary.[182] The atonement, then, is directed primarily to satisfying divine holiness and justice, a clear DML-J emphasis. As a result of achieving this, the atonement has positive benefits for mankind in the reconciliation of mankind to God, His holiness having been fully honoured by the divinely provided sacrifice offered by Christ on Calvary.

This satisfaction is tied into Who it is we believe Christ to be in His Person. So how we see Christ is singularly important, and it must be that which especially honours God's holiness.[183] The connection between the Person of Christ and God's holiness must be maintained, teaches Forsyth. He emphasises the holiness of God's love, and this differentiates his theology from theological liberalism, which speaks merely of God's love (love that smacks more of sentimentalism than of real love). His point of

---

[180] Forsyth, *Work*, 11-14.
[181] Forsyth, *Work*, 15.
[182] Forsyth, *Cruciality*, 5
[183] Forsyth, *Cruciality*, 6.

departure is that the first concern of Christ and revelation was not simply the fact that God's love was forgiving, but the purity of such love.[184] Sentimentality serves no one and only provides discouragement to those who read nothing but the literature of love. Forsyth sees the goal of such thinking gravitating towards a predominating attention being focused on a slushy love's morbid or immoral forms.[185]

Atonement is primarily the act of God; it alone makes any repentance of ours satisfactory to God and is an act of revolution so far as man is concerned.[186] This satisfaction, above all, meets the age in its need and impotence. It satisfies its need for a centre, for an authority, for a creative source, a guiding line, a north star, and a final goal.[187]

DML-J adopted these emphases and preached them regularly. DML-J's preaching replicates Forsyth's point that the atonement alone meets the needs of the present age. Outside of this, there is no hope for anyone. Man is lost and wanders about in his lostness, and he needs a fixed point, a true north.[188] God in the atonement provides this. He is critical of the then current religion, describing it as weak and opining that what it lacks is what the atoning cross supplies when viewed as the reconciling judgement of God towards the world.[189] We cannot separate God's holiness from the idea of judgement as the way through which grace becomes active. He speaks elsewhere of "holy grace and love" – another striking combination. This holy grace and love stir in the sinner's heart two important realities: self-judgement and self-condemnation. It also highlights the truth that Christ has accepted God's judgement on man's behalf.

In the New Testament's place for the atonement, Forsyth criticises the higher critics who involve themselves in theology that is gratuitous when it

---

[184] *Ibid.*
[185] Forsyth, *Cruciality*, 8.
[186] Forsyth, *Cruciality*, 7.
[187] Forsyth, *Cruciality*, 8.
[188] *Ibid.*
[189] Forsyth, *Cruciality*, 9.

seeks to create a combat of Jesus versus Paul, etc.[190] He rejects this approach without a second's thought. He views Jesus and Paul as preaching the same message and the one and only way of salvation – through the cross. He views Jesus' death as unique and inextricably joined with forgiveness, in opposition to the liberals. Man cannot atone for his sin, as the liberals so confidently affirm. Forsyth, with some justice, ridicules such teaching and sees it as removing Christ from the Godhead of grace and reduces Him to a mere though chief, means of grace to fellow seekers.[191] But, and here is vintage Lloyd-Jones in a sentence, a gospel church is not simply a band of professors, disciples or fellow-seekers. It is rather a community of believers in Christ, a fellowship of saints.[192] Forsyth does not view the Church as a "mixed multitude" of mere professors of religion, but as sinners who have experienced the redeeming grace of God in the Lord Jesus Christ. Neither Forsyth nor DML-J would have countenanced the idea that the church in Corinth is the model for the church in the twenty-first century. The only exception might be that many of the Corinthian church's problems concerned an overflow and abundance of spiritual life. Paul would not have to write such a letter to the churches in the West today, warning them of possessing and using too many spiritual gifts! That admitted, in some respects Paul's corrective letters demonstrate that the Corinthian church is not the model for church life today. Rather, they stand to bring the church under the discipline of the gospel in order that she will be conformed more closely to the divine ideal for the church on earth, including an abundant spiritual life. It is not the church as she existed in the first century that is to be our model in all things, but the teaching concerning the nature and composition of the Church found in the New Testament. The church on earth has within it the Body of Christ and is made up of members of His Body. Under God, it is repentance for sin and faith in the world's Redeemer that creates this membership. It is a cocktail of genuine believers and imposters, regardless of how diligent the eldership is in exercising loving church discipline. But the church must not hide behind the truth that man cannot see the heart of another,

---

[190] Forsyth, *Cruciality*, 13.

[191] Forsyth, *Cruciality*, 14.

[192] Forsyth, *Cruciality*, 14, 15; cf. Lloyd-Jones, *Knowing the Times*. (Edinburgh: Banner of Truth Trust, 1989), 28f.

therefore, let anyone who says they are Christians into full and practically 'irrevocable' church membership. However, and thankfully, I am not pursuing the issue of DML-J's ecclesiology because this is not the subject of this study.

In Forsyth's scheme, ecclesiology and soteriology are necessarily intertwined. In contradistinction to the new perspective on Paul 'movement',[193] Forsyth seeks to maintain the unity that these together display and require. When God reconciles a believer to Himself through the propitiation of Christ, he is by faith brought into the εκκλησια, the Church, the Body of Christ. Forsyth retains intact these two doctrines and does not seek to drive a wedge between them. Forsyth's ecclesiology demands that a church member has experienced God's saving grace. And that salvation is available only in the cross.

What, then, constitutes an evangelical church? Forsyth is forthright in providing the answer: it is a church that stands for the prime value of Christ's death as an atonement for sin made to a holy God. This truth elevates that death, he argues, above the greatest martyrdom or even the greatest witness to divine love.[194] The Church, then, is a body of the redeemed, of those who have personally entered by faith into the benefits of Christ's purchased redemption. Some writers have described the Gospels as the record of Christ's atoning death on the cross, with an introduction. Forsyth says that the Gospels stand at the very least on what Christ did in His atoning deed. The Gospels were written for a church that came into being with the power of the gospel coming into men's lives, and they give remarkable space to it.[195] Our Lord Himself gave the full meaning of the gospel (1 *Corinthians* 15:3; cf. 11:2). After his conversion to Christ on the Damascus Road (*Acts* 9), Paul received fuller instruction in the faith. He learned, in essence, that Christ died for our sins, and that His blood was shed so that those sins could be remitted. Paul learned that Christ's death established a new relationship with God, a new covenant

---

[193] This is linked with the name of N. T. Wright, and advocates a shift whereby justifying faith is moved from soteriology to ecclesiology,

[194] Forsyth, *Cruciality*, 15.

[195] Forsyth, *Cruciality*, 15, 16.

between God and men and that the entirety of Israel's history meant this, as do the Scriptures.[196]

Forsyth is clear on this point. The Christian faith with its unique understanding of the cross is a redemptive religion made in Heaven for the benefit of men on earth. This faith alone satisfies fully the holy righteousness of God and simultaneously deals with man's guilt. It does not consist in what Jesus taught, but in what He *did* in dying for the world's sins.[197] This emphasis comes through in DML-J's evangelistic preaching.[198] That Christ died for the world's sins was for him basic to the gospel. It was on this ground he was able to offer that salvation to the "whosoever," promising that it will be theirs on condition of repentance and faith. They would possess Christ as the Saviour, the new Creator. But "the Saviour" of what? Forsyth is clear on this. On Christ's death on the cross, he insists that Christians must learn that what was going on there was no less than God in Christ acting to reconcile the world to Himself. It certainly was not simply a display of magnificent heroism.[199] It was God intervening in Christ with a saving purpose. Paul bases this understanding on 2 *Corinthians* 5:19, his great passage on reconciliation.

Bearing all this in mind, Forsyth explained that the only cross the church can preach to the whole world is a theological one. Sentimentality has no place in the church's preaching. Contrary to the theological liberals who pollute many professing "reformed" and "evangelical" churches today, it is not good enough to preach the bare fact of the cross as a historical event. We must interpret the cross within its biblical context, and that interpretation must proclaim what *God* meant by the cross.[200] The emphasis here is on the cross, and Forsyth focuses on the cosmic application of the message of the cross as interpreted within its biblical

---

[196] Forsyth, *Cruciality*, 17, 18.
[197] Forsyth, *Cruciality*, 14.
[198] See, for example, the numerous such statements in his *Authentic Christianity* and in his other evangelistic sermons in the Appendix.
[199] Forsyth, *Work*, 30, 56, 57, 76, 82, 96, 99, 100, 108, 110, 114, 126, 133, 147.
[200] Forsyth, *Work*, 48.

context.[201] He makes the point that while salvation is a historical fact,[202] an event, it is not this that saves anyone. When interpreted theologically, it brings salvation to the world. As he wrote about this stupendous event, Paul could not but write emotionally about the cross. He could not have delivered a lecture on the cross because as he gazed upon it, he saw it through eyes that had been opened and cleansed by the Holy Spirit.[203] For him, the cross was a deeply emotional reality. DML-J saw this too. In his preaching, he put emotion into his proclamation of such a message, knowing that he could not preach it otherwise.

Forsyth goes on to explain the result of Christ's life-work (reconciliation) considered in its totality in permanently changing the relation between what he calls "collective man" and God.[204] He is not focussing on man as an individual, but on man understood collectively, generic man. It is mankind, humanity, the human race that Christ came to reconcile to God, through a reconciliation that has only one ground on which to rest – the atonement accomplished by Christ.[205] Further, this reconciliation has only one grand end – communion with God.[206] It is the world, considered as a whole, that Christ has reconciled.[207] This divine event succeeded in doing what nothing else in world history ever did – it reconciled the world to God. Reconciliation did not come about as a result of a process, however good.

Note the distinction that Forsyth indicates in his criticism of Hegel's philosophical position. In Hegel's mind, argues Forsyth, the world and everything in it was a process of God's grand idea. But it was merely a process. The fundamental distinction between a process and an act is that the former has nothing moral in it whereas the latter can be done only by

---

[201] Jones, *Reformation*, 50.
[202] Forsyth, *Work*, 53.
[203] Forsyth, *Work*, 51.
[204] Forsyth, *Work*, 54.
[205] Forsyth, *Work*, 56-58. See also the grand goal of reconciliation which is communion with God, 57, 68, 69.
[206] Forsyth, *Work*, 57, 68, 69, 94.
[207] Forsyth, *Work*, 65.

a responsible person. The act has in it the idea of will and responsibility, but a process is utterly devoid of morality,[208] as the political or peace process in Northern Ireland demonstrates so magnificently. This Hegelian notion of process lacks morality, says Forsyth. If Hegel is correct and the world is a process, then it does not need to be redeemed or reconciled to its Creator; nor is such reconciliation an historical and divine *fiat*. As a process, it is amoral, and the amoral has the tendency, when sinful man becomes involved, to degenerate into the immoral.[209] And this amoral process simply carries the world along. But an act is altogether different, because it can only be done by a moral agent, and involves the notion of will and personality and responsibility. Once you submit to this idea, 'process' cannot exist.

DML-J got hold of this idea, or rather this idea got hold of DML-J, and he presented it with power and conviction in his preaching ministry. He emphasised human responsibility for sin and also human responsibility for trusting the Christ of the cross. Forsyth recognised a *real* universalism inextricably linked to the Saviour's death for the world.[210] This *real* universalism is met many times in *The Work of Christ*. Forsyth's understanding of the atonement and its extent is fundamental to his theological position. The positive influence of Dale *vis-a-vis* the atonement may be traced in Forsyth's work with similar and at times identical phrases appearing throughout his work. Given that DML-J was also "taught" by both Dale and Forsyth, it is not surprising that we find similar and identical phrases being used by the Doctor in connection with the death of the Saviour.

---

[208] Forsyth, *Work*, 67.
[209] This point has been argued in relation to the Northern Ireland "peace process" - the amoral has degenerated into the immoral. Convicted terrorists were released under the Belfast Agreement of 1998 who then were given seats at the very top and heart of government, a reality that retraumatises their innocent victims.
[210] Forsyth, *Work*, 77, 85, 86, 93.

14

J. Denney's Soteriology

The book by Denney that influenced DML-J in his re-orientated thinking was his *The Death of Christ*. Calvin influenced Denney so far as his soteriology is concerned. Both these theologians saw the truth that Christ died for all men, for the world, as their written statements confirm. DML-J took on board Denney's treatment of the death of Christ, and the central tenets of his thinking found its way into DML-J's preaching. Examining his books, one cannot but be impressed with his biblicism. In this book, Denney proceeds similarly to Dale. In his introduction, he states that anyone minded to write on the death of Christ has to progress on the basis of two assumptions. One is that there is a New Testament, and the other, that Christ's death holds an important place in it. He says that accepting the factuality of the New Testament is the most important of the two, because denial of this means the denial of the place the cross has in it.[211]

Denney contended that there was such a thing as a New Testament. In his treatment of this central subject, he examines it in the synoptic Gospels, looks at the earliest Christian preaching in *Acts*, and then explores Paul's epistles. The epistle to the *Hebrews* is opened up, followed by the Johannine writings. He then scrutinises the importance of the death of Christ and examines how the modern mind views the atonement. Denney continues by investigating sin and the Divine reaction to it and concludes by evaluating the place of Christ and man in the atonement.

---

[211] Denney, *The Death of Christ*. (London: Hodder and Stoughton, 1902), 1.

This thorough piece of work paved the way for other scholarly treatments of this doctrine.[212] Denney writes freely of Christ in His death as being the atonement for the world's sin.[213] Christ gave His life for the life of the world, bearing on Himself its burden, and as the Lamb of God took away its sin. Indeed, the salvation of the world depends on what God has done in Christ. For Denney, and for the New Testament writers, Christ's atoning death corresponds to a universal need that then became the basis of a universal religion.[214]

God has provided this world with a Saviour Who will save it from its sin and also from sins' consequences. He says that Christ's death for all necessarily involved the death of all because of the inclusive character of that death.[215] In fact, Denney equates Christ's death with the death of all; in other words, when Jesus died, it was the death of all that He died.[216] Christ in His death on the cross thereby made the death of all men His own.[217] So Denney is clear about the cosmic dimension of the death of Christ – it was for the world, for the sins of the world, for all. Expounding Paul, Denney avers that God was actively engaged in Christ when He was reconciling the world – or rather as Denney elaborates it, nothing less than a world – to Himself.[218] But it was through Christ alone that that reconciliation became a reality. Without Christ in His death, reconciliation is voided. His atoning work was a work of reconciliation, and, in its global dimension, avails for no less than the world.[219] The good news is that the whole world may benefit from it. Denney concludes that God has reconciled the world to Himself because God in Christ has dealt

---

[212] For example, Leon L. Morris' *Apostolic Preaching of the Cross*, (Guildford: The Tyndale Press, 1972) and his *The Cross in the New Testament*, (Devon: Paternoster Press, 1976). Also J. R. W. Stott's *The Cross of Christ*. (Leicester: InterVarsity Press, 1986).
[213] Denney, *Death*, 217.
[214] Denney, *Death*, 118.
[215] Denney, *Death*, 141.
[216] Denney, *Death*, 142.
[217] Denney, *Death*, 143.
[218] Denney, *Death*, 144.
[219] Denney, *Death*, 145.

with the world's sin.[220] Christ on the cross took our place, and in so doing, identified with the world's sin.[221]

The sin of the world presented God with a problem.[222] Paul felt that this universal sin made a difference to God[223] because this sin was against God's righteousness. His righteousness had to be vindicated; God simply could not ignore this situation, and go on justifying men as if no problem had arisen on His part.[224] This point is most important, infers Denney. Sin affects God as well as man. As the Psalmist David expressed it, "Against You, You only, have I sinned and done this evil in Your sight" (*Psalm 51:4*). All sin is against God; it impugns His righteousness and holiness and is an attack on His honour and truthfulness. Denney reflects this in his soteriology. That's why Scripture defines propitiation in relation to the world's sin. God provided it so that He could maintain fellowship with man. Paul did not view the propitiation in terms of sacrifice or of it being vicarious,[225] he argues, but rather he taught that Christ understood in Himself the whole of humanity.[226] The implication is that through Christ's death humanity has suffered. It is the Son Who has taken the sin of the world to Himself and took it as all that it is to God. The result is that believers in Jesus can now be declared righteous. There is no restriction whatever in Denney's soteriology. He is clear: Christ died for us all, and that death that He took upon Himself is portrayed as the death of the whole sinful race.[227] God's love for the world is truly infinite, and it has now been made possible for the apostles of Christ and the evangelists to preach peace[228] to all men through Him. Denney asks if it is too rash to assume that there must be an intelligible connection between Christ's

---

[220] *Ibid.*
[221] Denney, *Death*, 149.
[222] Denney, *Death*, 173.
[223] Denney, *Death*, 168.
[224] *Ibid.*
[225] Denney, *Death*, 174.
[226] *Ibid.*
[227] Denney, *Death*, 147.
[228] *Ibid.* Cf. Ralph P. Martin, *Reconciliation*. (London: Marshall, Morgan and Scott, 1981) where he views 'reconciliation' and 'peace' as synonyms, 1981:139.

death and the sin of the world for which Christ in His blood is the propitiation?[229] It was this atoning death that demonstrated the great love of God for lost sinners.

That such a connection exists, Denney affirms somewhat indirectly. Looking at the cross, the New Testament bids us say, He bore our sins, He died our death, and only His infinite love can constrain us to confess this. Hence, it is in Christ's death that we find the *whole* secret of Christianity.[230] In His death, He takes the sin of the world on Himself and bears it away. By so doing, He has reconciled the world to Himself. In *Colossians*, when Paul refers to "the world" which is the object of reconciliation, it is no longer just the world of sinful men. It is the world on a much grander scale, and Paul presents the reconciliation of sinful men as part of this vaster reconciliatory work.[231] Denney affirms that Christ's person has undergone a kind of expansion from a historical to a cosmic significance and in line with the enlarged scope of the work of reconciliation.[232] His argument seems to be that if it is truly cosmic, then no problem exists for His not making atonement for the whole world. Hence, he can confidently affirm that through Christ in His death God has dealt effectually with the world's sin, accomplishing its removal.[233] This offering was made once for all,[234] necessitated the incarnation and is the explanation why God may remove the world's sin. Denney's frequent mention of "the sin of the world" is impressive and confirms God's will in sending the Redeemer to take responsibility for this work for the human race.[235]

The exclusivity of salvation is set forth clearly by Denney. There is salvation in no other than the Lamb because none but the Lamb was sent to take away the sin of the world. Hence, in Jesus Christ and Him crucified is the

---

[229] Denney, *Death*, 177.
[230] Denney, *Death*, 178.
[231] Denney, *Death*, 195.
[232] Denney, *Death*, 199.
[233] Denney, *Death*, 217.
[234] Denney, *Death*, 220.
[235] Denney, *Death*, 233.

entire hope of this sinful world.[236] So, the blood of Christ does something once for all, "all" being the operative term. It takes away global sin, Christ being the divinely provided propitiation for the world's sin (1 *John* 2:2). The object of God's love is the sinful world, and He has atoned for that world's sin. Denney affirms "where there is no atonement there is no gospel."[237] Evangelistically, Denney avers that this is the great gospel that wins souls. It alone tells of a sin-bearing, sin-expiating love that appeals for acceptance. It is this love that takes to itself the full responsibility of the sinner, and that unconditionally, without preparations, but with only one condition – that he abandons himself to it.[238]

This understanding is the biblical gospel. The moment sinners abandon themselves to the grace of God in Christ, that very moment God reconciles them to Himself. Only the preaching of a full salvation now has any promise of revival in it and refers to Wesley for confirmation.[239] Demonstrating his understanding of gospel appeal, Denney argues that what it comes to is that before God's mercy in Christ can be available to the sinner, the sinner must have a sufficient depth of penitence toward God. He must also be sufficiently earnest in his desire to be reconciled with the God Whom he offended by his sin, and desire holiness. There must also be a sufficient moral sincerity in the sinner. Otherwise, the marvellous grace of God would merely minister to sin.[240]

This point sounded strange when I read it, and Denney realised that this way of expressing it restricted the absolute freeness of the gospel. To him, it is to be explained only out of the love of God and the necessity of the sinner and not on the merits of men. He corrects this position by stating that Christ did not lay down His life for those who were sufficiently penitent for that would detract from His work as the propitiation for the whole world. Further, He bore all the sins of mankind that all might

---

[236] Denney, *Death*, 249.
[237] Denney, *Death*, 284.
[238] Denney, *Death*, 288.
[239] *Ibid.*
[240] Denney, *Death*, 291.

believe in Him and receive the gifts of repentance and forgiveness.[241] Preparationism of any kind was not part of Denney's scheme. Since Christ is the propitiation for the whole world, degrees of penitence or none at all, are irrelevant.

In any review of what experts say about the atonement, and in the context of DML-J's soteriology, not to take on board the soteriology of the Welsh Calvinistic Methodists would be awry. It is to this that we now turn.

---

[241] *Ibid*.

15

The Welsh Connection - John Jones, Talsarn (1796–1857)

John Jones of Tal-y-sarn was born in Dolwyddelan and brought up in a farming family with many connections with Nonconformist religion. He received no formal education and spoke only Welsh. Arriving to find work in Talsarn, Jones discovered his preaching gift and the Calvinistic Methodist Church ordained him to the Christian ministry in 1829, aged 33. Jones ministered in Talsarn until his death in 1857.

Alan Clifford asks,

> *Between his birth at Dolwyddelan to his death at Talysarn, was there any Welshman who brought more blessing to Wales through the preaching of Christ than he? Did any preacher present the Saviour of sinners more gloriously, eloquently and tenderly than he? Was there any minister whose heart throbbed with more love to Jesus and his fellow-men? Is there any better Spirit-anointed model for preachers today than the Christ-exalting John Jones Talsarn?*[242]

For Clifford, John Jones was incomparable – for his godliness, preaching ability, and sermon content, standing as he did within the great Welsh tradition of John Calvin's soteriology. Jones is well deserving of the epitaph

---

[242] Alan C. Clifford, in an article sent to me in September 2011, and used with permission.

"one of the greatest preachers in the history of Wales." It was men like John Jones, Talsarn who influenced DML-J's soteriology.

What, then, did John Jones believe the gospel message to be? The answer will provide an incontestable reason, under God, for the soteriology he adopted. Jones was extremely concerned about the theological and spiritual condition of his beloved Wales, and not least the Calvinistic Methodist Church in which he was a minister. In a letter requesting the help of Rev. Thomas Richard written in January 1841, Jones described what was happening in the church.[243] A culture of suspicion had arisen among the older generation of ministers towards John Jones' contemporaries concerning the content of their gospel preaching. Jones speaks of the spreading of rumours, party spirit, lying slanders, unfounded stories, gossip, suspicion, and the taking advantage of others.[244] They engaged in this behaviour at a time when God blessed the nation with a great evangelical awakening. The gospel preached by men like Jones was being owned and blessed of God to the salvation of numerous souls. It was in such a time of divine blessing that these pernicious things were happening. Countless people experienced great spiritual good at this time, as did the church in that land, yet how much more good would have been done had this anti-spiritual attitude not obtained among them.

What John Jones believed concerning the gospel and preached to all men everywhere was coming under serious criticism. This criticism was perpetrated by older Calvinistic Methodist ministers in North Wales and they were also subjected to unjustifiable criticism and condemnation, Rev. John Elias being the foremost of their critics.[245] John Jones describes Elias as someone who is prone to hot-headedness and to extremism in

---

[243] Jones, cited in Thomas, *Controversy*, 354.
[244] *Ibid.*, 327–354.
[245] *Ibid.*, 350.

everything he does.[246] Jones brackets Elias with three other unnamed individuals,[247] men of extremely narrow judgement.

That gospel "narrowness" exists is accepted. The Christian life is characterised by "narrowness" as is Christian doctrine. But there is a "narrowness" which exceeds biblical bounds and that exists where matters that are not clear in Scripture become the touchstone for those that are. Where philosophic and scholastic considerations become the method for interpreting plain Scripture, then biblical limits have been breached.

For John Jones and his ministerial brethren, certain older ministers were adopting a theological line that was damaging to evangelism. In fact, he charged them with promoting antinomianism. He said that they divided the Bible into two covenants in a most unfamiliar way. One covenant damned a portion of mankind, leaving it without any hope. The other covenant, however, safeguarded the remainder, before they even were conceived. He blamed the effects of these false beliefs for the many thousands of Welshmen who were decaying in antinomianism.[248]

Jones criticises this "division" very strongly and blames it on the high orthodox.[249] He highlights their preaching content and informs Thomas Richard that some ministers stress the necessity of preaching election, and emphasise the particular nature of the atonement. They stressed man's inability to do anything accompanying salvation, the covenant of works, and the imputation of Adam's first sin to his seed, etc.[250] The tone in which he catalogues these differences suggests that he rejected the preaching

---

[246] *Ibid.*

[247] *Ibid.* Cited in Thomas, *Controversy*, 350, D. E. Jenkins discovered that the three suppressed names were those of Henry Rees, John Hughes, Pontrobert, and John Jones, Tremadog. (M.A. Thesis, Liverpool University, 1924, p.178.

[248] John Jones, as cited in Thomas, *Controversy*, 351.

[249] It is at least arguable that high orthodoxy needs authentic Calvinism to provide the *raison d'être* for its very existence, just as in political matters consociationalism requires societal division as a rationale for its existence.

[250] *Ibid.*

content of those he criticises. Specifically, he rejected their view of the gospel that did despite to the gospel and the work of evangelism.

John Jones' theology and soteriology followed different contours. In evangelism, he saw it as unnecessary to stress election in preaching, even though election is what guarantees gospel success. He favoured a universal atonement such as was believed by Calvin and Amyraut. Regarding man's inability, Jones also complained of the manner of preaching by the older brethren. He described it as polemical and controversial and as being anti-evangelistic Their approach was not conducive to convincing a sinner of his spiritual and eternal danger or to pressing him to flee from God's coming wrath.[251] Angry preaching was not valuable in producing conversions. Pointing out the weaknesses in this approach, Jones believed that in order to demonstrate the wickedness and misery of man the preacher must emphasise certain truths. He must stress that the fault lies directly with the sinner and not in anything either in God or the atonement. To show the sinner how he became a sinner and then to point him to the covenant of works is to miss the point altogether.

When these older men preach the atonement, writes Jones, they stress the particularity of its design. Instead they ought to preach Christ and His cross as God's remedy for sin and urge sinners to flee to Him for refuge. Examined calmly, such preaching "quenches the Spirit" and undermines the very possibility of sinners being converted to Christ. When preaching on the work of the Spirit in a man's conversion, continues Jones, the emphasis is on man's inability to respond to the gospel until the Spirit commences His convicting work in the heart. They ought rather concentrate on pleading with lost sinners to seek Christ with all their hearts and give directions how to do this. Emphasising man's inability to come to Christ anaesthetises the sinner against any awareness of his spiritual and eternal danger and also against any urgency to run to Christ for salvation. This approach is deterministic in the extreme if not fatalistic – the sinner waits until God first touches him before he is under any obligation to trust the Saviour. If God does not touch

---

[251] Cited in Thomas, *Controversy*, 351.

his heart, then the reason is that God has not elected him to salvation. Therefore Christ had not died for him. That makes God, not the rebellious sinner, responsible for his eternal lostness in Hell. The motivation for preaching in the older men is to get their hearers to believe those things not necessary for salvation. Such preaching is spiritually fruitless. Jones complained of a cold orthodoxy that had gripped some older ministers, an emphasis on confessional correctness and an accompanying spiritual deadness. John Jones was broken-hearted because of this unacceptable ecclesiastical and spiritual situation, and the passionate way that he writes to Thomas Richard comes across in every line.

His second main concern was the desire in both parties to crave first place.[252] In his opinion, there was a drive to occupy thrones, to be pre-eminent. Ministers gathered around them "yes" men, who bowed to their every demand. This concern concurs with what Jones wrote about the content of preaching by these older men. If the preaching and message are sectarian, that is because those who do it are sectarian. And sectarianism pursues its paths in order to get what it wants, by whatever means and at whatever cost. They wanted to remove those brethren who were being used by God because they did not 'dot' *their* every 'i' and 'cross' *their* every 't' theologically. These older men were having a deadening effect on their congregations, believing this to be in agreement with reformed and biblical preaching. The younger ministers were effective evangelists, and their opponents suspected the genuineness of the work done under God's blessing by these gospel servants. This attitude approached speaking ill of the work of God's Spirit in the souls of convicted sinners.[253] So attempts were made to remove these servants legally; which attempts, thankfully, failed.

John Jones was a thorough gospel man, his great calling in life being to preach the gospel. To preach that, a man had to have a right grasp of the message of salvation. Jones feared that his ministerial colleagues had gone off on a tangent theologically that undermined the gospel. He knew

---

[252] Cited in Thomas, *Controversy*, 352.
[253] *Ibid.*

what he had to preach, and by God's enabling grace, he preached it. Had he been unconcerned about the preservation of the gospel, he would not have got into this doctrinal controversy. But, with Calvin, when someone attacks the gospel, a man would be an unfaithful servant if he did not rise to its defence.

Jones' ministry had a great appeal for and impact on DML-J, and many of John Jones' traits and attitudes are reflected in his ministry. Not least of these is that what those Calvinistic Methodists like John Jones believed and preached, DML-J believed and preached. Jones' soteriology was also DML-J's soteriology.

SECTION FOUR

Theology and Philosophy

16

DML-J - The Biblical Theologian

DML-J was pre-eminently a biblical theologian rather than a systematic theologian.[254] He had frequent conversations with his grandson, Christopher Catherwood, telling him that we must be "Bible Calvinists, not system Calvinists."[255] From 1952–1955 of his Westminster ministry, he delivered his Friday night lectures on the great doctrines of the Bible. After reflection, he concluded that it is better to teach and to learn Christian doctrine from the regular exposition of the text of Scripture.[256] Hence he changed his method to one in which he worked his way systematically through the text of Paul's letter to the *Romans*, commencing in 1955 and concluding in 1968, when he had reached *Romans* 14:17. This decision also explains the sermonic form of these *Romans* messages.[257]

DML-J's theology is essentially evangelistic – gospel-centred and gospel-focused. His evangelistic preaching is drawn out of the gospel as revealed in the Old and New Testaments. Like John Calvin, DML-J held as axiomatic the truth of *Deuteronomy* 29:29,

---

[254] Robert A. Peterson (Sen.), *Calvin and the Atonement*. (Ross-shire: Christian Focus Publications, 1999), 10.
[255] C. Catherwood, 2000:104. See also end note no.23.
[256] Lloyd-Jones, *God the Father*. (Eastbourne: David Cook Kingsway Communications Ltd, 2008). Note, no pagination in the early pages of this book.
[257] *Ibid.*

> *The secret things belong to the LORD our God, but those things that are revealed belong to us and to our children forever, that we may do all the words of this law.*[258]

Here, God's single will is *revealed* in a dualistic manner. His hidden will is inaccessible to fallen human minds, inscrutable to human thought processes and embedded deep within the eternal divine purpose. On the other hand, His revealed will is that which is made known in the gospel. This will can be accessed by men, and declares God's will for mankind (including the salvation of the human race).[259] This makes salvation certain to everyone who repents of his sin and trusts in the Lord Jesus Christ as his Saviour.

Delving into the unrevealed will of God is an exercise in philosophising and DML-J was very distrustful of philosophy in all its forms, because it claims to be able to answer all the questions of life. He saw no place for philosophy in a theological course, only apologetics, but even this in a curtailed way. To him, the doctrines of election and predestination are included in the "secret things" that we do not and cannot understand because we are not meant to understand them.[260] These "secret things belong to the LORD" and are, therefore, inevitable because of Who God is. To Him belong ultimate knowledge and wisdom and understanding, and for fallen human beings to try to understand this is not only to eat forbidden fruit, but is to make ourselves and our attempts utterly foolish.

The Doctor teaches that this inevitability is something in which to rejoice. That this great God has even revealed anything to us is a matter of praise, being under no obligation to tell us anything. By our sin we have given up any claim we imagined we had upon Him.[261] So far as he was concerned, he could think of nothing more amazing than that our God has let us into some of His secrets. However, his impatience with philosophers is

---

[258] NKJV (Nashville: Thomas Nelson Inc., 1982) is used throughout this book by the author unless otherwise stated.
[259] Selection #14, 94, 203, 238, 242, 243.
[260] Lloyd-Jones, *Living Waters*, 276.
[261] *Ibid.*, 277.

oft repeated in his sermons. He sees the philosopher as someone who maintains that he has the innate ability to understand all truth, so he conjures up a philosophical system that will embrace everything. This system must be complete with nothing left that he cannot explain.[262]

DML-J sees the drift into philosophy as an evidence of "the wiles of the devil" (*Ephesians* 6:11) and adds that philosophy is the single greatest enemy of Christian faith and truth.[263] His objection to philosophy is because of man's ultimate confidence in human reason. Man's conviction that the power of his mind to arrive at the truth and be able to understand it is what makes the claim so ridiculous. DML-J sees the ultimate problem being where final authority lies.[264] This emphasis on human authority challenges what DML-J holds as axiomatic for the Christian Faith by denying what the Scriptures clearly teach. The past 150 years or so have seen flesh being put on this idea with the emergence of the higher critical movement that emanated mainly from German scholarship. This scholarship saw the pride of man coming into its own with Scripture being made subject to human understanding and man sits in judgement on the Bible. This error says that men can decide what is acceptable and what is not.[265] It effectively subordinates Scripture to human reason. Like Luther whom he greatly admired, DML-J followed the advice of Staupitz to the budding Reformer when he counselled him to extract all his theology from the Bible alone. He was not to derive it from the systems of the schools.[266] The relevance of this to his disapproval of scholasticism is pertinent.

DML-J criticised Thomas Aquinas (1225–1274), the great Catholic thinker, despite his respect for him as a great theologian and philosopher. He lived when western culture was at a critical juncture. The Aristotelian *corpus* in Latin translation had just arrived, and this event reopened the question of the relation between faith and reason and called into question the *modus*

---

[262] Lloyd-Jones, *The Christian Warfare*. (Edinburgh: Banner of Truth Trust, 1976), 170.
[263] Lloyd-Jones, *Warfare*, 164.
[264] *Ibid*.
[265] Lloyd-Jones, *Prove All Things*. (Eastbourne: Kingsway Publications, 1985), 43.
[266] J. H. Merle D'Aubigné, *The Life and Times of Martin Luther*. (No place of publication: Moody Press, 1960), 41.

vivendi[267] that had obtained for centuries. DML-J accuses Aquinas of doing great harm to Protestantism by taking Aristotelian philosophy and attaching it to the Christian faith – something that theologians cannot do without serious results.[268] He denied that Greek philosophy can contribute anything to our understanding of the Christian faith. He went further claiming that it is a positive hindrance to such an understanding, even though Aquinas was able to satisfy most people that he succeeded in creating this marriage.[269]

The Doctor would have agreed heartily with Tertullian (c.150–225) who asked what Athens has to do with Jerusalem or the Academy with the Church? What he meant was that Greek thought and philosophy have nothing to do with Christianity and its biblical heritage.[270] The importation of Greek ideas into what were Hebrew thought-forms was not conducive to arriving at a true and accurate understanding of the biblical text. The New Testament was written in Greek, but the thought forms were essentially Semitic because the penmen were almost all Jews.[271]

However, DML-J sees as the explanation for this dalliance with philosophy the preoccupation of philosophers with "vain deceit" and "profane and vain babblings."[272] He proffers the view that the reason the church in the nineteenth century became "respectable" and better educated was that with these intellectual advances, people required a more cultured ministry. Proclaiming the simple and unvarnished gospel was not sufficient, and they had to illustrate their sermons by quotations from the Greek philosophers, the Latin classics, and the great poets. In mid-Victorian times, the church

---

[267] An agreement or arrangement which permits parties in conflict to co-exist peacefully, either indefinitely or until a final settlement is achieved.
[268] Lloyd-Jones, *Joy Unspeakable*, (Eastbourne: Kingsway Publications, 1984), 112. See also McGrath, *Christian Theology*. (Oxford: Blackwell Publishing, 2001), 226.
[269] *Ibid.*
[270] Tertullian himself provides a wonderful example of *the fact that denying* a connection puts one in a position in which one is *likely to make just such a connection without realising it.*
[271] Luke is the exception to this.
[272] *The Christian Warfare*, 168, 173.

wanted to be more intellectually respectable[273] so she set about training men of culture and intellect for the ministry, irrespective of whether or not they were Christians.

Again, he demonstrates his impatience with philosophy. When medieval philosophical method and content intrude upon what the Scriptures teach *vis-a-vis* the atonement, his impatience is intensified. The Scriptures must be allowed to speak for themselves and to reveal their God-inspired message to the world. Any interference of sinful man must not be allowed to blunt its cutting edge. For DML-J, the Bible must be central at all times, and what God revealed to mankind accepted as the sole and final authority in all matters of faith and practice. His point was that we have to be content with the revealed things, and not pry into those things that have been kept "secret." It was those matters that possessed an eternal significance that belonged to God alone while other eternally significant concerns He has revealed to men.[274] Into these matters, sinful human minds must not pry. Their rightful domain requires a wall to be built around it so that what God has been pleased to reveal suffices the believer.

DML-J's view and Calvin's show coalescence at its most impressive. Calvin preaches about the foolishness of the disciples desire to inquire into the secrets of God.[275] To make such inquiry into these eternal secrets, one must be God, and sinful human beings are not God, nor are they like Him. Indeed, the Reformer displays his wisdom when he says that it is best to ignore what God does not teach us in the Scripture and to stick to what He does.[276] Where Scripture is silent, we, too, must remain silent. This truth states the limit beyond which we must not pass.[277] Calvin also cautions against going beyond Scripture in any formulation of doctrine. While expounding Christ's correction of His disciples' wrong views about

---

[273] *The Christian Warfare*, 174, 175.
[274] G. T. Manley and R. K. Harrison, as cited in the *New Bible Commentary Revised*, Eds Guthrie, et al, (London, InterVarsity Press, 1970), 225.
[275] Calvin's Sermons, *The Deity of Christ*, Ed. Leroy Nixon. (Grand Rapids, Eerdmans, 1950), 223.
[276] *Ibid.*, 222.
[277] *Ibid.*, 225.

the establishing of the Kingdom of God, Calvin expands his teaching and application. They and we must be satisfied with what God reveals, and to live by that. To do otherwise is confusion. There is even to this day forbidden fruit that God tells us not to eat. What we need to know, He has made known.[278]

Calvin warns that those who wish to delve into the forbidden fruit of God's secrets are no different to those who wish to outsmart Him.[279] This statement agrees totally with the position of DML-J. His calling as a gospel preacher was to go as far as Scripture allows, but no further. There must be no anxiety to inquire beyond God's revealed will in Scripture, because, argues Calvin, this is nothing but foolish curiosity and sinful inquisitiveness. In his gospel preaching, DML-J, agreeing with Calvin, went fully as far as Scripture went, but no further. DML-J states that the main feature of Calvin's thought is that he bases everything on the Bible without borrowing from the worldly wisdom of men. He refuses to create an admixture of Aristotelian philosophy and Scripture, the effect being that philosophy and Scripture become regarded as equal and cited Aquinas' *Summa* as an example. DML-J contended that for Calvin, the Bible was the only authority and the only 'philosophy' he permits is that which is drawn directly from Holy Scripture.[280]

DML-J insists that our understanding of Bible truth is logical and that one thing flows from the other. "Logical necessity" is a term he uses.[281] There is a logic that is proper, and such logic leads to conclusions that are consistent with the clear teaching of Scripture.[282] He draws this logic out in his sermons. For example, he states that God is in control of everything

---

[278] *Ibid.*, 226.

[279] *Ibid.*

[280] Lloyd-Jones, *Times*, (Edinburgh: Banner of Truth Trust, 1989), 35.

[281] Lloyd-Jones, *Let Everyone Praise the Lord*, (Bridgend: Bryntirion Press, 1999), 111.

[282] I am indebted to the Rev. Eric J. Alexander who taught me this during his preaching visit to Northern Ireland while I was assistant minister in Ballymena, Co. Antrim that "biblical doctrines must lead to biblical conclusions, and not necessarily to logical ones." This valuable lesson has stayed with me for these four decades, and has been my bedrock on many occasions.

and that all things and men are in His hands. The "logical necessity" that flows from this, he asserts, is that it is incumbent upon us to know the truth about God, the Bible being the truth devoted to that theme.

However, there is a logic that is improper and leads to conclusions that are, at times, inconsistent with the clear teaching of Scripture and at others appear to contradict that teaching. Take, for example, the doctrine of the atonement, which is the focus of this study. When the Bible states, "Behold! The Lamb of God who takes away the sin of the world!" (*John* 1:29), logical consistency requires an interpretation that affirms the Lamb of God did something on the cross that had a bearing on the sin of the world – He took it away. Logical inconsistency will say it was the sin of the 'elect' world that Christ took away, not the sin of the world, as John the Baptist affirms. Such exegetical fallacies are commonplace in some Reformed writing.[283] Further, logical inconsistency will say that because the Lamb of God has taken away the sin of the world, all will thereby be saved. DML-J will have none of that false logic because it is exegetically indefensible. It is this "human authority" that challenges what DML-J holds as axiomatic for the Christian faith by denying what the Scriptures clearly teach.

DML-J understands the term "secret" as what provides the ultimate explanation of things,[284] and this is not something that concerns him. If the Bible does not reveal it, it is not important for us to know it. What is important for us to know, God has revealed in the Scriptures. In humility, he is quite prepared to leave this with God and is not interested in theological speculation because that does not help anyone to become or live as a Christian. Nor does it help a preacher declare the gospel. In fact, it imposes serious limitations on him especially when he comes to expound texts such as *Isaiah* 53:6, *John* 1:29; 3:16, 17; 4:42; 1 *Timothy* 4:10; *Hebrews* 2:9; 2 *Peter* 3:9; 1 *John* 2:2; 4:14, to select at random a few examples of the Bible's universalistic texts. Indeed, speculation, by definition, is not Scriptural doctrine. Therefore, it is a major obstacle to true evangelistic preaching.

---

[283] E.g., John Owen's *Death of Death*. (London: Banner of Truth Trust, 1983 rpnt).
[284] Lloyd-Jones, *God the Father*, 6.

17

Dr Martyn Lloyd-Jones and Limited Atonement

DML-J's self-understanding as "an evangelist" is extraordinarily important in this study. He also defined himself pre-eminently as a biblical rather than a systematic theologian.[285] Additionally, and according to Rev. Dr R. T. Kendall when he was Minister of Westminster Chapel he spoke to DML-J about his views on the atonement. While engaged in his doctoral research, Kendall contacted DML-J and sought his views on John Calvin's theology of the atonement. When DML-J examined Calvin's commentaries for himself,[286] he expressed surprise at finding "how frequently universalistic Calvin's statements were."[287] During a two-week period, being excited by his discoveries, DML-J phoned Dr Kendall repeatedly and exclaimed, "I've found another one!" During one such discussion with Kendall, referring to the doctrine of limited atonement, he confessed, "I never preached it, you know ... only once on *Romans* 5:15 and I was in great difficulty when I did so." Mrs Bethan Lloyd-Jones was present when he said this to Kendall, and interjected, "I have never believed it and I never will."[288] One can reasonably conclude that these together serve to

---

[285] C. Catherwood, as stated in Lloyd-Jones, *Joy Unspeakable*. (Eastbourne: Kingsway Publications, 1984), 12.

[286] Elwell in Elwell (Ed), *Evangelical Dictionary*, 99, is incorrect to limit Calvin's teaching on general to his *Sermons on Isaiah's Prophecy of the Death and Passion of Christ*. If he looks carefully he will see numerous references to the universal aspect of the atonement throughout his writings, and not least in his evangelistic sermons.

[287] Alan C Clifford, *The Good Doctor* (Norwich: Charenton Reformed Publishing, 2003), 273/4.

[288] *Ibid*. Like her husband, she too was a medical doctor.

consolidate the view that DML-J did not believe in "limited atonement,"[289] as understood and defined by scholasticism-influenced theologians, such as Dr John Owen and his followers.

However, a point of clarification and correction is required at this point. When we examine DML-J's sermons, we discover that he made a mistake when he said that he ever only preached on limited atonement once. This lapse of memory concealed the fact that he preached on limited atonement in his sermon on *Ephesians* 5:25, claiming that Christ "died for the church. He died for nobody else."[290] It is important to note that these sermons were preached between 1959 and 1960 and at the same time as he preached his *Romans* 5:15 sermons. So this idea was evidently in his mind at that time. This time was also the year (1959) that the Banner of Truth Trust published John Owen's *The Death of Death in the Death of Christ*. This convergence is interesting. DML-J was a founder of the Banner of Truth Trust, and clearly he did not wish to cause a theological or commercial stir at a time when the Trust was in its infancy. So it appears that he provided that particular limited atonement emphasis at that time, despite this emphasis being well out of sync with his view of the atonement as demonstrated in his published sermons. Prior to and after this date, his gospel emphasis was on the universality of the gospel provision for the world. In fact his references to the universality of the atonement are ubiquitous throughout his writings, so this statement in *Ephesians* 5:25 is uncharacteristic of his view on the atonement. This point will be considered in greater depth later.

Just after the completion of his doctoral research at Oxford University but before its acceptance in 1977, Kendall was called to be visiting minister at Westminster Chapel, London for a period of six months. It was at that time that the Westminster Conference invited Kendall to

---

[289] Rev. J. J. Murray asserted that DML-J did believe in limited atonement at a conference marking the 31st anniversary of the death of Lloyd-Jones in Larne, Northern Ireland in March 2012.

[290] Lloyd-Jones, *Life in the Spirit*, (Edinburgh: Banner of Truth Trust, 1973), 145.

read a paper entitled *John Cotton – First English Calvinist?*,[291] and chaired by DML-J. Kendall discloses that he made public some of his findings on John Calvin's treatment of the extent of the atonement in that paper. The expectation among attendees was that Cotton would confirm the widely held view that Calvin believed in a "limited atonement." Kendall continues, alleging that only Dr Lloyd-Jones and he were prepared for the stunned reaction of those present at that conference.[292] There was a clear 'reaction' within the ministers of the Reformed world to the contents of Kendall's paper that questioned the 'received wisdom' regarding Calvin's soteriology. Kendall claimed that DML-J held his paper in high regard. Both the reaction of ministers and the approval of DML-J guaranteed that Kendall's work would be widely read and studied. Clearly, then, as with Calvin, DML-J would find it difficult to view, as his theological heirs, those who embrace limited atonement as expressed historically in the TULIP acronym. Indeed, the same applies also to the various shades and derivatives of Westminster theology.[293] So there is a clear difference between DML-J's view of the atonement and that held by other Reformed preachers who are convinced Westminster soteriology men. It also highlights a difference between DML-J's soteriology and that taught in the Westminster standards.

---

[291] R. T. Kendall, (1997). *Calvin and English Calvinism to 1649*. (Oxford: Oxford University Press, 1981 and Carlisle: Paternoster Press, 1997), v.

[292] *Ibid*.

[293] When DML-J was asked about the advisability of the Westminster Confession of Faith being used as the doctrinal basis of a newly founded Reformed church at Gateshead in the north of England, his enquirers were met by, "No, no. That's much too Calvinistic." By this he meant that it was theologically too extreme in its orientation, and not sufficiently close to the evangelistic preaching of John Calvin. This information was furnished by Rev. Dr Alan C. Clifford, minister, Norwich Reformed Church, England, who was privy to this conversation, and is used with permission. It is rather telling, if not a bit strange, that Gary Brady in his "Lunch Time Lecture: A Few Words about Forewords" on the "The Shorter Writings of Dr Martyn Lloyd-Jones," delivered on Monday 17 May 2010 in London, said, "That was an ideal for Lloyd-Jones 'loyalty to the Truth as expressed in the Westminster Confession of Faith with a marked catholicity of spirit.'" Had Brady known of the above conversation, he would not and could not have written what he did. Indeed, had he read with care DML-J's published sermons, he could not possibly have drawn that unwarranted conclusion.

What is it that accounts for this difference in view? Being aware that the antinomy concerning the secret and revealed will of God is unfathomable to the sinful human mind, DML-J accepted this divine antinomy and dichotomy[294] with impressive ease. This philosophy tends to prefer everything nicely tied up and with no 'loose ends,' and is a characteristic of Aristotle's philosophy. He never allowed his preaching to be restrained by his grasp of the secret will of God (or lack of it!). He preached the gospel and offered Christ as the Saviour of the world to everyone. Regarding the atonement, the revealed divine will is both universal and conditional, but His secret will is particular and unconditional. In all its facets, the gospel relates to the revealed will of God. Election and predestination relate to God's secret will, or eternal counsel, both of which DML-J accepted and taught in due proportion and where appropriate in the course of his methodical expository preaching ministry. Indeed, in keeping with most Reformed preachers, he did not believe in preaching election and predestination to unbelievers. The only exception he allowed to this was when he wanted to humble the proud Pharisees and educate them about the absolute sovereignty of God in salvation. So when DML-J preached the gospel, following Calvin, he presents the gospel message of the cross of Christ as a universal call to all to repentance and faith. This message was what he preached without exception or distinction – in line with what God has revealed in the Scriptures. But, and here's the encouraging point for all gospel preachers, what guarantees the success of the gospel is the fact that the message will be efficacious in the elect, according to God's hidden counsel. Election and predestination guarantee gospel success.

It was this truth that undergirded DML-J's evangelistic ministry. He constantly affirmed that we cannot save ourselves, and if ever we are to be saved and reconciled to God, He must do it. At no time did he speculate about who was elect or non-elect. Nor did the order of the divine decrees

---

[294] Clifford, *Calvinus*, (Norwich: Charenton Reformed Publishing, 1996), 7.

bother him.[295] He preached the everlasting gospel in the power of the Holy Spirit and left the outcome with the Lord, the textual context determining the particular emphasis. Unlike some of his ministerial colleagues who were scholastic in orientation, he preached and offered Christ to all who heard him in the hope that they will respond in faith to Christ. He offered Christ's salvation to all and left the results with God. That explains why he never kept an account of those who professed conversion under his ministry, nor did he call sinners to come forward in order to receive Christ. Alter calls and emotional appeals were not part of his *modus operandi*.

DML-J was anxious to point out that, given fallen man's spiritual deadness and frailty, he is unable to understand what God is doing. Therefore, it is always best not to become tormented by what we cannot understand. He is truly a foolish man who allows what he is unsure of to rob him of that of which he is sure.[296] In any case, it is good to know that God knows more than we do![297] The inscrutability and incomprehensibility of God to the human mind ought to keep us humble, and that man is foolish who tries to unravel the divine immensities and infinities. Indeed, the truly humble position in the light of the doctrine of God's absolute sovereignty in salvation, is to accept this "delicate balance"[298] in humility and with a sense of awe, gratitude and wonder. DML-J would describe the proper attitude before such mysteries in the words of Charles Wesley where the believer is to be "lost in wonder, love and praise."[299]

---

[295] In an email from Dr Clifford, dated 30th September 2014, and used with permission, he writes concerning the order of the divine decrees that in the view of Amyraut, there is no sequential order. He continues, "Amyraut made this clear during his 'heresy' trial at the Synod of Alençon (1637): '...though...this Decree [is] diverse, yet it was formed in God in one and the self-same moment, without any succession of thought, or order of priority and posteriority. The will of this most supreme and incomprehensible Lord, being but one only eternal act in him;...' (John Quick, *Synodicon in Gallia Reformata* (1692), ii. 355)." DML-J held this view too, and would have heartily commended Amyraut's understanding.

[296] Attributed to one of the Puritans whose name I have not been able to trace.

[297] This sentiment has been attributed to C. H. Spurgeon by Dr John F. MacArthur.

[298] Clifford, *Calvinus*, 7.

[299] Chas Wesley, from the hymn *"Love divine, all loves excelling."*

DML-J had no difficulty in preaching to the unconverted sinner, telling him, "God loves you, and Christ died for you." High Calvinists argue that this is language that ought not to be used, on the basis that we do not know if God loves that particular individual or if Christ has died for him, or not. In other words, the sinner being preached to has first to ascertain whether or not God loves him and Christ died for him before he could venture on Christ for salvation. In DML-J's view, this is perverted logic as well as very bad biblical theology.

18

Reformed Scholasticism

Preaching a loving, God-appointed Saviour for the world (in line with *John* 1:29; 3:16; 4:42; 1 *Timothy* 4:10; *Hebrews* 2:9; 1 *John* 2:2; 4:14), is surely one of the highest privileges that can come to any man. But to make this agree with the particularistic interpretation, the term "world" has to be re-interpreted to mean "the world of the elect" or "the world of believers." In some cases, to fit the particularistic model, "the world" has to be understood as "the church."[300] This specific re-writing of the truth has sadly convinced many who accept it as gospel. High Calvinists do not appear to have the theological capacity to accept the plain wording and teaching of the revealed will of God. They feel obliged to force the text of Scripture into the scholastic mould invented in medieval times by philosophers such as Aristotle. For example, Owen re-interprets Paul's "all" to mean "elect individuals of all sorts." But there is nothing in the text of Scripture to warrant such a re-writing of the apostle's words, and certainly no exegetical necessity for doing so. This indefensible and unjustified exegetical fallacy has neutered evangelism in every church that accepts this as God's truth.

DML-J did not follow Owen in this regard but was a faithful follower of Calvin in his interpretative practice, refusing to introduce speculative classifications as limiting factors in his understanding and presentation of the gospel. Such dubious and flawed methodology has done enormous and incalculable damage to the cause of the gospel in the world and has

---

[300] Elwell as in Elwell (Ed), *Evangelical Dictionary*, 99.

left the church impoverished as a result. I can identify two manifestations of this flawed approach that effectively destroyed the "finely-tuned biblical balance" of Calvin's thought. (1) The ultra-orthodoxy of Calvin's successor in Geneva, Theodore Beza (1519–1605), and (2) the unfortunate response of Jakob Arminius' (1560–1609) sub-orthodoxy.[301] Bezan rationalistic ultra-orthodoxy, because of its insistence on the application of strict logic to Calvin's biblical theology, led to hyper-Calvinism, with all its strangling effects. It did this by focusing on what he believed to be the character of God's secret will. On the other hand, the strict logical rationalism of Arminius denied divine election and substituted instead an emphasis on free-will that made *man* the captain of his eternal destiny, rather than the sovereign God. Had that antagonism not surfaced, the Reformed Church might well have fewer divisions, together with less "bad blood" between brethren, than it possesses today, and the church a much healthier one.

Since DML-J did not have formal theological training, it is difficult to argue that his exegesis is faulty so far as his understanding of the content of the gospel is concerned. He was clearly a man raised up by God at a particular time and to do a particular work in His Kingdom. The accurate exegesis of the plain text of Scripture by the Doctor is clearly biblical and soundly Calvinistic. While appreciating some of Owen's points, he is much happier in the company of men like Richard Baxter, John Davenant, Matthew Henry, and a host of other like-minded brethren, not to neglect the Welsh Calvinistic Methodist Fathers. It is rather surprising and incongruent that, having founded the London Theological Seminary, the research centre should have been called the John Owen Centre, but that's just one of life's anomalies!

One of the marks of DML-J's preaching ministry is his acceptance of the Reformed principle, namely that Christ's reconciling work on the cross was sufficient for all but efficient only for the elect. The "sufficiency/efficiency"

---

[301] Clifford, *Calvinus*, 11.

paradigm,[302] is accepted as axiomatic within the Reformed churches.[303] This theory provides albeit an imperfect means for understanding the outworking of God's will. It teaches that Christ's death purchased and made available to the whole world a great salvation, while simultaneously guaranteeing the eternal salvation of God's elect people on condition of faith. Faith is not the cause of justification, but the condition, a point made by Prof. Dale Ralph Davis.[304] In his commentary on Judges, Davis makes exactly this point with reference to repentance, faith's conjoined twin. Similarly, as in Calvin, faith is the God-appointed condition for receiving His salvation, but it is certainly not a cause of it. The cause of faith-received salvation must surely be God's great heart of compassion towards lost mankind. DML-J repeatedly calls sinners to turn from their wicked ways in repentance and trust Christ alone for salvation, in line with Davis' point. It is not, then, election or predestination that Scripture reveals is the pathway to salvation; rather salvation is received by faith in Christ alone and this is the pathway to it. This paradigm combines the universal and the particular in a way that tries, despite its weakness, to help fallen sinners make some sense of the biblical balance of the gospel.

In DML-J's theological scheme, the gospel is 'for all,' is to be preached 'to all' because Christ died 'for all,' and God's great salvation is offered 'to all' because Christ has made it available 'to all' who will repent of their sins and trust in Him alone for salvation. DML-J preached this mighty missionary and evangelistic message with all the spiritual energy the Holy Spirit supplied, holding nothing back. He offered to and pleaded with and urged sinners, *qua* sinners, to come to Christ in faith, depending on nothing but His great mercy and His call to them to come. The elect have God's salvation guaranteed to them, but the same remedy for the same malady is made available to all. Whoever believes the gospel will enter into the exprience and reality of God's salvation.

---

[302] Calvin accepted this paradigm as applicable generally, though he denied that it was applicable as an explanation of 1 *John* 2:2. See his commentary on this verse.
[303] This paradigm, linked with the names of Peter Lombard and Thomas Aquinas, is challenged by some Reformed theologians, on which see the discussion below for further details.
[304] Dale Ralph Davis, *Judges*. (Ross-shire: Christian Focus, 2000 (rpnt. 2007)), 134.

Scholasticism had in effect driven the Scriptures from their proper place into a mystifying darkness.[305] Reformed scholasticism had delivered a similar disservice to the church. It is but an evangelical expression of the old liberal rationalism of a bygone age. It is that attempt to explain everything there is about God. Neo-rationalism and its reformed counterpart take the mystery out of everything – out of life and out of worship.[306] When they have taken the mystery out of our religion, they have taken God out because God is the Ultimate Mystery. Or, as the philosophers put it, He is the *Mysterium Tremendum*; evangelicals, on the other hand, refer to Him as *"the God and Father of our Lord Jesus Christ."*[307] The result is an absence of awe and wonder when worshippers come into His presence because liberal Protestants have reduced God to a few philosophical propositions. He is a 'god' in name only. Reformed scholasticism has the tendency to deplore loose ends in theology, preferring philosophical exactness of definition and leaving no room for unanswered questions, or mystery or astonishment or wonder. In the atonement debate, rationalists have engaged in this and have created a form of Calvinism that is anti-evangelistic as well as being anti-evangelical. They enjoy debate about matters not essential to salvation; they engage in theological philosophy that has some effect but only on the mind. They deplore emotion or feelings in religion, which probably explains why their services are so dull, boring and cold. They are theologically "orthodox" but utterly lifeless. This dead orthodoxy, they argue, is true Reformed worship.

How different were the convictions of DML-J! True, he was an exact exegete and theologian who shunned sloppiness and carelessness. But he knew the place the emotions occupied in religion and gave proper expression to the emotions in his preaching, praying and worship. If religion does not touch the heart at the deepest level, it is not Christianity, he would assert. He preached about "knowing God" which meant coming into a personal saving relationship with God through faith in

---

[305] J. H. Merle D'Aubigné, *The Reformation in England*. (London: Banner of Truth Trust, 1853/1971), 89.

[306] Aiden W. Tozer, *Worship – The Missing Jewel*. (n.d., 3).

[307] Paul in *Romans* 15:6; 2 *Corinthians* 11:31; *Ephesians* 1:3; *Collosians*.1:3; and Peter in 1 *Peter* 1:3.

our Lord Jesus Christ. Intellectual knowledge of God and ourselves is fundamental to becoming Christian believers.[308] But accompanying this is the experiential aspect. When sinners come to know God truly, this is profoundly experimental; they experience something deeply spiritual – God's grace and mercy in bringing them to salvation. Salvation does not touch just the mind; it touches the heart also, and the will. There is intellectual knowledge of God but there is also emotional knowledge of God, and these two must not be separated. Let us never forget that there is emotional intelligence in the spiritual realm just as there is in management and psychological circles. Scholastic Calvinists appear to have forgotten this altogether. So for them, the atonement is merely about theories, debating the pros and cons of the various offered theories of the atonement, and refuting the theories that do not reflect their philosophical mindset. For them, it is the particular theory of the atonement that saves sinners, not the atonement whose benefits are received by faith in Christ alone. R. W. Dale taught DML-J this crucial lesson that it is not any particular theory of the atonement that saves sinners, but Christ in His death on Calvary. The Doctor never forgot the importance of this lesson.

DML-J greatly admired Luther, whose opposition to scholasticism is acknowledged.[309] In his later years, scholastic divinity was Luther's *pet aversion*. D'Aubigné tells us that he trembled with righteous anger whenever Aristotle's name was spoken in his presence. He even went so far as to allege that if Aristotle had not been a man, he should have taken him for a devil.[310] The dry teaching of the Schoolmen disgusted him.[311] The church of his day highly revered their outputs. In fact, he preferred the mystics to the schoolmen. Aristotle's "works righteousness" was anathema to him.[312] His heart rejoiced when the biblical training of young theologians would be inclined to discredit Aristotle.[313] So strong was his hatred of

---

[308] Cf. Calvin's opening words in his *Institutes of the Christian Religion*.
[309] D'Aubigné, *Luther*, 192.
[310] D'Aubigné, *Luther*, 19.
[311] *Ibid.*, 68, 184, 278.
[312] *Ibid*, 70.
[313] *Ibid.*, 83.

Aristotle that Luther went so far as to place Aristotle with darkness and divinity with light.[314] He rejected the empty systems invented by the Schoolmen, preferring the plainness of gospel teaching instead.[315] When Cajetan set about refuting Luther's "errors," he stated that he would not go to the works of the scholastics but to Scripture. However, he forgot his stated intention and went straight to the council of the popes and to the schoolmen.[316] In fact, D'Aubigné writes that the finger of blame was pointed at the English Reformers accusing them of preaching heresy because they "set the Scriptures in the supreme place within the life of the church."[317] This practice of making Scripture supreme is still not cherished by the church today. Today, Reformed scholastics do exactly the same when debating with biblical theologians. For them, Scripture patently is not a sufficient and authoritative source from which to dig their theology but has to be supplemented by writings of human origin. Indeed, some Reformed churches so strongly repudiate the use of man-made compositions in their worship that it is rather ironic that they place such importance on man-made confessions when it comes to summarising what they believe. As a matter of principle, they would not have compositions of human origin used in the sung part of public worship. As another matter of principle, they elevate their Confession of Faith to a level practically above Scripture.[318] When the schoolmen set about explaining the doctrine of the church, D'Aubigné affirms that by the time they had provided their explanation, it was unrecognisable.[319] It is rather telling that when Thomas Cranmer became professor of divinity at Cambridge University in the 1530s, he instructed his ministerial students, "Christ sendeth his hearers to the Scriptures, and not to the church."[320]

---

[314] *Ibid.*, 85.

[315] *Ibid.*, 180. See also, D'Aubigné, *Reformation England 1*, 350 where the translation of the Bible into the vulgar tongue was viewed as the springboard from which church divisions emerge.

[316] *Ibid.*, 203.

[317] D'Aubigné, *Reformation England 1*, 153.

[318] Cf. D'Aubigné, *Reformation England 1*, 262.

[319] *Ibid.*, 264.

[320] D'Aubigné, *Reformation England 1*, 437.

The two great adversaries of Christianity are hierarchism and rationalism, and the reformers attacked these enemies. Rationalism is how the Schoolmen[321] went about their philosophising and theologising, resulting in confusion rather than clarity. Luther was pleased that in his discussions with Dr Eck, "the scales of scholastic theology ... fell then entirely from before my eyes..."[322] Bilney also testifies that at a certain point in his life when he became a Christian, he "began to smell the word of God, and forsook the doctors of the schools and such fooleries."[323]

DML-J imbibed Luther's position on rationalism and scholasticism and made it his very own. He was as intolerant of this dangerous diversion as was Luther. He saw how Romanism had almost entirely hidden the gospel under the debris of scholasticism and feared that this had been happening in his day.

---

[321] D'Aubigné, *Reformation England 1*, 151 where Erasmus was described as a schoolman not a believer. The author adds an interesting sidelight into the mindset of the schoolmen when he wrote about Erasmus, "He wanted the people to obey the church and not trouble themselves about the Scriptures. ... Nothing terrifies the defenders of human traditions so much as the Word of God."
[322] *Ibid.*, 281.
[323] D'Aubigné, *Reformation England 1*, 204.

19

Lloyd-Jones the Evangelist

The Reformed constituency around the world regards DML-J's preaching very highly. His preaching and teaching ministry has built up countless believers in their "most holy faith," and has been the means under God of bringing many into His Kingdom. It has sustained many Christians, including ministers, who have found the going tough at times. God used DML-J's preaching ministry to call many men into the Christian ministry.[324] Their hearts have been lifted up within them and brought to fall down before the infinite majesty of the living God in adoring worship. He has mentored, without knowing it, countless ministers around the world. Further, he has been the most effective trainer they had as to the content and method of the Christian Reformed Faith. He taught them what the gospel is, how a sinner becomes a Christian, and what the church is meant to be, the why, how and what of preaching, etc. DML-J has been instrumental in these, and in many other, ways.

However, given the clarity and power with which he preached the gospel, it is noteworthy if not regrettable that many of those who admire him, would not share the Doctor's soteriology. In the house of his friends, there are those who believe that he believed and taught the doctrine of limited atonement,[325] and who would argue the case despite voluminous evidence

---

[324] It was my reading of his *Preaching and Preachers* that God's call to me into the Christian ministry was crystallised, validated and confirmed.
[325] Rev. J. J. Murray made this statement publically and in my hearing at the Puritan and Reformed Conference in Northern Ireland in 2012.

to the contrary. Perhaps one reason for this is that many of the Doctor's earlier publications were "teaching" sermons rather than evangelistic sermons. This created the impression that DML-J did not believe that Christ died for the sins of the world, for all mankind,[326] for the whole universe.[327] It created the wrong notion that he opposed offering Christ as Saviour to all,[328] that He is the Son of God the Saviour of the world,[329] that God appointed him as the Redeemer of the world,[330] and that He does not desire the death of the sinner but that he might come to Him and live. Many refuse to see that DML-J followed closely in the footsteps of John Calvin, who had a message of salvation for all mankind. Even his "teaching" sermons do not convey the impression that he believed in and taught limited atonement.

Another reason for this attitude to DML-J's theology is the same as that used to teach that Calvin believed and taught limited atonement. Many of the advocates of this theory have read anything and everything but Calvin's writings – his sermons, commentaries and Institutes. They have studied the writings of later Calvinists (arguably, a misnomer in some cases) and have concluded, on the basis of a second-hand religion, that Calvin believed as Beza and Owen believed. But how mistaken they are. The Banner of Truth Trust published most of DML-J's major writings. It either regards Amyraldianism as being within the Reformed Faith and church (as evidenced by the number of Amyraldian authors whose works it has published). Or it suffers from theological schizophrenia and does not know it. It is a staunch "five-point" Calvinist publishing house. Therefore only those authors who subscribe to the human mnemonic, TULIP, have their books published by it. Nothing could be further from the truth, however. The Trust embraces both true Calvinism as well as Owenism; it embraces Amyraldianism as well as Bezan theology;

---

[326] See #71, 115, 138, 358.
[327] See #119, 257, 265, 275, 302
[328] See #30, 32, 35, 36, 48, 49, 63, 70, 103, 105, 127, 143, 145, 183, 314, 319.
[329] See #4, 6, 60, 88, 89, 90, 91, 95, 96, 99, 100, 116, 117, 118, 167, 169, 170, 172, 174, 179, 184, 187, 189, 209, 232, 236, 238, 261, 271, 280, 283, 286, 298, 308, 315, 317, 327, 331, 335, 345, 346, 357.
[330] See #248.

Baxterianism as well as Helmism. So it is wrong to assume that because the Trust publishes a particular man's works, that he necessarily belongs to the Trust's theological camp. In the case of DML-J, it is abundantly clear that he does not belong to the Owenite camp but dwells happily within the camp of John Calvin, Amyraut, Baxter and their followers. In other words, DML-J is an authentic Calvinist, who promotes authentic Christianity by preaching an authentic Calvinistic gospel.

It is also most telling that DML-J spoke only once or twice at the Banner of Truth Ministers Conference held each Spring at Leicester University. This absence provoked the questions, such as, why was this, and why did he not speak at the conference after 1963?[331] One reason is that DML-J did not think that a book publishing Trust should be involved in organising conferences for ministers. One can't help thinking that there may be more to his absence from the Leicester conference than meets the eye. The work of publishing good Christian literature was the *raison d'etre* of the Banner of Truth Trust, and this was DML-J's understanding of its purpose. The Christian public must be thankful to God that the Trust published 'good' Christian literature, not least that of the Doctor's.

Iain H. Murray, one-time assistant to DML-J at Westminster Chapel, London, and long time friend, was given the task of writing the official biography of the Doctor. His words are of inestimable interest at this point. Murray writes:

> *To the critic there is inconsistency in ML-J's gospel preaching. He preaches man's inability and absolute dependence upon God but then he speaks of the arms of divine mercy thrown open to all, of the love of God in Christ ready to embrace all, of an atonement freely offered as a gift for all. But such an 'inconsistency' belongs in Scripture itself. Certainly there is a universal love revealed in Scripture and its wonder is not to be belittled. But the love that saves is the love made known to those who, having heard of their lost*

---

[331] Email from Dr Alan C. Clifford (used with permission) who attended Westminster Chapel between 1963 and 1966, and was present at the Leicester Ministers Conference on the last occasion when the Doctor spoke. This was July 1964..

condition and entire undeservedness, are ready to be saved by grace alone. One emphasis in preaching belongs to men unhumbled in their natural pride and another to those who have come to an end of themselves. When it comes to addressing the latter the preacher has to be as unfettered as Scripture is unfettered in the proclamation of salvation to all.[332]

Murray recognises the "apparent" inconsistency in DML-J's gospel preaching, but he freely admits it is those who are critical of the Doctor's gospel preaching that hold this view. Unlike his critics, DML-J could live with the paradoxes of Scripture and give each aspect of truth its due weight. He made no attempt to suppress these antinomies, or to re-write Scripture to comply with man-made canons of confessional correctness.[333] The preacher holds that God is sovereign in salvation and that it is His work exclusively; it is monergistic. He also holds, in harmonious tension, that the provision of the gospel, as revealed, is for all men indiscriminately and is to be received by faith in Christ alone – Calvin's precise position.[334] Like Calvin, DML-J speaks of the arms of divine mercy being thrown wide open to all with God's love ready to embrace all. Salvation belongs to the Lord (*Jonah* 2:9), but God extends His saving love to all because He wants all to be saved. Murray is correct; DML-J is simply following the inconsistency of Scripture because he too is "captive to the word."[335] High Calvinists recognise Scripture's "inconsistencies" but they try to fix them by removing these "apparent" Scriptural "inconsistencies." The result is something sub-biblical. In his preaching, DML-J was as unfettered as is Scripture. This freeness in preaching the gospel is as it should be.

The raises the question: how unfettered are Reformed preachers in preaching Christ, the Son of God, the Saviour of the world? How free is their offer of Christ as Saviour of all? For DML-J, he did not know, nor did he care, whether or not a man was of the elect when he preached Christ. He knew he was a sinner, of the world, lost, guilty, godless, without strength, and that was enough to offer Christ to him as his Saviour. In

---

[332] Iain H. Murray, 1995:xxx.
[333] Clifford, *Atonement*, 111.
[334] Wendel, 273
[335] Martin Luther's unforgettable phrase.

this, he was reflecting Thomas Chalmers' position. Nor did the sinner have to know, first of all, that he was of the elect before he could come to Christ in repentance and faith. High Calvinism implies that possessing this knowledge is a necessary prerequisite before the sinner can come to Christ for salvation, since, according to it, Christ died only for the elect. This prior knowledge erects an unnecessary obstacle to the poor lost anxious sinner! It engenders hopelessness! The scholastic Calvinists give the very clear impression that this is the case, as do hyper-Calvinists. If the sinner is in Adam, as all men *are*, then Christ died for him.[336] That is sufficient warrant for the preacher to offer Christ to him as a complete Saviour, and it is sufficient warrant for every sinner to come to Christ in repentance and faith.

Happily, this was "the beloved Doctor's" approach. It is the approach that gospel preachers must take today if the churches are not to disappear into oblivion. Following the Doctor in this regard will restore to the churches the only message that glorifies God and that He blesses to the salvation of His elect.

---

[336] He "bled for Adam's helpless race," as Chas. Wesley put it in his hymn, *"And can it be that I should gain...."*

SECTION FIVE

Doctrinal Issues And Controversies

20

The Atonement – a Controversial Doctrine

That atonement doctrine has become a controversial one none will deny. That said, it is a fact that all theologians agree that the Church is to proclaim the gospel to all nations (*Mark* 16:15).[337] But what does that mean? Does it mean that Christ in His death is a sufficient Saviour for the whole human race? What does *that* mean? Is the gospel to be preached in the full knowledge that Christ's finished work is, by design, sufficient to save the world? Are ministers to preach it knowing it is now available to all and is effectual to save all who believe in Christ? Or was Christ's death sufficient only for the salvation of the elect?

Indeed, did DML-J mean by "sufficient for all" what the limited atonement advocates mean? This camp sees it as a "bare sufficiency," making it merely adequate to cover mankind's sin, having the potential to cover the sins of all men. But something can be sufficient for a purpose without it being designed for that purpose. Douty's illustration helps here. Imagine a multi-millionaire moving into your street with sufficient wealth to pay the debts of everyone living there. However, he decided, despite that, that his wealth would be of no help to them because he had previously decided it was only for the relief of his friends who lived elsewhere.[338]

This illustration explains clearly the logical fallacy of the limited atonement understanding of "sufficiency." Of what use is a "sufficient for all"

---

[337] Here Mark speaks of preaching the Gospel to every creature.
[338] Douty, *Death of Christ*, 35, 36.

atonement if God has not designed it for all? It is surely a miserly God Who would provide atonement that is "sufficient for all" but not intended for all. But our God deals in super-abundance, liberality, generosity. If the atonement is sufficient only for those for whom it is efficient, then the use of "sufficient" is redundant. Such a naked sufficiency, propounded by Beza and followed by Owen,[339] is of no use to guilty sinners because they in effect "deprive the universal sufficiency of the atonement of all its value."[340] Smeaton adds his point that Christ's "sacrifice was of infinite value, and sufficient to cancel sin, though infinitely great."[341] Again, here is naked sufficiency that in effect tells us nothing. What particular redemptionists mean is merely that Christ's death had intrinsic sufficient value, that this is what was intended and that therefore it was sufficient, in and of itself, to cover mankind's sins.[342]

Irish Archbishop James Ussher (1581–1656) gives an illuminating description of a limited atonement preacher. He is a comprehensively deceived man because he thinks that by preaching what he describes as a bare sufficiency in Christ's death yields a sufficient ground of reassurance to the distraught soul.[343] Ussher's point is powerful. A provisional sufficiency for all but not intended for all is not sufficient for all after all. If God had designed it that Christ came to die for the elect only, then how could a sacrificial death of infinite worth, in itself, afford any basis for offering salvation to all?[344] Dr John Davenant (1576–1641), a representative at the Synod of Dordt, agrees with Ussher on this point. If a thing is merely sufficient, it cannot on that basis avail for all.[345] The sufficiency/efficiency paradigm of Christ's atonement, properly understood, is critical for Davenant.

---

[339] Clifford, *Atonement*, 74. This idea was originally propounded by Peter Lombard in the 12th century.
[340] *Ibid.*
[341] Smeaton, 1871/1991:48.
[342] Douty, *Death of Christ*, 35.
[343] Ussher, as cited in Douty, *Death of Christ*, 35.
[344] Douty, *Death of Christ*, 35.
[345] Davenant, *Dissertation on the Death of Christ*. (Shropshire: Quinta Press, 1832/2006), 79.

Refreshments were being offered to the small congregation after the evening service. A lady asked me what kind of tea I wanted, and named Darjeeling, Earl Grey and English Breakfast tea. This offer of any tea was as wide open as it could be, despite the examples. I opted for Darjeeling tea. The lady searched for a Darjeeling tea bag, but to her embarrassment, found none. That got me thinking about the gospel. Do limited atonement men realise what they are saying when they hold *that* understanding of the atonement alongside making a free offer of the gospel to all men? If so, they would realise that they were doing exactly what my friend was doing with the tea. She made a totally genuine offer of any variety of tea to me but did not know that there was no Darjeeling tea. She was rather discomfited at finding this out. The limited atonement men say they *know* Christ did not die for all men, but proceed to offer Christ freely to sinners for whom the Saviour did not, in their view, die. This position is clearly contradictory if not hypocritical; in fact, it is worse because these men are knowingly offering a Saviour to sinners for whom, in their view, He shed not a drop of His blood. That is deceptive. Their defence is that they do not know who the elect are, so they offer the gospel freely to all. But that is no defence because they freely admit that Christ did not die for all, yet they proceed to offer a Christ Whom they believe did not die for all, to all. Those contradictions are strong arguments in favour of Calvin's soteriology of universal atonement and of that also held by Baxter and by DML-J.

Davenant claimed that the schoolmen never thought to defend a sufficiency only and to deny, as some of them do, that Christ died for all,[346] a most pertinent point, if true. The Middle Ages Schoolmen's paradigm presents a helpful, though not flawless, explanation of the distinction between what God had intended and what actually resulted. They taught, that in the intention of God, Christ died sufficiently for all, but not all believed the gospel, save the elect. Hence, there is no necessity to opt for the one or the other when both biblical emphases can be accommodated most adequately.[347] DML-J did this in his preaching. With other Christian

---

[346] Davenant (rpnt), 2006:52.
[347] See Clifford, *Atonement*, 74.

preachers, he believed that Christ died for all, for mankind, but only those who believed in Christ were saved, the elect.[348] He avoided all rationalism and speculation, yet provided a rational interpretation of all the Scriptural data. Douty suggests that what the ultra-reformed men do is to transfer the expression "sufficient" from Christ's intention in dying to the mere intrinsic value of Christ's death *per se*. He sees this as a new idea and not one supported by the great swathe of church history.[349] This understanding suggests that those who followed the Beza/Owen line were promoting a novel idea not found in Calvin or in Scripture. Indeed, many Reformed theologians[350] maintain a universal dimension to the death of Christ in keeping with the Lombardian paradigm. The inevitable conclusion is that no gospel preacher can be authorised to offer salvation to all men if Christ did not die for all. To do so is to offer something that is simply not designed for them nor available to them. Hence, before ever coming to Christ for salvation, the sinner must first ascertain whether or not he is of the elect.

Thomas Chalmers faced this paradox as a theological professor in Scotland. Clifford quotes from his *Institutes of Theology* where the first Moderator of the Free Church of Scotland provides the aptest illustration.

> *'If Christ died only for the elect, and not for all'* then ministers *'are puzzled to understand how they should proceed with the calls and invitations of the gospel. ... Now for the specific end of conversion, the available scripture is not that Christ laid down His life for the sheep, but that Christ is set forth as a propitiation for the sins of the world. It is not because I know myself to be one of the sheep, or one of the elect, but because I know myself to be one of the world, that I take to myself the calls and promises of the New Testament.*[351]

Chalmers makes a most important point of evangelistic theology. Preachers are not to concern themselves with who is or is not the elect but are to

---

[348] See Selection #163, 164, 165, etc.
[349] Douty, *Death of Christ* 36.
[350] For example, Rev. Profs John Murray and Donald Macleod, etc.
[351] Chalmers as cited in Clifford, *Amyraut Affirmed*, 63.

view every hearer as being by nature "of the world" therefore in great need of Christ. Nor are they to be so cautious that they refuse to offer Christ's salvation to all if they believe, for fear that the non-elect might believe and be saved! They are not to delve into eternal mysteries or even into the eternal counsel of God. Rather they are to declare the revealed will of God to their hearers, and that is, says Chalmers, that Christ died as the "propitiation for the sins of the [whole] world" (1 *John* 2:2).

God's revealed will could not be clearer. God loves the world and sent His Son to die for it. Therefore, there is salvation for all who turn from their sin and trust in the Lord Jesus Christ alone for salvation. Hearers are not to concern themselves with whether or not they are of the elect or are accounted among the sheep, for these are impossible quests prior to conversion. Rather they are to see themselves as guilty worldlings who urgently need the Saviour, and then to see that God has provided such a Saviour for the whole world, and to flee to Him without delay.

Davis concurs with Chalmers on this point. The Old Testament scholar recognises that sinful man cannot plumb the depths of God. When there is recognised "tension" in God's dealings with the sinful race, this, too, must be acknowledged. Davis notes the tension that exists in God's bosom,[352] the tension between judgement and grace. That there is tension in Scripture between them no one denies. This is "revealed" tension. This tension is not confined to the text of Scripture but is integral to God's holy character.[353] Davis explains that Jehovah (YHWH) is the God whose holiness demands He judges His people. The heart of this same God moves Him to spare His people the judgement they so richly deserve.[354] It is a further illustration of dualism in God's will. He wants to judge all people for their sinful rebellion against Him, His holy nature demanding such a response, yet He also wants to save them by His grace. What His secret will is in this matter is something about which Scripture remains silent. But it does shut us up to believing what He was pleased to reveal in Scripture.

---

[352] Davis, *Judges*, 135.
[353] *Ibid.*,
[354] Davis, *Judges*, 134, 135.

Reformed theologians have readily accepted the existence of God's secret and revealed wills. They have also acknowledged, albeit with qualification, the "sufficiency/efficiency" paradigm given by Peter Lombard and used by Reformed theologians ever since though not uncritically. That it has its detractors is freely admitted; however, they have not offered any better paradigm to explain the antinomies of Scripture *vis-a-vis* the atonement, its difficulties notwithstanding. Furthermore, finding a suitable model that satisfactorily accommodates all the Scriptural data may prove to be elusive, and a possible better approach is to draw from various models those aspects that support a biblical interpretation.

An illustration from the world of science might help to explain this contentious subject. Scientists debate whether or not light is made up of particles or waves. It appears that if light is the one, it cannot at the same time be the other. Scientists work on the basis that light can be and is understood as being both particles and waves, and can perform the necessary experiments to prove this. Scientists use this working hypothesis to explain virtually mutually exclusive features of light. The wave-particle duality does not seem to provide any problems, both metaphors being happily accepted within the world of quantum mechanics as reasonable ways of understanding light. It explains ideas that allegedly are mutually exclusive and mutually contradictory. Particles have mass but waves transfer energy. Light does both these things. Thanks to Einstein in 1905 we can now with confidence accept this duality – a duality created by God and discovered by men. Einstein found that light is not only a photon, it is also a continuous field of waves. Although apparently contradictory, this discovery is what made Einstein the genius he was. Light is by nature mysterious and in his scientific work, he chose which metaphor best suited the problem with which he was then working. Light sometimes acts like a particle and sometimes like a wave. Both are demonstrably true and one part of this duality separated off from the other is in reality a half-truth. As J. I. Packer so rightly puts it, "a half-truth masquerading as the whole truth becomes a complete untruth."[355]

---

[355] Packer's introductory essay to Owen's *Death of Death*, 2.

In common idiom, we talk about the general and the particular, and we understand how these are related. The particular is in the general, so if a thing is generally true, any particular of it is also true. Or we could say that the particular is a manifestation of the general. Nor do we have difficulties in the dualism of believing in the special love a man has for his wife and children and also the general love he has for his neighbours. God commands both for His people, obliging them to exercise both kinds of love.

Emil Brunner makes interesting points on this issue when he writes about spiritual men learning to reconcile God's wrath or anger, with sinful man. He argues for the indispensableness of this dualism. Only where God is known as One Who, outside of Christ, is angry, but Who in Christ is pure love, does faith in Christ become a real decision, and Christ's atonement a real turning-point. For Brunner, the dualisms of holiness and love, revelation and concealment, mercy and anger must go together and must not be dissolved without serious consequences. These include the destroying of the seriousness of what occurred at the cross where mercy and wrath, love and grace, punishment and forgiveness married in an indissoluble union. Where this dualism is not believed to be in line with the facts, the sheer mystery of Calvary would be destroyed.

It is difficult to believe that the acceptance of dualisms such as mercy and wrath residing within the same God together with the rejection of universalism and particularity also within the same God's plan of redemption, is so complex an issue to accept with equal ease. Unless, of course, there are plots afoot to defend a particularistic dogmatic position over against a more biblical one. To depart from the balance of Scripture is to depart from the God Who breathed out Scripture, a serious accusation.

We can only satisfactorily understand the atonement debate when we give both the universal and the particular their proper place. As Dr Clifford so rightly said,[356] if scientists have no difficulty in accepting the Einsteinian theory of dualism within their spheres, why cannot Owenite theologians

---

[356] Email to me on 15th February, 2014. Used with permission.

accept the much less problematic idea of duality that is so clearly taught in Scripture? DML-J had no difficulty understanding this divine duality; nor was he conscience-stricken as a preacher because he offered a real salvation to real sinners *qua* sinners, believing that Christ had died for all men. He warned sinners not to turn their backs on the salvation Christ purchased for them.[357] God demonstrates His overflowing generosity to all men in His gracious attitude to mankind as displayed in the death of Christ. The limited atonement camp has cast a dark cloud over the goodness of God to all mankind. They had diminished, if not removed altogether (in some cases), common grace, and disparaged God's extraordinary liberality when He sent His Son to save humanity. God is not less bountiful than He declared Himself to be. His sovereignty over all things, including the salvation of sinful men, must not be allowed to diminish His countless acts of goodness to all (*Psalm* 145:9). And the highest good He shows them is surely in sending His Son to die for all, namely, for those who deserved the very opposite. To do or believe otherwise is to detract from His glory.

Contrary to A. W. Pink's (1886–1952) extreme statement that God does not love those who despise Him, even a worldling such as Judas who then betrayed the Saviour was called "Friend" by Jesus in Gethsemane (*Matthew* 26:50). So extreme is Pink's soteriology that it is difficult to spot any likeness in it to that presented in the New Testament. It is also difficult to see much resemblance between Pink's theology and the theology of DML-J. Reading his chapter on the sovereignty of God in salvation[358] was something I experienced as claustrophobic and depressing despite the numerous proof texts he used to make his argument, a practice Helm condemns. His Trinitarian approach does nothing to allay these feelings. Unlike other Reformed writers who can take the broad sweep of Scripture, Pink focuses exclusively on those texts that support the conclusions he wishes to draw.[359] The sovereignty of God in salvation is a doctrine that

---

[357] Selection #67, 169, 212, 221, 229, 272.

[358] A. W. Pink, *The Sovereignty of God*. (London: Banner of Truth Trust, 1961), 45–73.

[359] G. I. Williamson, *The Westminster Confession of Faith*. (Philadelphia: Presbyterian and Reformed Publishing Company, 1964), 81, does similarly, if not somewhat unconvincingly, when he tries to explain the biblical texts that bear on the universal aspect of the atonement.

DML-J held and preached regularly. But he was a big enough intellect and heart to know that God holds much of the teaching on His sovereignty within His bosom, and He has not revealed that to men. What he did do was to take what God had revealed in Scripture and expound that without entering any caveat whatever. He allowed Scripture to speak for itself, and to be its own interpreter.[360] His reading of the biblical text was identical to that which any reasonable man reading it would take from it.

But Pink, starting from a limited redemptionist position, selected those texts that favoured that viewpoint and marshalled them to draw an inevitable conclusion. His conclusion is that Christ in His sovereignty did not love all, did not die for all but only for the elect, and that Christ's atonement was necessarily limited.[361] In effect, he started knowing the conclusion he wanted to draw, discarded the evidence that did not take him in that direction, and selected other suitable data as evidence for that conclusion. This truly is a suspect method if ever there was one. It is amazing, from one viewpoint, that the Banner of Truth Trust published such a methodologically and theologically flawed work. However, from another, it was a foregone conclusion that this is the type of book it would publish, confirming, as it does, its limited atonement Owenite position.

What is strange is that Pink with his trenchant particularism seemed to allow for a slender universal aspect to the atonement when he wrote that

> *The glory of God consists not merely in that He is Highest, but in that being high He stooped in lowly love to bear the burden of His own sinful creatures, for it is written, 'God was in Christ, reconciling the world unto Himself' (2 Corinthians 5:19).*[362]

He is careful, of course, to counterbalance this with a quotation from *Acts* 20:28 where God is said to have purchased His church with His

---

[360] WCF, 1:IX. See also Philip, *Confession*, 17. See also William Cowper's hymn, *God moves in a mysterious way*, where he makes the same point.
[361] This methodology is followed by limited redemptionists, as in Williamson, *Confession*, 81.
[362] Pink, *Sovereignty*, 151.

blood.[363] This tactic is used so as not to convey the impression that he fully endorsed the universalist emphasis of Paul in 2 *Corinthians* 5:19. It is probably a case of Pink and authentic Calvinists such as DML-J using the same vocabulary but working to a different dictionary. They use the same terms but put different meanings into them. Pink illustrates this when he understands the term "the world" to mean "the world of the elect."

---

[363] *Ibid.*

21

Donald Macleod (b. 1940)

Prof. Donald Macleod (b. 1940) is held in high esteem within Reformed circles both as a preacher and as a theologian. His numerous articles and his many books identify a man with a fertile mind and an impressive critical facility. As a Presbyterian, he is committed, on paper, to Westminster soteriology, which demands a limited atonement view. Critical of DML-J on various fronts,[364] Macleod interestingly holds to a broader soteriology than the Westminster Confession of Faith (WCF) would allow. While committed to limited atonement in its design and application aspects, he is also committed to the universal aspect of the atonement as revealed in Scripture, in which all who believe in Christ will be saved. Macleod holds that the eternal God loves the whole world, the world for which the Saviour died. Hence, God calls us to imitate that depth and breadth of love for humanity that God the Father demonstrated when He gave His only Son for it (*John* 3:16).

Macleod argues that after Jesus invited nothing less than the whole world to come to Him, he imagines the situation where the human race comes to Him. He asks if the Saviour can keep His promise to give them rest, answering in the affirmative. He says that Jesus can teach them all and carry all their burdens. He alone is the One Who can meet their deepest needs and deliver them from every anxiety they will ever have. He can

---

[364] His lack of formal theological training/education, his views on the Holy Spirit, his doctrine of the sacraments, his ecclesiology and churchmanship, to name a few areas.

restore them to wholeness and make them free. The One Who can do this is not only the Messiah of the Jews but also of the whole world. In this, our Lord was calling Israel back to her true vocation as the vehicle through which God would bless the world. God is the universal Saviour.

Provided Macleod is not imposing Aristotelian or scholastic limitations on the meaning of the words used, he is making clear in these statements a number of important things. *First*, God's love for the world has a depth and a breadth that is unmatchable. *Second*, His gospel invitations are addressed to the whole world. *Third*, He has the wherewithal to meet every need that mankind has and presents to Him. And, *fourth*, Jesus the Messiah was anointed for the whole world, and it is the whole world that God will bless through Israel.

This way of explaining it is authentic Calvinist, or Amyraldian, language and doctrine because it is Scriptural language. DML-J uses exactly this language when preaching the gospel and also when teaching the saints.[365] He does not force the texts of Scripture through some confessional sieve but allows them to speak their own God-breathed message. It was this factor that, under the Holy Spirit's blessing, accounts for the authority with which DML-J preached the everlasting gospel.

In his book, *From Glory to Golgotha,* Macleod re-affirms, without confessing so much, that his understanding of the atonement is authentically Calvinistic; his soteriology is not Owenite. How he squares this with his subscription to the WCF is a matter for another day.

But notwithstanding his cutting criticisms of Amyraldianism – which view he unashamedly adopts – Macleod's understanding of the atonement differs nothing from that espoused by Calvin. Where Macleod's soteriological views depart from that of authentic Calvinism, as taught by Calvin, Amyraut, Daillé, Baxter, etc., then I'd be very interested in seeing. As for me, I see no clear blue water between their views on the atonement and his.

---

[365] See the Appendix.

In his published criticisms of Amyraldianism, Macleod is doing what he knows best – stirring the theological pot in order to get a reaction. It is here that he manifests a level of theological confusion. In a review article in *Evangelical Quarterly*,[366] Macleod consistently confuses Amyraldianism with Arminianism, at times giving the impression that this is deliberate.[367] This ploy cannot be because of a lack of theological knowledge or insight, but betrays, sadly, a dogma-driven rather than a data-driven *modus operandi*. Amyraldianism is as different from Arminianism as it is from high Calvinism. It alone maintains, not only the balanced biblicism of John Calvin, but of the Bible itself. He also confuses authentic Calvinism with the high orthodoxy of later Calvinism, even in his weighty and well-presented opposition to Amyraldianism.

In his opening salvo, he mistakenly portrays Amyraldianism as the biblical middle way, offering what he calls a balanced alternative to both Calvinism and Arminianism. To be fair to the professor, he acknowledges that Amyraldianism is biblical and offers a needed corrective to the extremes of both (high) scholastic Calvinism and Arminianism. Because of his high regard for Calvin's balanced biblicism, Macleod is acknowledging further that Amyraldianism is authentic Calvinism and reflects the Bible's middle way between the extremes that have arisen post-reformation, namely, high Calvinism and Arminianism.

Macleod is correct when he avers that reformed theology has at no time ruled out such language as that God loves all men and Christ died for all.[368] As a respected Reformed theologian, he offers a most welcome admission and corrective. That is precisely the point made by authentic Calvinists. Sadly, not a few professing Reformed preachers frown on such statements, and "demonise" those who hold such an authentically Reformed view. We commend Prin. Macleod for emphasising this point,

---

[366] EQ, 81:3, 2009:210.
[367] Williamson makes the same mistake (*Confession*, 80).
[368] Taking an almost contrary view is Dr Matthew McMahon who describes Amyraldianism, or authentic Calvinism, as an error, and incorrectly and without foundation links it with the Pelagian heresy (*Amyraut and Hypothetical Universalism*, The Puritan Hard Drive, 2004:2, 3).

one that many Reformed evangelicals must surely appreciate and accept. It is thrilling to see him articulating this biblical truth so well.

That 'Christ died for all men' is obvious within authentic Calvinism. The Owenite position that Christ died only for the elect is, according to Macleod, "profoundly non-evangelical," and, I might add, profoundly non- or, worse, anti-evangelistic. Sadly, many lesser theological thinkers proclaim a message that is designed by them not to give the slightest impression that Christ died for all men. They do not want to tell sinners that God loves all men, "the world," (*John* 3:16). This misunderstanding has robbed Reformed evangelicalism of its verve and warm-hearted compassion for the lost. Baptist minister, R. E. O. White says with conviction, the Christian pastor believes that it is possible for every living creature to be redeemed. White calls every man to surrender himself to Christ who loves everyone he had made.[369] DML-J's son in law, the late Lord Catherwood, at a Christian Union meeting I attended while a student at Leeds Polytechnic in the early 1970s, made the point that every man is redeemable. Such compassion reflects a wider and more biblical doctrine of the atonement than is held by many 'Reformed' ministers.

On the critical issue of evangelism, Macleod states that there are "Calvinists" who have a distorted view of biblical Calvinism. He adds that it would be better if the church unshackles such men. Indeed, he even suggests that they are "exterminated."[370] It is factual that such preachers in theoretically Calvinistic churches are non- or anti-evangelistic! Perhaps a personal illustration will help. At an evangelistic mission in a congregation within a Presbyterian congregation in Northern Ireland, I never once heard the universal love of God for mankind mentioned or even hinted at by the preacher. Now, either the evangelist was not an authentic Calvinist and believed he was. Or, if he was a true Calvinist, he did not believe those precious Scriptural truths Calvin believed and Prin. Macleod affirmed! But whatever the reason, he missed the whole end of the gospel of Christ as he had understood it, and that was disappointing. Preachers like this abound

---

[369] White, *A Guide to Pastoral Care*. (Pickering and Inglis Ltd, 1976), 2, 3.
[370] Macleod, *Evangelical Quarterly*, (Exeter: Paternoster Press, 2009, Vol. 81:3), 220.

within such professing 'Reformed' denominations and are shackled by a theological system that is sub-biblical. Or, as Macleod argues, perhaps they are shackled by their misunderstanding of what they have subscribed – in its historical context. This situation raises the uncomfortable question of what ministers are taught at theological college when such a serious misunderstanding of the gospel persists. Let us assume, rightly or wrongly, that their lecturers teach the true authentic Calvinism of the Scriptures. However, it would appear that some of them have come under the clogging influences of high or even hyper-Calvinism. Macleod has pointed out this "core dogma" with his usual clarity.

But what lesser Reformed preachers do is to ignore this "core dogma" at the cost of authentic evangelism. If Macleod was to faithfully and consistently apply such discipline within professing Reformed denominations, there would be few ministers remaining because most would be "instantly jettisoned." Authentic Calvinism is in danger of being destroyed through lack of accurate understanding of what it was the great Reformer taught. Indeed, the drive for an educated and cultured ministry has meant that evangelistic preaching has ceased, being the rightful domain of street preachers and mission hall evangelists, but not for the institutional church. To many reformed preachers, alas, the gospel has been relegated to a footnote at the end of their sermons. In many churches, even that would represent a massive step forward because of the sheer paucity of gospel preaching done in them.

Let me give a flavour of Macleod's preaching at his evangelistic best. He declares that the personal cost to Christ when He made Himself a propitiation for the sins of the whole world was beyond calculation.[371] He teaches that the resurrection dominion of Christ extends over the whole world. That being the case, the New Testament defines evangelism as the proclamation of the gospel to every creature that Christ Jesus is his Lord. Further, it is essential to the proclamation that this Lord wants all men to be saved, and quotes 1 *Timothy* 2:4 as his authority.[372] On the

---

[371] Macleod, *From Glory to Golgotha*. (Ross-shire: Christian Focus Publishing, 2002), 125.
[372] Macleod, *Golgotha*, 136.

dominion theme, Macleod states that He Who sits on the throne is the Saviour. It was He, Who, as the Lamb of God took away the sin of the world, referencing this with (*Revelation* 5:6).[373] Listen to Macleod again as he focuses in on the heart of God towards mankind. God wants no one to perish in Hell; rather, He wants all men to be saved.[374] Or again in this longer passage,

> *But surely the most important fact about Hell is that none of us need ever experience it. All the persons of the Trinity are seeking your salvation. Let me make it as personal as I can. They are seeking your salvation. God the Father gave His own Son. God the Son laid down His life. God the Holy Spirit loves us. How then can we go to Hell? Not when there is such love in God! Not when there is such salvation in Christ! Not when all the persons of the Trinity are seeking your salvation! That will be the most terrible thing of all: the moment when God calmly asks, 'Did you hear of my love? Did anyone ever tell you that I sought your salvation? Did anyone ever tell you that My Son and My Spirit also sought your salvation? Did anyone ever tell you how I gave My Son to be your Saviour? Did anyone ever tell you how it would pain and grieve Me to condemn you? Did no one warn you not to put Me to that grief and pain?' What will your answer be?*[375]

Macleod urges Christians never to forget that they are primarily bearers of the gospel, evangelists. It was to them that Jesus said "Go and preach the good news to every creature" (*Mark* 16:15). They are to tell every man that he has good news, not bad news, for him.[376]

Observing the balanced biblicism of Calvin demands that preachers press sinners immediately to enter the Kingdom of God. It is not a 'take it or leave it' situation at all. All are to be pressed to come to Christ in faith because all are in dire need of what He has done on the cross for all mankind. The preacher will know that those who come to the Saviour have had something real offered to them and received by them. He will

---

[373] Macleod, *Golgotha*, 137.
[374] Macleod, *A Faith To Live By*. (Ross-shire: Christian Focus Publications, 1998), 283.
[375] Macleod, *Faith*, 287. Emphasis mine.
[376] Macleod, *Faith*, 288.

also know that the Holy Spirit has done a special work of saving grace in their souls. There is no difference here between those who embrace Calvinistic theology. Whatever our theory might be in this regard, a <u>real offer</u> of a <u>real Christ</u> promising a <u>real salvation</u> is made to <u>real sinners</u>, that is, to all mankind. The moment they believe in Christ, they are saved. This message is true evangelistic preaching as done by all good Calvinists, and DML-J is an excellent example of such preaching. This message is God's revealed will in the gospel. What God's decretive (secret) will is, is not our concern. I know that what a man thinks determines what he is and does, so cognition is important. But each of us must leave room for those who see things a little bit differently for the sake of the authentic gospel and evangelism.

Prof. Macleod might as well have been quoting directly from Calvin or Baxter or DML-J when he penned those words. How refreshing that a Reformed theologian of his stature confirms and agrees with authentic Calvinism as expounded by Calvin and his true interpreters, and not as taught by those who followed the theological arc set by Beza and promoted by Owen! How Macleod squares these views with the WCF is mysterious, but no doubt, he can synchronise them to his satisfaction.

The Canons of Dordt in this regard truly are seminal concerning the atonement, and much more biblical than Westminster theology. Dordt is not a theological curiosity, as Macleod states without giving his reasons. The fact is that Amyraldian soteriology is significantly closer to Dordt than Dordt is to the WCF. Had it been less reactionary and tunnel-visioned, it would have adopted Dordt's language, and spared generations of theologians and preachers from falling into the spiritually destructive hyper-Calvinism error.

Macleod is wrong, however, when he states that only those who advocate the free and unfettered offer of the gospel are regarded as Amyraldians.[377] Amyraldians are delighted that many of those who are not professedly Amyraldian in their soteriology feel unfettered in their offering the

---

[377] Macleod, *EQ*, 221.

benefits of Christ's redemption to all men. Thomas Chalmers is a case in point, as are Whitefield and Spurgeon.

Macleod's mind moves effortlessly from saying that Christ offers redemption to the whole world to referring to what His death would mean to His people, His mind being preoccupied with an exclusive love for His own. Macleod accepts that Reformed believers and preachers can say with confidence that Christ died for you and that He died for sinners. In saying this, they are affirming that, since all are sinners, He, in that sense, died for all.

What Macleod thinks about this central gospel doctrine is clear. He speaks of Christ's decision to exercise clemency and show pity to a lost race,[378] a statement that does not sit well with Westminster soteriology, but is faithful to Scripture. On seeking to answer the big questions of life, he asserts that Christ Himself is the cure for man's deepest problems, for the Saviour calls on the weak and heavy-laden to come to Him. As the Lord understands Himself, He is able and willing to hold out "rest" to the whole world. He "dispenses" rest to everyone regardless of age or gender – to every man, woman and child. Christ says this, adds Macleod, knowing full well the sheer magnitude of the problems facing humankind, and He Himself so visibly frail and vulnerable. He extends to the world a redemption that can rescue it from its tyrannies and anxieties.[379]

Macleod's hypothetical universalism is clearly discernible in these statements. He states his inclusivism of each and every one unambiguously. As we examine his writings, we will discover that he has some sympathy, if with justifiable reservations, for the Lombardian principle that the death of Christ is "sufficient for all, efficient for the elect." This paradigm makes reasonable sense of the apparent contradictions within the gospel. There are very many universalistic texts about the design of the atonement in the Scriptures and there are texts that state that Christ died for His people. The deliberate ambiguity in Lombard has enabled men of a different view to

---

[378] Macleod, *Glory*, 59.
[379] Macleod, *Glory*, 61. Contra Williamson, *Confession*, 79.

accept this form of words, thus facilitating the spread of the true gospel.[380] The same ambiguity occurs with the word "world," and facilitates gospel proclamation. Macleod strikes the proper balance in his books; may all Reformed preachers "go and do likewise" (*Luke* 10:37).

Macleod is abundantly clear that the true understanding of the gospel and the atonement is that held by Calvin and, I might add with great confidence, preached by DML-J. The Trinity loves the world and desires the world's salvation. In the heart of God, there is no wish for the eternal perdition of any sinner. He wants all to be saved. Notwithstanding Macleod's criticisms of DML-J, there is no difference in the gospel they proclaimed.

---

[380] Clifford, *Atonement*, 74.

22

John Murray (1898–1975)

Theological professor, John Murray (1898–1975), has a clear place in his theology for the universal aspect of the atonement despite his allegiance to high orthodox Westminster theology. We can expect this viewpoint from any man whose supreme authority is the Holy Scriptures. Throughout his writings, Murray demonstrates his limited atonement position but feels compelled to proffer a wider understanding of the atonement when Scriptural exegesis demands it. It is important to see what he writes in support of a more general atonement granting the 'givenness' of his limited redemptionist position. Murray approaches this question from the position that the advocacy that Jesus renders and the propitiation that He is, are complementary, but without explaining why this is the case. If he were prepared to go as far as the apostle John (1 *John* 2:2) and say that He is the propitiation for the whole world, then an explanation would have been provided. But Murray does not go that far. He holds back because John's statement is at variance with his. He admits we can see quite readily that Scripture uses universal terms in relation to the atonement. But we cannot then assume that these very words establish the doctrine of universal atonement.[381] To draw such a conclusion is bizarre.

Does the Bible's universal language, used under the inspiration of the Holy Spirit, not teach truths that have at least some connection with universal atonement? If the Bible does not teach universal atonement, why would its writers use such "confusing" language? And why do

---

[381] Murray, *Redemption*, 75.

theologians feel the need to "re-write" the Bible in their preaching and writing to ensure that those reading the Scriptures do not end up believing in universal atonement? Does the Bible mean what it says? If the Bible's language, taken in its natural sense, does not mean what the words mean, which parts of the Bible have to be radically re-interpreted to secure a limited atonement interpretation? Do they feel compelled to engage in Bultmannian demythologising of the biblical text so that it says what best suits their theological prejudice? Surely John Murray knew better than most that his argument is extremely weak when he claims that universal language cannot be used to establish universal atonement. Contrariwise, and by the same token, particularistic language cannot be appealed to to establish particular atonement either. This careless "illogic" is most unworthy of the good professor.

If this has to be done, then one product is to secure the need for professional theologians to interpret the Bible properly for non-theologians. It also guarantees the jobs of theological professors and lecturers and theologically trained ministers, because ordinary people cannot read the Bible for themselves and arrive at its true meaning, a rather Catholic idea. This "sophistry" establishes the need for a Protestant *magisterium* and explains why the Protestant churches no longer publicly criticise the teachings of Roman Catholicism.

If Murray wishes to follow Lewis Carroll's dictum (*"a word means what I want it to mean, no more and no less"*), so be it.[382] For him, words mean what he *wants* them to mean, and not what they *actually* mean. He follows this practice especially where Scripture is clearest as to the design and scope of the atonement. Prof. Murray uses, perhaps, abuses, language in order to promote a dogmatic rather than a biblical message. He has all the standard Bible dictionaries, lexicons and linguistics against him. So for his soteriology to be acceptable, he would had to have re-written all these standard works and add to them those ideas that support his particular interpretation, had he been alive.

---

[382] Murray, *Redemption*, 1979 rpnt.

On the basis of Murray's theological/philosophical presuppositions, he is consistent and right to write-off universal atonement teaching. But, his argument is weak when he contends that universal atonement men can appeal in an off-hand manner to only "a few texts," a criticism also made by Helm, and by Kennedy.[383] Why this should be a problem for these scholars is difficult to see because Murray is a strong WCF man with its Larger and Shorter Catechisms. All of these documents are attended and supported by and dependent upon carefully selected proof texts. This discovery exposes Helm's confessional position to the same criticism. Further, the Canons of Dordt are suitably referenced from Scripture, so to criticise universal atonement men for pointing to, not a few, but many texts of Scripture is mean-spirited, if not slightly hypocritical. In any case, if appeal cannot be made to the Scriptures to found any particular doctrine, this begs the question as to where exactly the framers of the confessions and catechisms found the contents of their documents. Saying that such a method is unworthy of the serious Bible student, Murray states, in effect, that his understanding of the atonement and redemption is the proper one. It is the one that he will proceed to teach in his books. His own cavalier treatment of the text is more worthy of his conclusion than those against whom it is directed. Thankfully, he exhibits better exegetical skills on the whole in his commentary on *Romans*.

What, for Prof. Murray, is the source of our understanding of the doctrine of the atonement? Without equivocation, he answers that it is the Bible. What previous generations have understood the Bible to teach is surely a blessing of divine providence, there being no need to "re-invent the wheel"! However, since the Bible is not sufficient for extreme Reformed theologians, recourse has to be made to some of the creeds and confessions of mainly seventeenth-century England, normally those that support the conclusions they hold. The use of this extra-biblical material is not to condemn or even discourage such consultation with historical sources, but rather to support such a task. It urges carefulness

---

[383] Kennedy as cited in James Stewart, *A Man in Christ*. (London: Hodder and Stoughton, 1964), 15. Kennedy accuses those who use "solitary proof texts" as having "wrought more havoc in theology than all the heresies."

because these human compositions are to be kept at best in a subordinate position to Scripture[384] and where they depart from Scripture's teaching, we should depart from them. One has to ask in this regard whether or not their interpretation agrees with Calvin's, and for that matter, DML-J's?[385] Murray and Helm would answer that it does, but they need to demonstrate how this is the case.

---

[384] Richard A. Muller, *Post-Reformation Reformed Dogmatics*, (Grand Rapids: Baker Books, 1993), 341.
[385] See Appendix.

23

Human Responsibility Denied

It is enlightening to note where objections to universal atonement sometimes come from and what reasons objectors offer as to why this understanding is allegedly wrong, or sub-orthodox. The limited atonement lobby affirms that Christ in His death atoned only for the elect, and no one else. This decision was taken by God in eternity, and, therefore, unchangeable. This belief implies that the non-elect cannot be saved because God has decided beforehand not to save them. So the fault for their lostness is God's, not theirs.

In the Garden of Eden, a similar situation is described where, after man's fall into sin and disobedience, the blame game started. Adam blamed God for giving Eve to him as wife, and Eve for the tragedy he brought on himself; then Eve blamed the serpent (*Genesis* 3). Adam sees the woman as "the secondary cause" of the problem and God as "the primary cause."[386] It is all God's fault.

So, if God had already decided to save only the elect unbelievers before they had done either good or bad, the logical implication is that the non-elect unbelievers have no possibility of being saved. God had made a prior decision to pass over them.[387] Therefore, their eternal lostness is not their fault, but God's. Austrian neurologist Sigmund Freud's position is that the cause of all of man's problems lies at God's door, not man's.

---

[386] Adams, *Competent*, 214.
[387] In theological parlance, this is known as preterition.

This position gives rise to the reluctance to hold man responsible for his actions, decisions, and behaviours. Ultimately, the problem was caused by God because man had "no choice in these matters."[388] Compare this viewpoint with that held by the Owenites in their soteriology and one is compelled to arrive at a similar conclusion. If man is not saved ultimately because the gospel has been preached to him, then it is God's fault. Further, if God, from eternity, did not love some men and Christ had not died for them, what is the point in evangelism? Why preach the gospel to every creature, as Jesus commanded His disciples? It will not change anything. If what Christ did on Calvary saves sinners, what need is there for repentance and faith? The one group will infallibly be saved just as the other group will infallibly be lost. Clearly, the counsel of Freudians and Owenites amounts to much the same thing – a counsel of utter despair. It is hopelessness both psychologically and spiritually. It holds out no hope for anyone – the elect will be saved and the non-elect lost without either having to respond to Christ as He is freely offered in the gospel. Perhaps that is why there is so little passionate gospel preaching in those churches that hold to the Owenite/Freudian composite. Does this not explain why it is no longer emphasised in many sermons the need for sinners to be saved? Instead, they are given lectures in theology and their minds filled with often good material, but they leave with their hearts untouched by the grace of God in Christ. The coldness of such services is criminal. There is no fire in the preaching and sinners are not being "nailed to their seats." They leave services discussing, not God's message, but the weather and the cost of living, even politics. No burning desire in them has been stirred to repent and get right with God immediately. The need for decision now is not pressed upon their consciences. They are given no warning that this might be the last opportunity they have to get right with God. Nor are they reminded that God's Spirit will not strive with man forever (*Gen.* 6:3). Sinners are allowed to leave church services with no stirring of their responsibility to trust in Christ alone if they are to be saved. The effects of high Calvinist theology and Freudian psychology, separate and combined, are far-reaching and such a cocktail is perhaps the most dangerous potent that anyone could dispense or ingest.

---

[388] Adams, *Competent*, 213, f.n.1.

Such ministers are the darlings of the churches, a protected species, an honoured grouping and viewed as very good churchmen. Evangelicals who preach a clear gospel message in the power of the Holy Spirit, are opposed, persecuted, rejected, deposed, excommunicated from church privileges, and ostracised by their former colleagues. The unwritten sign stands clear above many congregations: *"Evangelists need not apply."* The churches discriminate against them, are deprived of preaching opportunities, and cast on the scrap-heap, because they face their congregations with their responsibility to trust Christ alone for salvation. But those who studiously avoid pointed preaching and application of the demands of the gospel to their hearers are applauded and sheltered by church authorities. Church members do not leave their services feeling guilty because of their wrong relationship with God, so no complaint is made against ministers to the church authorities. But, based on what DML-J famously said, what is the value of maintaining a religious denomination if loyalty to the gospel is the price to be paid for such loyalty?[389] There is no other way to describe this but institutional maintenance, or corporate protection, at the cost of gospel faithfulness. Protecting the institution is surely a seriously misplaced religious activity. Truly John Owen and Sigmund Freud, each in his own way, have done their worst to cut the umbilical cord of serious evangelism. The sad thing is that so few see it.

---

[389] Lloyd-Jones, *Times*, 241.

SECTION SIX

The Soteriology Of Dr D. Martyn Lloyd-Jones

24

Did DML-J's Gospel Involve Double Payment For Sin?

DML-J's soteriology comes directly from the text of Scripture, as did that of Calvin, Amyraut, Baxter, etc. Luther was advised by Staupitz "to get rid of the systems taught by the Schools and derive all [his] theology from Scripture,"[390] and DML-J followed him in this. Further, his gospel message is the result of careful and "disinterested" exegesis. DML-J never saw himself as tied to confessional statements, and at times, while appreciating them, criticised their use and abuse. He had a message for the whole world because it was for the whole world that he believed that Christ had died. If the Saviour had not died for all, he held, there is no gospel for all. If the gospel is to be preached to all (*Mark* 16:15), then it is because Christ died for all.

DML-J viewed the cross as "God's way of saving the world."[391] The entire human race stands guilty before God (its default position), and urgently needs deliverance from the divine wrath. The world is in active rebellion against God and His law, and since God had saved *him*, He could equally well and equally easily save the whole world.[392] There is no lack of power or intention in Almighty God to do this. The fact that the world needs salvation implies that the world is in great spiritual and eternal danger – it stands under the wrath of God (*Romans* 1:18). The world is "lost" and in danger of eternal perdition. It is God's world, so He found a way by

---

[390] D'Aubigné, *Luther*, 41.
[391] Selection #107.
[392] Selection #5.

which He could reconcile it to Himself (2 *Corinthians* 5:19). Reconciliation of the world to Himself is why God sent His own Son, Jesus Christ, as the divinely provided Substitute for that world. By dying in its place, Christ bore its sins, making them His very own. Now, if Christ bore the punishment due to the world for sin, is God not acting in an unjust and immoral manner if He then punishes us for sins already punished in Christ? Will a just God punish sin twice – first in the Saviour from sin on the cross, and then in the unrepentant sinner in Hell? Indeed, if Christ died for all men, and any perish, not only is God demanding double payment for sin but Christ could not have died for all men, but only for the elect.[393] The logic seems irrefutable. A. M. Toplady's hymn has these words: *"Payment God will not* twice *demand,* First *at my bleeding Surety's hand, And then* again *at mine"* (emphasis added). These sentiments are closely associated with the limited atonement camp that believes that this is an unanswerable position to take on the atonement, and one that essentially demolishes the universal atonement position.

Richard Baxter, greatly admired by DML-J, answered the double payment proponents who put forward the hypothetical question, Is it not unjust to punish him that Christ died for, even one sin twice?[394] In a series of arguments, the Puritan denied that this is the case. He said that the Law bound no one to suffer but the offender, the guilty Hell deserving sinner. Christ is not the offender, therefore, what Christ suffered was not the same punishment that the Law threatened, but it was satisfaction instead of it, which is the *tantundem* not the *idem*. Baxter draws a helpful distinction between the *tantundem* and the *idem*. The former, he teaches, indicates that just the right amount was paid, an amount of equivalent value, whereas the latter expounds the idea that what Christ did on the cross was exactly the same. Had Christ paid what our sins deserved exactly, He'd still be in Hell. But He's not!

Baxter says this was the only intention Christ Himself had in suffering. Therefore whoever tramples upon the precious covenant blood by which they were set apart for God, deserves a more severe punishment. Whoever

---

[393] Clifford, *Atonement* 127.
[394] Richard Baxter, *The Scripture Gospel Defended*. (1690). Cont.28, pages 47, 48.

treats the blood of Christ as an unholy thing, and who offends thereby the Holy Spirit of grace, should suffer much more severe punishment (*Hebrews* 10). This teaching declares Christ's decided will and He will judge those who reject His atoning sacrifice. He will inflict this punishment on them for their contempt of redeeming grace. Clifford's conclusion on this point is appropriate. "Christ therefore suffered the *tantundem*, not the *idem*. Baxter does not deny that Christ was 'cursed' instead of sinners in a penal, substitutionary sense; he only denies that his sufferings were identical in every respect with the 'curse of the law' (Galatians 3:13)."[395]

This attempt by the limited atonement lobby is designed to invalidate the Amyraldian position held by DML-J. God in Christ died for all the sins of all mankind, and that atoning death leaves unrepentant sinners without a reasonable answer. Since this was DML-J's soteriology, it is incumbent on me to try to 'rescue' the Doctor from the accusation that his position necessarily implies a double payment for sin. Such a position would be unjustifiable and intolerable as well as immeasurably unjust; if true, this would be to question, if not deny and insult, the character of God as just. How can this be done?

The most reasonable answer is to move away from the pecuniary, or commercial, theory of the atonement drawn up by Anselm of Canterbury (1033–1109) and adopt a forensic metaphor.[396] This change will find the problem largely solved. What Christ did on the cross[397] was deeply personal.

---

[395] Clifford, *Atonement* 130, 131.

[396] A metaphor may be defined as a figure of speech in which an implied comparison is made between two unlike things that actually have something in common. The ideas used to explain them are metaphors. The theologian's task is to choose the metaphor that best fits the biblical data and which helps us make good sense of that data. In this case, the forensic metaphor is preferred to the commercial theory in that it gives a better account of the biblical teaching on the atonement.

[397] William Cunningham teaches that the sufficiency/efficiency paradigm is "sound in some sense" (quoting Calvin, 1862:397, n*). Cunningham then proceeds to draw a distinction between "what Christ did" and "what His death was." But surely the Person and Work of Christ are indivisible and both aspects are inextricably linked. Therefore to draw such a distinction is without precedent in reformed and biblical theology.

Therefore, it was not just an impersonal matter of paying someone's debt caused by his sin, though this was involved. Business-like transactions can degenerate into grossly impersonal activities. Further, it draws too rigorous a parallel between "debt" and "sins" and this theory does not acknowledge "the map is not the territory."

However, if we adopt a forensic position, which is the approach adopted by the apostle Paul in *Romans* in his courthouse scenarios, the great Judge has a level of discretion so that He can decide to remit the debt or not. It all depends on what He finds in the debtor. It is profoundly personal in character and the sinner knows that it is profoundly personal.[398] And the moment he puts his trust in the Saviour, his sin and guilt are cancelled. But if he refuses, his sin and guilt have been atoned for but because he has not applied the remedy to his own case, his guilt remains on him. For him to receive any benefit from Christ's death on Calvary, he must accept that He is guilty and plead with the Judge for mercy.

This double payment matter is a strong objection to the soteriology of DML-J, and one of which he was not altogether unmindful. Hence the very rare occasions when he made what seemed like limited atonement statements.[399] The double payment objection to universal atonement (and therefore to the soteriology of DML-J) is sometimes offered as a solution to this problem. Now if that understanding is the correct one, then the inevitable consequence is that sin is being punished twice – once at the Saviour's hand on the cross and again by the unforgiven sinner in Hell. DML-J answered the double payment objection convincingly, in his

---

[398] Cf. *Psalm* 53:4. This is how the courts in the civilised world do their business. If a defendant pleads 'guilty,' his sentence is reduced to reflect that plea. But if he refuses to plead guilty, then despite the provision being there to reduce the sentence on condition of admission of guilt, his sentence is as it stands in law.

[399] See his expository sermons of *Romans* 5 and on *Ephesians* 5. According to both Revs Iain H. Murray and John J. Murray, these two cases demonstrate that DML-J believed in limited atonement. The implication is that the hundreds of universal statements made by the Doctor are to be interpreted in the light of these two statements, a rather strange methodology indeed. Ought it not rather to be the other way round, that his alleged limited statements are to be interpreted in the light of his numerous universal statements.

Ephesians series. He preached, "God and His holy law are fully satisfied and pleased, and *man is reconciled to God and can be forgiven.*"[400] By His atonement, the necessary reconciliation between God and man has been accomplished and "man is reconciled to God." His view is that reconciliation has been achieved yet man, the sinner, remains in an unforgiven state and condition. Forgiveness for him is possible – man "can be forgiven." So the situation is that through Christ's atonement, redemption has been accomplished for the sin of the world. But until the Holy Spirit applies the benefits of that redemption to the sinner's heart, that sinner is still under the wrath of God, his default position. Redemption then can be achieved for all yet the sinner remains unpardoned. This explanation provides one very forceful answer to the double payment objection to universal atonement as preached by DML-J.

DML-J never quoted Amyraut so far as I know. Like Bunyan, DML-J's approach was not to be system dominated but dominated instead by the main gospel themes that he discovered in Scripture.[401] It was this discovery that gave him the liberty to preach a full gospel to a lost humanity. Like Bunyan in his pre-prison years (1656–1659) in which he distanced himself from an unbiblical emphasis on predestination, DML-J also distanced his thinking from that of theologians such as Dr Boettner who viewed predestination as the key that unlocks the gospel. Bunyan did not consider predestination as the central doctrine that determined how his soteriology would take shape.[402]

Studying DML-J's numerous universal statements does not give any suggestion that he was contrasting the universal with the particular.[403] He simply preached the biblical gospel as it stood without entering any caveat to control his meaning. DML-J held to universal statements regarding the atonement because these convinced him that only if this were true could a genuine offer of blood-bought salvation be made to all men.[404]

---

[400] Lloyd-Jones, *Darkness and Light*, 307. Emphasis added.
[401] Wenkel, as in the *Scottish Journal of Theology*, 58/3/2005, 338.
[402] *Ibid.*
[403] *Ibid.*, 339.
[404] *Ibid.*, 348.

Wenkel concurs with those like Prof. John Murray, who draw what is a valid distinction between redemption accomplished and redemption applied. Now that Christ in His death has accomplished redemption for all men, they have to lay hold of Christ by faith in order to benefit personally from this great salvation. This understanding places faith as the pivot between being saved and being lost. When the gospel is preached, the assumption is that the unregenerate hearers will assume by faith that what Christ did on the cross was for them personally.[405] They will also assume that God loves them in a saving manner.[406] This is what appears to be the understanding in that spiritually real, existential context. Any study of the DML-J sermons will convince readers that his hearers were called on continually to put their trust in Christ alone for salvation; so faith was for him the crucial matter for deciding their eternal destiny.

In DML-J's theology, two parallel threads ran together – particularity and universality. This dualism is evident in his soteriology and the universal aspect is ubiquitous in his evangelistic preaching. DML-J makes no obvious attempt to reconcile these twin truths for to do so would make him break his *modus operandi* that was to allow the text of Scripture to speak for itself. As in Bunyan's pre-prison ministry, DML-J makes no concession whatever to semi-Pelagian or Arminian synergistic theories of the atonement. When he preaches the everlasting gospel, he does so with the conviction that God is "not willing that any should perish but that all should come to repentance" (2 *Peter* 3:9). God's desire is that all might be saved by a personal appropriation of the merits of Christ's blood and the redemption that it purchased for the lost. Only on such a foundation can any genuine offer of salvation be made to the unsaved. To do otherwise is to act in a most hypocritical manner.

Wenkel states in the clearest terms what he believes the Scriptural position to be. He says, "While God's will is to be viewed as hypothetically universal – willing all to be saved – there is also a strong particular aspect to God's will."[407] DML-J also held this to be the biblically authentic way

---

[405] *Ibid.*, 341.

[406] *Ibid.*, 345.

[407] Wenkel, as in the *Scottish Journal of Theology*, 58/3/2005, 346.

of understanding what God has revealed in Scripture. He preached the gospel as God's available remedy for the sin of the world, and he also believed that salvation is of the Lord and that it is the Lord in His grace Who saves believing sinners. Christ in His death for the elect secured their salvation when they appropriated its benefits by faith in Christ; it was also a death that accomplished redemption for the whole world. It was this message that DML-J proclaimed throughout his ministry. Bunyan believed in the substitutionary theory of the atonement; this is the theory that DML-J thinks best suits all the available biblical evidence and shows greatest fairness to the doctrine of God's justice.[408]

Wenkel uses a phrase that is unfamiliar to me – "Eternal propitiation" – which he got from Bunyan's *The Doctrine of Law and Grace Unfolded*.[409] What Bunyan meant by this term is not explained except to say that "eternal propitiation" was accomplished by Christ in His death. This point may imply that God has been propitiated from eternity and that His wrath has been appeased from before the foundation of the world. It may also imply that once Christ made propitiation, it is then effective for all eternity. What "eternal propitiation" means in effect is rather obscure. The concept does not, from one perspective, seem to fit in with this soteriology, though from another, is does. Nor is it a discernible biblical idea. It falls into the same category as "eternal justification." Perhaps I'm wrong.

In these early days of his ministry, Bunyan believed that the extent of the atonement refers to its application not to its design.[410] This view also coheres well with the Doctor's position. The atonement's design is general and universal, but its application is particular and specific. This dualism does justice to all the relevant biblical data on this doctrine as well as to how God has revealed His will for the world. During this period of Bunyan's ministry, it could be contended that his soteriology, like that of DML-J, was at odds with that of his compatriot, John Owen. Owen founded his particularism and his rejection of universal redemption on

---

[408] Lloyd-Jones, *God the Father*, 317–327.
[409] Wenkel, as in the *Scottish Journal of Theology*, 58/3/2005, 348.
[410] Cf. Wenkel, as in the *Scottish Journal of Theology*, 58/3/2005, 348.

a refusal to accept a dualism in either God's will or the design of God in the atonement.

Wenkel makes an interesting point about Bunyan's sources for his soteriology. He affirms that it is most unlikely that he either followed or read any of Amyraut's works, seeing the latter wrote only in French. Wenkel admits that while Amyraut was a source of provocation within Reformed circles, "he was also a figurehead of a larger stream of thought within Reformed theology."[411] These points within Reformed Christianity are rejected by many. While DML-J was a widely read theologian, no evidence comes from his books that he read Amyraut's works. Certainly, he never quoted Amyraut in his books, etc. So no "direct" influence came on DML-J from Amyraut's theology. Given his convictions, he could only have arrived at his soteriology by his careful study of Scripture and by independent thought. Like DML-J, Amyraut was a controversial figure within Reformed circles. DML-J became a "leader" of that constituency that saw him as its mentor. Indeed, he was the *de facto* leader of a wider evangelicalism as testified to by claims Pentecostals made to his influence on their thinking.

It is however immensely significant that the academic contributors to the recent theological tome, *From Heaven He Came and Sought Her*,[412] made no reference to DML-J's soteriology. One possible, if not probable, explanation is that his soteriology did not fit with the limited atonement presuppositions of the book. Had the editors believed that DML-J held to limited atonement as understood by the Owenites, then it is very likely that his soteriology would have featured to some extent in the book. Many of the writers were great admirers of the Doctor. Unwittingly they have validated the thesis of this book that DML-J was not in their soteriological camp.

---

[411] Wenkel, as in the *Scottish Journal of Theology*, 58/3/2005, 351.

[412] *From Heaven He Came And Sought Her.* Eds D. Gibson and J. Gibson. (Illinois: Crossway, 2013).

25

Dr D. Martyn Lloyd-Jones on Romans 5:15

Speaking with Rev. John J. Murray on the occasion of the thirty-first anniversary of the death of DML-J,[413] he said, "Dr Lloyd-Jones believed in limited atonement." Mr Murray was formerly an editor of the Banner of Truth Trust in London and Edinburgh. Quizzing him about this assertion, I requested the grounds on which he made it. He assured me he taught this in his exposition of *Romans* 5:15. I was slightly taken aback by this because everything I had read of the Doctor's denied me any reason to think that this was what he believed. Contrariwise, his position was identical to universal atonement. Even a cursory reading of his evangelistic sermons on *Acts* will demonstrate this. Soon after, I was in Belfast's Evangelical Bookshop, Northern Ireland, and I discussed this with the manager, John Greer. He agreed to phone Rev. Iain H. Murray, co-founder and one-time editor of the Banner of Truth magazine, to ask him about this. Mr Murray confirmed that DML-J believed and preached limited atonement, giving as sources his sermons on *Romans* 5 and *Ephesians* 5. These, he confirmed, proved that the Doctor held limited atonement as the proper soteriological understanding.

These men tried, in vain, to claim that DML-J held an understanding of the atonement that they and other high Calvinists shared, namely that Christ died exclusively for the elect. Furthermore, they did this on the basis of *two texts* on which DML-J preached sermons on this doctrine. Disappointing for the two Murrays, what they were doing is what DML-J

---

[413] March 2012.

rejected out of hand – "isolating a text or idea and building up a system around it, instead of comparing Scripture with Scripture."[414] The Murrays were isolating two texts on which DML-J preached sermons on limited atonement and constructing the idea that he believed *their* version of limited atonement, despite an avalanche of sermons to the contrary. These two Christian gentlemen departed from the Doctor's position, a practice that he would not endorse because it portrays his soteriology inaccurately.

Having re-read the relevant sermons from these studies, I found the following to be the case. Despite at least 350[415] direct quotations from DML-J's published sermons that teach directly and clearly imply universal atonement, this contrary viewpoint surprised me. So what exactly did he say about *Romans* 5:15? DML-J preached two sermons in the *Romans* series on *Romans* 5:15 around February/March 1958. The second sermon found him focusing on that teaching that attracted some misunderstanding. It concerned the meanings of "all" and "the many."[416] After affirming that "sheer literalism" makes "all" in this verse mean "every individual person in the world," he discounts this methodology as wrongheaded and "unintelligent."[417] He proceeds to demonstrate that

> *'all' and 'the world' and 'many' and so on, as used in Scripture, quite frequently do not mean every individual in the world ... they do not mean every single member of the human family.*[418]

His thoughtful qualification, "quite frequently," keeps the door open to his belief that "quite frequently" they do mean "every individual in the world." It is easy to see why he adopts this language and approach and

---

[414] Lloyd-Jones, *Knowing The Times*, 11.
[415] I also have, in addition to these, twenty-four other direct quotations from DML-J which substantiate my understanding of his soteriology, but for which copyright permission proved impossible to secure because of self-imposed publication deadlines. These quotations were taken from his *Plight of Man and the Power of God*, and his two volume work, *Living Water*.
[416] D. M. Lloyd-Jones, *Assurance* (Edinburgh: Banner of Truth Trust, 1971), 240-252.
[417] *Ibid.*, 241. Baxter also endorses DML-J's exegesis here, 1694:3.
[418] *Ibid.* George E. Ladd, *A Theology of the New Testament*. (London: Lutterworth Press, 255) has a similar understanding of this issue.

gives examples of how this is not the case, referring to *Luke* 2:1, and *Acts* 2:18 quoting *Joel* 2:28.[419] His message was leading up to a denial of stark universalism, and he dismisses as ridiculous the idea that this means everyone, including the ungodly.

DML-J rejects the "foolish literalism" that makes the meaning of "all" in Scripture inclusive of everyone on every occasion,[420] for Scripture limits the meaning of this and similar terms by placing conditions on them. In so doing, he is exposing and opposing universalism *per se*, the kind promoted by naked universalists. He holds that only believers are justified,[421] in contradistinction to the 'new perspective on Paul' teaching current at this time.[422] DML-J opposes and condemns without reservation universal salvation. Because Christ died for all, all will finally be saved, is both false and foolish. The falsehood has only to be stated to be recognised for what it is, and the foolishness contradicts the observable facts, and no time will be wasted in refuting these errors. However, DML-J is not opposing universal atonement. He criticises and rejects naked universalism, not hypothetical universalism, not Amyraldianism. His condemnation is of those who teach that "all" will be saved eventually by God's love.

DML-J does not teach one thing in his *Acts* sermons and something different in his *Romans* sermons. In fact, limited atonement is not even mentioned in these *Romans* 5:15 sermons. Nor is it a theory of the atonement he espoused in his printed sermons. Unfortunately no digital recording of his two sermons on *Romans* 5:15 is available on the ML-J website,[423] despite his sermons on *Romans* 5:12 being followed by his sermon on *Romans* 5:16, 17. DML-J confessed that when he preached this theory, he found himself in great difficulty when he did so. DML-J knew that such a theory has no basis in Scripture. His confession of being "in great difficulty" when

---

[419] D. M. Lloyd-Jones, *Assurance*, (Edinburgh: Banner of Truth Trust, 1971), 242.
[420] Lloyd-Jones, *Assurance*, 243.
[421] Lloyd-Jones, *Assurance*, 244.
[422] Prof. N. T. Wright claims in essence that Paul teaches that we are justified by *belonging* (to the church) and not by *believing* (the Gospel).
[423] The website is at www.mljtrust.org and was accessed on 15th August 2013.

preaching it is a strong argument against the view that DML-J believed in limited atonement in the way high Calvinists assert that he did.

When he preached this 'contentious' sermon on *Romans* 5:15 is unknown, but this theory does not appear in his published expositions of this verse. What may have happened is the subject of speculation. While he might have said he believed this doctrine during preaching on *Romans* 5:15, when the *Romans* 5 book, *Assurance,* was eventually published, this reference, if he made it at all, was redacted from the printed sermon. Or, what is also equally likely, he had preached on this verse on another occasion and at a different venue, and experienced the difficulty referred to in his conversation with Kendall. Further, if DML-J did preach on or refer to limited atonement during his sermons on *Romans* 5:15, he may well have asked that the Chapel destroy the recording so that the wrong impression of his theology is not given. However, admitting this may be a reasonable explanation for their absence, it is pure speculation on my part. I will leave it to the reader to decide. Whatever the explanation for its non-appearance in his published sermons on *Romans* 5:15, or in the ML-J archive,[424] he admitted he was quite uneasy when he preached limited atonement from that or any other text. Whatever he might have said in private, this emphasis does not appear in his published sermons. These sermons were edited for publication either by him or by his widow (who did not believe in limited atonement) and daughters after his death, a fact that confirms the accuracy of his statement to Kendall.

DML-J criticises a wrong understanding of what Paul was writing in this letter. He asked the following three rhetorical questions about what this means:

> *If it does not mean universal salvation, does it mean that what the Apostle is teaching here is that the opportunity or the possibility of justification is to be offered to all? Is he saying that in Jesus Christ there is the chance or the opportunity for all to justify themselves if they believe and accept the message? Is it the possibility for all, if it is not a fact concerning all?*[425]

---

[424] The ML-J archive contains some 1,600 digitally re-mastered sermons of the Doctor's.

[425] D. M. Lloyd-Jones, *Romans,* (Edinburgh: Banner of Truth Trust, 1974 rpnt), 246.

He states with his usual clarity what he thinks Paul means. Paul is emphasising the certainty of salvation for believers, not its mere possibility. However, salvation is possible for unbelievers, on condition they trust in Christ alone. Before men became believers, they were unbelievers, and the same possibility of salvation was held out to them. His emphasis is not on the atonement as such but focuses on the Christian's assurance of salvation. The publishers entitled the book in which these studies appeared, *Assurance*. He is clear that the benefits of redemption can only be received by faith in Christ alone; however, it is not faith *per se* that justifies, but God.[426] So, like Calvin in his theology, faith unlocks the soteriology of DML-J.

How, then, does DML-J interpret the terms "all" and "the many"? His general position is typical – we must "allow Scripture to speak for itself."[427] He is at pains not to introduce philosophy, given the natural tendency of humans to do so. His explanation is that Paul is contrasting the "all" who are in Adam with the "all" who are in Christ.[428] Paul's interest is not in numerics but is in fundamental principles.[429] Fallen mankind is by nature connected with Adam, and we all died in Adam, but by grace all believers are in Christ, and they live in Him – all of them. Paul speaks here about individual salvation, not universal salvation, so he marshals his arguments to teach that salvation is certain for all believers in Christ, those who know God's ongoing forgiveness, as Calvin teaches. Moreover, Calvin's understanding of this verse steers away from a literalist interpretation. He says in his commentary on *Hebrews* that the taking away of sins equates with freeing sinners from the guilt their sin incurred. Calvin asserts that the sins of many equates with the sins of all, as in *Romans* 5:15.[430] The editor of Calvin's commentary on *Hebrews* adds that it is characteristic of Paul's style to use different words, while quite often he wishes to convey

---

[426] *Ibid.*

[427] *Ibid.* See WCF 1:IX. Philip, *The Westminster Confession of Faith* – Part 1, Chapters 1–8. (Dundee: Didasko Press (?), 1966), 17.

[428] These terms are burrs under the saddles of high- and hyper-Calvinists who simply cannot accept them as they stand written.

[429] D. M. Lloyd-Jones, *Romans*, (Edinburgh: Banner of Truth Trust, 1974, rpnt), 246.

[430] Calvin, *Comm. Hebrews* 9:28. Emphasis his.

the same idea. A specific case in point is where Calvin avers that "many" means "all." In his *Romans* commentary, Calvin writes about how Paul makes grace common to all men, not because it reaches all but because God offers it in His mercy to all. He takes it as axiomatic that Christ, in His death, suffered for the sins of the world, and He offers the benefits of this sacrificial death without distinction to all. The sad fact remains that all do not receive Christ.[431] The editor of Calvin's *Romans* commentary makes the point that Calvin held the doctrine of general redemption.

DML-J sounds a cautionary note to the effect that

> *we must never proceed to draw deductions beyond what is stated in Scripture. ... All we can do is to read the Scriptures and observe what they teach, and submit ourselves entirely to that.*[432]

So the natural meaning of Scripture was his guide in all branches of theology, and this was so clearly demonstrated in his sermon on *Romans* 5:15. Interestingly, high Calvinists find it difficult to accept Scriptural language especially when it tends to undermine their pet theory of the atonement. They make what can only be described as an amazing claim that these universal terms refer to "all kinds," "all classes," or "all categories" of people, rather than deal with Scriptural data as they stand. Not one provided any exegetical evidence for this claim, and readers received no justification explaining why they did this. Indeed, it can be argued that no justification exists for such a cavalier attitude to the Sacred writings. Additionally, no Bible translator translates the word "world" as "world of the elect" or "world of believers" or even "church." Translators have been honest in their dealing with the text and have not translated "all men" as "all classes of men." The textual evidence simply does not exist for such practice. Such a "translation" converts a concrete term – "all men", into an abstract one – "all classes of men." An abstraction can exist only in one's mind, not in reality. Abstractions neither need nor are capable of receiving the salvation that was purchased by Christ. The spurious attempt to re-home universalistic terms where they belong – in the world

---

[431] Calvin, *Comm. Romans* 5:15.
[432] *Ibid.*, 250.

of Scriptural reality — sees limited atonement men creating the clumsy phrase "some men of all classes." But such a phrase can make no serious claim to being a translation of the New Testament Greek text, nor is it a viable interpretation. We must be eternally grateful to Bible translators for their scrupulous honesty in dealing with the biblical text, a fact that should challenge and shame high Calvinists who take such liberties.

For gospel preachers, when they make such additions to the Scriptural data, these texts are powerless to command obedience and acceptance. They rob the texts of their force and the implicit obligation on "all men everywhere to repent" is lost. Is that why so little evangelistic work is done in many Reformed churches today? When the preacher explains that a particular text means not "all men" but "some people of all classes," they reduce it to absurdity. Fancy telling a congregation that God now commands some people of all classes to repent. The truth is that the Mediator in His office as King has the right to make demands on all His creatures, whether they acknowledge it or not. He requires the submission of all to His Kingship.

How does DML-J deal with this matter? He takes the texts as they stand and presses the urgency of the gospel call on the consciences of all those who listen to him. Nowhere does he resort to unwarranted expansions of the biblical text, a practice he repudiates strongly. He never squeezed the biblical text into any confessional Procrustean bed. See the Appendix for his own preaching statements for proof of this assertion.

So his sermon on *Romans* 5:15 does not reveal that the Doctor believed in or preached limited atonement. He took the verse as it stood and allowed it to speak its own message.

26

Dr D. Martyn Lloyd-Jones on Ephesians 5:25

Reflecting on what J. J. Murray and I. H. Murray affirmed, I searched DML-J's sermons on *Ephesians* 5 and found that he addressed the atonement issue within the context of Christian marriage. The atonement was not his major focus at this point, however, but on the Christian understanding of marriage. He positioned this within the context of the Christian's responsibilities in marriage, the family and at work (*Ephesians* 5:21 - 6:9). Even when addressing marriage, Paul cannot exclude the consideration of doctrine, especially the doctrine of salvation.

Preaching on *Ephesians* 5:25–33 his primary task is understanding the love of God. He sees it both in particularistic terms and in its universalistic breadth. He writes, "It is the same sort of love wherewith Christ loved the church; indeed, wherewith God loved the world."[433] He draws attention to the fact that this is the same Greek word that both John and Paul used for God's love (αγαπαω) both in *John* 3:16 and in *Ephesians* 5:25. The love with which Christ loved the church is identical to the love with which God loved the world. DML-J demonstrates particularism and universalism in his choice of words. The love with which God loved the world is one that loved the ugly, vile, ungodly, sinful, weak, guilty and condemned. This love moved outward to another. It is not a sentimental love, but a love that acted for the good of another/others; it was a love that gave, and bore away sin.

---

[433] Selection #107.

Paul uses the illustration of Christ's love for the church to explain how husbands are to love their wives – they constantly give.[434] Baxter holds that Paul teaches husbands to imitate Christ in loving their wives, as He did His church. He gave Himself in a special sense for her by His death, in order to sanctify her before God, and to cleanse her from sin and unrighteousness.[435] Paul emphasises the special love of Christ for His church, but not to the exclusion of His love for all. When a minister at a wedding counsels the groom to love his wife as Christ loved the church and gave Himself for her, he is not implying that the husband's love is to stop there. His wife is the main, though not the exclusive, focus of his love. Paul uses the state of marriage to illustrate his doctrine of the atonement as much as he uses his soteriology to illustrate marriage. Christ's love is a giving love; it is redemptive love. His love has a particular object – the church. Christ had already loved the church and had given Himself for her. God loved the world and gave His Son for it, indicating that it was the same love each time. What He did for the world, He also did for the church, and *vice versa*. In personalising what He did for the church by giving Himself for her salvation, DML-J proceeds to apply this to the individual. He adds, "[Y]es but also 'for me', for every one of us as individuals."[436] "Every one of us as individuals" is included in Christ's atoning work on Calvary.

Bearing in mind that the context here is Christian marriage and the character and quality of the exclusive love a husband ought to show to his wife, DML-J reiterates what he describes as "supreme doctrine ... no higher doctrine." A Christian husband is to love his wife sacrificially and without self-interest. His love for her is to be exclusive of all others,

---

[434] Calvin in *John Calvin's Sermons on Ephesians* (Edinburgh: Banner of Truth Trust, 1562/1973, rpnt 1979), comments in his sermon on *Ephesians* 5:22-26 is apposite. On page 575, Calvin preaches that "...our Lord Jesus Christ was ... unmindful of himself, and did not regard his own person, when it was a question of our salvation." He gave Himself for our salvation, to sanctify the church and to make her a glorious church. He goes on to employ *John* 3:16 as confirmatory of his point.

[435] Baxter, *A Paraphrase of the New Testament*, on *Ephesians* 5:25.

[436] D. Martyn Lloyd-Jones, *Life in the Spirit in Marriage, Home & Work*. (Edinburgh: Banner of Truth Trust, 1974), 145.

a particular love. I remember Dr John MacArthur[437] translating 1 *Timothy* 3:2, saying that an elder should be "a one-woman man," more familiarly, "the husband of one wife," an exclusive relationship.

DML-J says, "- all that the Lord Jesus Christ did, he did for the church." There is no dispute here on either side of the soteriological debate, and DML-J is reflecting what Paul had written. Continuing, "He died for the church; He died for nobody else."[438] These clear words from the Doctor, out of their context, spell an equally clear particularist understanding of the atonement. But his supreme purpose in writing this is to demonstrate from the highest possible source the quality of love with which husbands ought to love their wives. It is a particular love that focuses on their spouses. Christian men are to choose their love, and then to love their choice – exclusively in that sense. That there is a particularity in God's and Christ's love is not disputed, and Paul brings this out here. By extension, there is also a particular love of a husband for his wife. Calvin emphasises the same point in his sermon on these verses.[439] His entire focus is on marriage and uses his soteriology as an illustration of how husbands ought to love their wives. Election undergirds what the apostle is writing, and election has to do with prior choice.

When DML-J speaks about Christ dying for the church, the accompanying phrase, "for nobody else," in this sermon context, has the potential to point in the direction of particular redemption. Why, then, did DML-J use this form of words here? It was to show how Paul was teaching these Ephesians, and therefore us, the exclusivity and particularity of married love. He uses this term in the sense that those whom Christ loved with this particular love and for whom He died effectually received incalculable benefits from that atoning death – He atoned for their sins and guilt. Wives also receive great benefits from being loved in that exclusive way by their husbands. This explanation affirms that DML-J believed in an atonement that benefitted the elect. It is the quality of the divine love that he emphasises. Husbands are to show quality, exclusive love to their

---

[437] The meeting was held in Belfast, Northern Ireland in the early 1990s.
[438] *Ibid.*
[439] Calvin, *Ephesians*, 564–576.

wives. They are not to show that quality love to another woman – that's the Doctor's focus in these sermons.

But, and returning more directly to the atonement, DML-J had a great place in his evangelist's heart for those who made up the rest of mankind. He teaches that Christ also had a real, compassionate love for all men, and for these He died and made atonement. To enter into the benefits of that atonement, they had to trust the Saviour. For DML-J, Christ's death was not a mere commercial transaction, a mere pecuniary act on His part; rather it was essentially forensic in character because it dealt with personal sin and guilt. In fact, in the same paragraph, DML-J uses the Lombardian paradigm to explain what he meant by these particularistic remarks.

> *His death, as Calvin and other expositors remind us, because it was eternal and because He is the Son of God, is sufficient for the whole world; but it is efficient only for the church. His purpose in dying was to redeem the church. He gave Himself for the church, for all who belong to her when she will be complete and perfect and entire. All was known to God from eternity, and the Son came, and gave Himself for the church.*[440]

It was in this sense alone that "He died for nobody else." Paul safeguards the proper breadth of the gospel, and DML-J does likewise. Selective reading of the DML-J corpus is natural to dogma-driven theologians, but it is unacceptable for them to do so. To infer that he believed about the atonement what Owen believed is quite erroneous, if not mischievous. DML-J's soteriology is balanced and gives due weight to the particular and universal emphases that are in the actual text with which he is dealing. This fact demonstrates his method when expounding the text of Scripture. He sticks to his text and says all it has to say. And he does this with every text he handles, thus revealing the true emphasis of that text.

Interestingly, J. J. Murray and I. H. Murray could identify only two passages they say indicate that DML-J believed in limited atonement, and even this is open to serious enquiry. Even if he held to Owen's understanding of

---

[440] Lloyd-Jones, *Life in the Spirit*, 145, 146.

limited atonement, his use of almost ubiquitous universalistic language could not then be interpreted as particular redemption. To do so is to use a seriously flawed methodology that will lead to the drawing of erroneous conclusions. A careful reading of his sermons will demonstrate otherwise. Care must always be taken that we do not attribute to another man's beliefs what we wish was there, and isn't. Unfortunately, DML-J went beyond what was written when he made this statement, "He died for nobody else," a practice against which he constantly warned and a principle that he contravened here.

The text of *Ephesians* 5:25 reads, *"Husbands, love your wives, just as Christ also loved the church and gave Himself for her..."* In commanding husbands to love their wives, Paul was not prohibiting them loving anyone else. The apostle did not tell them to love only their wives, for this would have been to contradict his other universal statements and his teaching in 1 *Corinthians* 13. It would also contradict the love that parents ought to have for their children, etc., and Paul did not do that! Sadly, and clearly, on this point DML-J departed from his oft-repeated dictum, not to go beyond Scripture. It is arguable that he allowed his mind to run off on a tangent, preaching as he did from the scantiest of notes; this happens to preachers sometimes, especially those who preach extemporaneously. This sermon is the only place that I know of where he made such an uncharacteristic statement on the atonement, despite DML-J's ubiquitous universalism.[441] Furthermore, in his *Ephesians* 5:25 sermon,[442] Calvin quotes *John* 3:16 to confirm the point he was making which was, despite the appearance of particularism, Christ died for the whole world.

Since one (or two) swallows do not make a summer, the Murrays seem to think they do. They have tried, in vain, to create a wrong DML-J position on the atonement. This attempt is similar to what Pharaoh did to the Hebrews in Egypt where they were expected to make bricks without straw.[443] The Murrays may have a little bit of clay, but they have no straw, and they didn't end up with any bricks, either!

---

[441] Dr Alan C. Clifford in an email dated 17 August 2013. Used with permission.
[442] Calvin, *Ephesians*, 575.
[443] *Exodus* 5:18.

Further, DML-J sees our salvation as something that God does for us and to us. It is experiential in character, and he describes it in this sermon as our being "rescued" and "redeemed."[444] Had it not been for the sufficiency of Christ's death for all and its efficiency for the church, we would still be in our sins. Once the sinner trusts in Christ's finished work on Golgotha, he experiences God's gracious salvation. Because predestination[445] and election are not experiential in nature, it is not these that bring sinners into possession of the benefits of redemption; it is God's requirement for faith in Christ that does it. DML-J believes it was the "precious blood" of Christ that purchased redemption for the world, but it does not automatically become the possession of the elect. The salvific benefits of Christ's blood have to be applied by the Holy Spirit and appropriated by the sinner through faith, which is the conduit for receiving it.

Dr Clifford explained why he thought DML-J used this uncharacteristic language ("He died for nobody else.") in his 1959/1960 exposition of *Ephesians* 5:25. Just then, the Banner of Truth Trust was being set up, and DML-J was keen to avoid any rifts with this new Reformed movement. In an email to me, Clifford suspects that caution drove him at this juncture. "Whatever he published on paper, it remains true that he was 'uncomfortable' with LA [limited atonement]. In short, he didn't believe it."[446]

So, the two passages alleged by the Murrays to confirm that DML-J believed and preached limited atonement have been found unconvincing. Their statements have been weighed in the balances of Scripture and found wanting (*Daniel* 5:27). Some could argue this as the Murrays do if they take it out of context. But kept firmly within the context of this passage and these sermons, it is clear that there was a breadth in DML-J's soteriology that neither of these men embraced. Hence, it is pushing language too far to claim that they and DML-J are on the same side of this controversy.

---

[444] Lloyd-Jones, *Depression*, 146.
[445] These undergird and guarantee the success of the Gospel in the world.
[446] Alan C. Clifford, dated 27th July 2013. Used with permission.

SECTION SEVEN

Scriptural Exegesis – To the Word and To the Testimony

27

What Do The Scriptures Teach?

Let us now examine DML-J's frequently quoted Scripture passages within their biblical context. These texts will be exegeted to determine their meaning. The Bible text will be allowed to speak for itself with no attempt to press it into confessional conformity of any kind. Reading DML-J's evangelistic sermons we see how frequently he uses these Scriptures to demonstrate the universal scope of the gospel message and also its remedy for "the sin of the world" (*John* 1:29).

> Isaiah 53:6 – ...And The LORD Has Laid On Him The Iniquity Of Us All.

DML-J quotes this verse repeatedly in his evangelistic preaching, especially the last part of the verse, *"and the LORD has laid on him the iniquity of us all."* What does this verse mean? The context is the people of Israel who, Douty states, represent all mankind,[447] without explaining how this is the case. It focuses directly on the Suffering Servant of Isaiah. Calvin in his sermon on this passage identifies this Individual with Christ in His death.[448] Vos sees in it "the vicariousness of [the Servant's] suffering

---

[447] Norman F. Douty, *Death of Christ*, 55, 56.
[448] T. H. L. Parker, *Sermons on Isaiah's Prophecy of the Passion and Death of Christ*. (Cambridge: James Clarke & Co, 1976).

unto death," and that "being of the flock he can suffer for the flock."[449] Disappointingly, Payne does not deal with this verse in his treatment of the work of the Messiah.[450] Leupold is prepared to mention that up to then, the hope of rescue for mankind was non-existent,[451] suggesting that for him, the implication is that mankind stood in need of being delivered, redeemed. Unfortunately, he does not tie this in with this verse and say the Lord laid on the Servant the iniquity of us all, but the implication is there nonetheless.

The Geneva Bible notes say the punishment of our iniquity was laid on Him. In expounding this phrase, hyper-Calvinist, John Gill, states that God has laid on His own Son Jesus Christ, the sins of all His elect. Gill contends that these words may infer that the term "laid" teaches that God made the sins of us all to meet on Christ, "us all" referring to God's elect everywhere. He sees their sins as coming from all compass points, as meeting in Christ their suffering Representative. Gill is doing more than just limiting the teaching of this verse. He is re-writing it and then interpreting the re-written form to suit a particular dogmatic position. Nothing in *Isaiah* 53:6 suggests a limitation in what the Servant of the Lord came to do. Unlike Calvin, Gill does not see it as applying to the whole world of men. He quotes R. Cohana (favourably) when he says that King Messiah's calling is to bear the sins of the whole world, quoting *Isaiah* 53:6c.[452] This exposition is inconsistent with Gill's stated position, yet he includes it in his comment on this verse. Of course, Cohana's understanding of Isaiah's universal language possibly agrees with Gill's position. However, Gill still quoted it in his comment on *Isaiah* 53:6, with Cohana's explanation referring it to "the sins of the whole world."

---

[449] Gerhardos Vos, *Biblical Theology*. (Edinburgh: Banner of Truth Trust, 1948/1975), 325. See also H. C. Leupold, *Exposition of Isaiah*. Vols 1 & 2. (Darlington: Evangelical Press, 1977), 229.

[450] J. Barton Payne, *A Theology of the Older Testament*. (Grand Rapids: Academie Books, Zondervan Publishing House, 1962), 271–284. One disappointing feature of Payne's otherwise very helpful book is the lack of a Scripture index at the back.

[451] Leupold, *Isaiah*, 229.

[452] Apud Galatin. de Cathol. Ver. l. 10. c. 6. p. 663, and Siphre in ib. l. 8. c. 20. p. 599.

Gill's interpretation contrasts with Calvin's who preaches (in his sermon on *Isaiah* 53:4–6) that Christ was every sinner's Substitute. He concludes that what we see is our Lord Jesus Christ bearing all our sins.[453] Calvin gives no hint that he meant by that "sinners of all kinds," or "sinners from all parts of the world." Calvin's oft-repeated phrase "the death and passion of Christ" is used to point to what He has done for all men on the cross. Indeed, Calvin preaches that Isaiah includes the word "all" to rule out all exceptions,[454] adding that Christ has enough to satisfy the real needs of us all.[455] He is gracious enough to approach because His sacrifice is sufficient for us all.[456] Calvin's inclusivity regarding Christ's redeeming work is set out in his exposition of *Isaiah* 53:6. In fact, he contends that this entire passage (*Isaiah* 53) is exclusively about the death and passion of Christ for us all.

Presbyterian commentator, Matthew Henry, wrote that it was the iniquity of us all that God laid on Christ because He is sufficient to save all. Hence, a genuine offer is made of that salvation for all without exception, excluding none that do not exclude themselves. There is no other way of salvation for anyone. Sinners are justified by having their sins laid upon Christ, and regardless of how many or how serious these sins are, Christ can bear their full weight. His exegesis is abundantly clear. He does not limit "of us all" but takes the words in their normal and natural senses. Introducing the idea of sufficient merit for the salvation of all in Christ, Henry includes the gospel offer of that salvation that God makes to all, an offer that excludes none and invites all. Because God laid on Christ the penalty of sin for us all, there is universal provision in the Saviour's atonement which the Lord offers to all who hear the gospel.

Dabney thinks this interpretation is open to less objection than other interpretations. "God sent His Son to provide a vicarious satisfaction for the sin of all whom His providence intended to place under the gospel

---

[453] Calvin, *Isaiah Sermons*, 70.
[454] Calvin, *Isaiah Sermons*, 78.
[455] Calvin, *Isaiah Sermons*, 81.
[456] *Ibid.*

offers."[457] This exposition makes great sense of the biblical data and ensures that preachers do not cut the umbilical cord of evangelism and world mission by mistake.

Wesley's Notes on the Old Testament give a similarly clear interpretation. He holds that if Christ had not been fully and truly God and fully and truly man, He would have sunk under that colossal load of mankind's every sin.[458] Wesley demonstrates his closeness to Calvin in his understanding of the universal terms used by Isaiah and highlights the substantial distance he was from Gill and that Gill was from Calvin.

When expounding the phrase "of us all," Rawlinson explains the universality of the atonement in terms of redemption being, potentially, as universal as the sin. Christ was a sacrifice that was full, perfect and sufficient for the sins of mankind.[459] Scripture is taken in its natural, common-sense, meaning. There is in the atonement provision for all. Therefore none need die without an available and sufficient Saviour. Calvin agrees: there is enough in Jesus Christ to satisfy us all because He is sufficient for all.[460] Calvin's "alls" display the inclusiveness of the atonement without limitation.

Presbyterian theologian, Albert Barnes uses language that expresses the thought that Christ suffered for all people. The atonement is naturally universal and sets out the notion that God has not restricted the number of those for whom the Saviour died.[461] Clearly, the universal aspect is to the fore in Barnes' exegesis and concurs with that of other careful exegetes, such as Calvin.

---

[457] Dabney, *Systematic*, 519, 520.
[458] Wesley's Explanatory Notes on *Isaiah* 53:6.
[459] G. Rawlinson, *The Pulpit Commentary – Isaiah*. (London: Funk and Wagnell, 1906), 296.
[460] Calvin, *Isaiah Sermons*, 81. In his commentary on *Isaiah* 53:6, he writes, "Our sins overwhelm us: but they are laid on Christ, by whom we are unburdened. Therefore, when we were perishing, and, alienated from God, were hastening to Hell, Christ took upon Himself the filthy depths (*colluviem*) of our sins, to rescue us from eternal destruction …" (p.67).
[461] Albert Barnes, *Notes on Isaiah*, (Grand Rapids: Baker Book House, 1972), 271.

The high Calvinist, Dr Alec Motyer, in his commentary on *Isaiah* writes,

> <u>We all</u> and <u>each</u> expresses both common culpability and individual responsibility ... Over against the common herd, and matching the individual need, there stands <u>him</u> on whom our iniquity has been laid. By the divine act, the Servant was the meeting point for <u>the iniquity of us all</u>.[462]

Motyer accepts the exposition that "each sin of every sinner would be like a separate wound in the heart of this man of sorrows." Inclusivity is innate to what Isaiah says, and Motyer brings this out quite clearly. He continues,

> *The Servant is not ... one moved by personal compassion and voluntariness; he is the provision and plan of God, who himself superintends the priestly task (Lev. 16:21) of transferring the guilt of the guilty to the head of the Servant, giving notice that this is indeed his considered and acceptable satisfaction for sin.*[463]

The guilty are all those deemed to be so by the law of God, namely, every son of Adam. The whole world is accountable to, and guilty before, God (*Romans* 3:19). So God has transferred to the head of the Servant/Saviour the whole world's guilt (Cf. 1 *John* 5:9 and *Romans* 3:19). Now if the limited atonement position is correct, and only the elect are guilty and godless, it could be argued that the non-elect have no need of a Redeemer. After all, atonement is not required where there is no sin. It further implies that they will go to Heaven in any case. Particularistic language makes nonsense of the biblical text and makes language incapable of being understood, requiring those who have been initiated into the deeper mysteries of such religion to explain its true meaning.

---

[462] J. Alec Motyer, *The Prophecy of Isaiah*. (Leicester: InterVarsity Press, 1993), 431. The author's original emphases have been retained.
[463] *Ibid.*

DML-J was with Calvin, Wesley, Barnes and Motyer (on this point) when he preached

> *In view of the fact that salvation is of God and therefore supernatural, although we cannot understand it, it holds out a hope for all. ... There is literally hope for all. ...It is God's work, and because it is God's work, it is possible for all and can be offered to all. ...There is literally hope for all.*[464]

Or again,

> *It is God who sent his Son into the world, it is God who sent him to the cross, it is God who 'laid on him the iniquities of us all,' Isa.53:6. It is God who has taken your sins and put them on him and punished them in him and is offering you a free pardon; it is God who has done it.*[465]

> *Here is 'the Lamb of God which taketh away the sin of the world,' Jn 1:29. Here is the one who has never sinned; here is one who is spotless; here is one who has never broken a commandment, never defied his Father. He has pleased his Father in all things and in all ways. And, 'God has laid on him the iniquity of us all' Isa.53:6.*[466]

> *He sent his only Son into this world 'for the suffering of death ... that he by the grace of God should taste death for every man' Heb.2:9. God's Son took our sins upon himself: 'He hath laid on him the iniquity of us all' Isa.53:6.*[467]

These four quotations demonstrate clearly DML-J's interpretation of *Isaiah* 53:6. Clearly, he follows Calvin, Wesley, Henry, Barnes, and, at this point, Motyer rather than Gill, or even Owen as we shall see.

Owen states, conjoining *Isaiah* 53:6 and *John* 3:16, that God out of his mere free grace and mercy, has found a way to redeem His elect. Owen is

---

[464] DML-J, selection #49. See also #9.
[465] DML-J, selection #183.
[466] DML-J, selection #188.
[467] DML-J, selection #208.

interpretatively particularistic when dealing with the Bible's universalistic statements.[468] For DML-J, hope is held out for all because the gospel offers it to all without exception. Because God has sent His Son to Calvary to bear the sins of all, a free pardon can now be offered to all. If He had not taken the sins of all upon His Body on the cross and died for them, how could a free and utterly sincere offer of salvation be made to them?

It was "the sin of the world" that God laid on Him, "the iniquity of us all." DML-J did not subscribe to the narrower view of the atonement as espoused by Gill and Owen. Subscribing to that narrower view would have hampered his evangelistic preaching, leaving him with nothing to offer the lost. The biblical teaching handed him something real to offer to real sinners — a real salvation that would become theirs on condition of faith in Christ.

Davenant reinforces this important gospel point in *Isaiah* 53:6 by reference to the church Fathers, quoting them as saying that the precious blood of our Lord Jesus Christ is itself the ransom of the whole world.[469] Quoting from David Paræus, Davenant indicated that what lay at the heart of Christ's passion was the removal of the reality of divine wrath against the sin, not of some selected men, but of the entire human race.[470]

One looks in vain for any treatment of this verse in Smeaton when he refers to *Isaiah* 53. He references vvs. 3,7,12, but makes no reference to 53:6.[471] Obviously he had his reasons why he avoided this verse, but its omission is significant, implying that Smeaton had difficulties with the truth contained in it. Disappointingly, Clifford, who is rigorously accurate

---

[468] I am reminded of Lewis Carroll's character, Humpty Dumpty, who said scornfully, "When *I* use a word ... it means just what I choose it to mean — neither more nor less." Alice (in Wonderland) then asks "whether you *can* make words mean so many different things." "The question is, "said Humpty Dumpty, "which is to be master— that's all." He believed that he could impart meanings to words that suited his purpose.

[469] Davenant, *Dissertation*, 33.

[470] Davenant, *Dissertation*, 35.

[471] Smeaton, 1871/1991:81, cf. 497.

in his exegesis of Scripture, makes reference to *Isaiah* 53:4, 5, 12 but omits verse six. Had he treated this pivotal verse, he would have thrown more light on its actual meaning. Douty, however, teaches that Christ's atoning suffering was on behalf of all men.[472] He demonstrates that the "all" at the end of this verse requires the same understanding as at the opening of the verse, both being true of all men, not only the elect.

Clearly, these few quotations indicate that there is a division between those who embrace the scholastic doctrine of limited atonement and those who follow the Scriptures, understood in their natural meaning. It is also clear which interpretation DML-J prefers, and it is not that of Gill and Owen.

---

[472] Douty, *Death of Christ*, 56.

28

Mark 10:45 –A Ransom For Many.

When Jesus says He came to give His life a ransom *for many,* what does He mean?[473] The 1550 Stephanus Greek Text says, και δουναι την ψυχην αυτου λυτρον αντι πολλων. Αντι, when used of persons, denotes something that is done 'for the sake of' or 'on behalf of.'[474] Hendriksen says it means 'in the place of,' and adds, without explanation, "Not in the place of all but many."[475] Λυτρον comes from a Greek root meaning "to loose," and refers to the payment made for those who are to be redeemed, loosing them from their bondage and setting them free.[476] Zodhiates explains that in this context, the term applies to the ransom that Christ paid to deliver men from the bondage of sin and the certainty and tyranny of death. This view could have the particularistic interpretation that many attribute to it, following Owen, but this is not the only viable or natural interpretation of this passage. From the spiritual perspective, who are "captives" and who are in "bonds"? All men are. All are the slaves of sin and are in bondage to iniquity. A particularistic interpretation is not necessary and Calvin does not follow it. He uses this text to refer to humanity.[477] Jesus refers to a numberless number. Some may argue that it is a number nevertheless

---

[473] Cf. *Matthew* 20:28. The 1599 Geneva Bible translates it: "for the ransom of many."

[474] Spiros Zodhiates, *The Complete Word Study Dictionary New Testament.* (Chattanooga: AMG Publishers, 1992), 190.

[475] William Hendriksen, *Mark.* (Edinburgh: Banner of Truth Trust, 1975), 415. He may have been using this verse when he wrote these words, but in explaining αντι, he was taking it in its normal usage without reference to this verse.

[476] Zodhiates, *Dictionary NT,* 930.

[477] Calvin, Comm. on *Matthew* 20:28.

therefore it is finite. Others say that because it is a large number (many), it is as good as meaning "all," as Calvin teaches.[478] For Calvin, the atonement is unlimited, but it carries no benefits for those refusing to believe in Christ alone for salvation.

William Lane reverts to a "high view" interpretation of this verse and introduces the thought of substitution.[479] When Jesus gave His life, Lane says that Mark qualifies this by saying that it was "a ransom for the many." Neither the Westcott and Hort Greek text (1881) nor the Stephanus Greek text[480] (1550) has the definite article in their text of this verse. So for Lane to add this is gratuitous and is to take unwarranted liberties with the text of Scripture. The Greek text says simply "a ransom for many," not "*the* many." What Christ did in giving His life on their behalf spared them suffering it themselves, he argues. Continuing, Lane states that Jesus gave His life in the place of those who had forfeited their lives.[481] He posits a level of definiteness in the relation between "the many" and Christ. But who, according to Lane, have forfeited their lives? He could answer in one of two ways. He could say that "the many" equates with "the elect" (as Hendriksen, Owen, Gill, etc. argue). Or he could say with Calvin that "the many" refers to all those who have forfeited their lives because of their sin, namely all mankind. Jesus in His death on Calvary paid the ransom price that sets men enslaved by sin and guilt free, he contends. However, he appears to understand "men" as referring to definite individuals, rather than as a generic term that includes all humanity.[482] He posits an indissoluble link between Christ and the community of people He came to ransom and concluded that this idea matches perfectly the most important thought of *Isaiah* 53. Apparently, Lane did not study Calvin's commentary and sermons on *Isaiah* 53, and if he had, he has taken a deliberately different interpretative route from Calvin thus explaining

---

[478] Calvin, Comm. on *Romans* 5:15.

[479] William L. Lane, *The Gospel According to Mark*. (Grand Rapids: Eerdmans, 1974), 384.

[480] Also known as the *Textus Receptus*, or the *Elzevir text*.

[481] Lane, *Mark*, 384.

[482] Philip *Confession*, 86 agrees: "He became man for our sakes - not merely 'a man' (though He did become that), but 'man.'"

his particularistic exposition. DML-J would have parted company with Lane at this point, preferring, as he did, to expound *Mark* 10:45 in clearly Calvinist terms. In his gospel sermon, he preached, "Do you sincerely believe that Jesus Christ the Son of God came to rescue and ransom you from your sin and to reconcile you to God?"[483] Again, he proclaimed,

> *He came to give his life a ransom for you. God delivered him up for you, whatever you may have been, whatever you may have thought of him to this moment. … So repent and believe on the Lord Jesus Christ and you shall be saved.*[484]

Or again,

> *… the only way even he could save anybody was by giving his life a ransom for us, by dying for us, to 'bare our sins in his own body on the tree' (1 Pet 2:24).*[485]

DML-J is clear that "many" in *Mark* 10:45 is as good as "all," as Calvin teaches. He preached his evangelistic sermons to mixed congregations (believers and unbelievers), and DML-J happily told them all that Christ gave His life a ransom for them, to ransom us. Also, several of Paul's letters were written to churches, but that does not mean that every single member was a true Christian; false believers were in membership in first-century churches.[486] He makes it particular to those to whom he was preaching so it is doubtless that what Christ did, He did for them. For them to benefit from Christ's work, they must trust in the Saviour. DML-J's Amyraldianism is "in your face" in these sermon extracts where *Mark* 10:45 is the text of reference. This method of interpretation also reflects Calvin's exegesis of this text.

---

[483] Selection #27.
[484] Selection #177.
[485] Selection #319.
[486] The churches at Corinth and in Galatia, for example, had false believers within their membership, otherwise his admonitions are meaningless.

29

John 1:29 – The Lamb Of God Who Takes Away The Sin Of The World.

John the Baptist spoke these words, "The Lamb of God who takes away the sin of the world," as the daily sacrifice did for all Israel. The Old Testament remedy was universally applicable to that particular people, Israel. But here is the *true* Lamb of God that takes away the world's sin. Ryle quotes Calvin approvingly, remarking that John "extends this favour indiscriminately to the whole human race, that the Jews might not think he had been sent for them alone."[487] Mankind is under divine condemnation, and God's remedy is offered to all without exception on condition of faith, as Calvin taught.

Baxter urges believers to look carefully at this Man Whom God has appointed to be sacrificed to Him, just as they sacrificed lambs in the OT. God established this atoning system that all who believe in Him might have their guilt absolved. Taking the plain meaning of the text, Baxter, along with Ryle, brings out what was in the original speaker's/author's mind. For Ryle, John uses the singular number, referring to "the sin" and not "the sins" of the world. Says Ryle,

> *The expression seems to me purposely intended to show that what Christ took away, and bore on the cross, was not the sin of certain people only, but the whole accumulated mass of all the sins of all the children of Adam.*[488]

---

[487] J. C. Ryle, *Expository Thoughts on John*. Vol.1. (Edinburgh: Banner of Truth Trust, 1869/1987), 63.
[488] Ryle, *Thoughts*, 61.

Neither Calvin, Baxter nor Ryle places any restriction on the meaning of the text because Scripture does not. Believing that Scripture is clear on these important matters, the natural meaning of the words is good enough for them, and, therefore, followed. To limit the author's intent is to do injustice to his thought, and Calvin, Baxter and Ryle eschewed that vigorously. Ryle delves into the hidden purpose of God in the cross when he mentions His intention for Christ in His death. Clearly, it was to atone for the sins of all men, not a limited few (relatively speaking). It was all-encompassing in its intent and limited only to the "whosoever believes," in effect. Ryle confesses, humbly, his limited understanding of things divine when he states that he rested in the inscrutableness of the divine will and purpose when Christ by His death atoned for the world's sin.[489] It is inclusive of all. Ryle, in repudiating the idea of "universal salvation" as a "dangerous heresy," and "utterly contrary to Scripture," asserts that "the lost will not prove to be lost because Christ has done nothing for them. He bore their sins, He carried their transgressions, He provided payment."[490] Since He has done that for all, no one can be said to die without an offered and available, willing and able Saviour (*Hebrews* 7:25). This understanding is true because God provided atonement out of love for all of His fallen creatures.[491] Their stubborn refusal to trust Christ is the cause of their eternal lostness, not any pre-creation decree passed by God. As Ryle preaches, "He set the prison door open to all, but the majority would not come out and be free."[492] So, for Ryle, it is the unbelieving attitude that damns sinners, not any insufficiency or inadequacy in the atonement. "Christ's atonement is a benefit which is offered freely and honestly to all mankind. ... the true meaning [is] that the Lamb of God has made atonement sufficient for all though efficient unquestionably to none but believers."[493]

---

[489] Ryle, *Thoughts*, 62. Grimm-Thayer says the word translated "takes away," which is used again in 1 *John* 3:5 means "to remove." Arndt-Gingrich adds that it means "to blot out." The issue of 'wastage' – where those for whom Christ died perish in their sins – is dealt with by Ryle at this point.
[490] *Ibid.*
[491] Smeaton, *Christ*, 45.
[492] Ryle, *Thoughts*, 62.
[493] Ryle, *Thoughts*, 62.

Calvin's exposition of this central gospel truth and that expounded by Baxter and Ryle are identical. For Calvin, the salvation that Christ brought is common to all men since Christ is the Author of salvation.[494] This point answers those who claim that while Calvin might be universal in his sermons, we cannot say the same of his Institutes, but that is not the case at all. Listen to the Reformer again, when he contends that so long as the Saviour remains outside our hearts, our sin and guilt separates us from Him. This fact implies that everything that He has suffered for the salvation of the whole world remains of no use to or value for us.[495] The convergence between Calvin, Baxter and Ryle on this point is impossible to miss, their exegesis is identical in content. DML-J believes the same and is also in this happy band of godly preachers.

The Geneva Study Notes on *John* 1:29 stick closely to the text and emphasise the universality of the atonement without adding any limitations to it. The Lamb of God is Christ and in His death He has made "satisfaction for the sin of the world." This word, αιρων, is in the present tense and signifies a continuous act of "carrying away." This Lamb has this power to take away the sin of the world, both now and forever.

Matthew Henry writes that the teaching of this verse is most encouraging to our faith. He asks the obvious question, if Christ takes away the sin of the world, then why not my sin? Why not indeed? He views Jesus as the world's Saviour. Here "the world," means humanity, all mankind. David Brown confesses that the Lamb here referred to points, beyond all doubt, to the death of Christ, and also refers to its sacrificial character. He adds that the sin (singular) denotes the Lamb bore both the combined burden of our sins, as well as its comprehensive efficacy. It was not for Jews only – as the morning and evening sacrifices were, but in contrast it was for the whole world. It was "the sin of the world" that the Lamb of God carried away, not just that of one particular nation. This sacrifice was not exclusive, but one that was/is sufficient for the whole world. Pastorally and evangelistically, Brown teaches that wherever a sinner lives in the world

---

[494] Inst.II.xiii.3.
[495] Inst.III.i.1.

and sinking under that overwhelming burden of sin, he shall find this "Lamb of God" more than able to carry that load.[496]

A. T. Robertson affirms that Jesus is the Lamb of God for the whole world, and not just for Jews.[497] The combining of "the world" and "the Jews" (as a particular nation) suggests that in distinction to "the Jews," "the world" is the κοσμος in all its rich universality. On κοσμος, Zodhiates understands the noun to include, among other things, the whole mass of people who live lives that are indifferent to and even hostile to the gospel and Christ's followers.[498] This hostility marks all mankind by nature because all fit this description. It is this world of humanity that is dominated by the evil one, and which is further the object of God's wrath and judgement, and also of His mercy. All men are the objects of divine judgement individually and collectively. The κοσμος, here, equates to all men. So the Lamb of God takes away the sin of all men.

Ladd points out that John's description of the Baptist differs from that given in the Synoptics. Here, he describes Christ in a specific way[499] – as "the Lamb of God who takes away the sin of the world." The Baptist's preference is for the soteriological aspect of Christ's work[500] rather than the eschatological, the theological rather than purely historical. When the New Testament uses the word κοσμος for mankind, the context is always the κοσμος as the object of the divine redeeming love and salvation. Ladd's words about how John sees the world in relation to Christ in His death are worth quoting.

> *God loves the world (3:16) and sent his son to save the world (3:17a; 12:47). Jesus is the Savoir of the world (4:42); he came to take away the sin of the world (1:29) and to give life to the world (6:33).*[501]

---

[496] David Brown, *The Four Gospels*. (Edinburgh: Banner of Truth Trust, 1864/1969), 352.

[497] A. T. Robertson, *Word Pictures of the New Testament*. http://www.biblestudytools.com/commentaries/robertsons-word-pictures/john/john-1-29.html

[498] Zodhiates, *Dictionary*, 882.

[499] Ladd, *Theology*, 43.

[500] Ladd, *Theology*, 249.

[501] Ladd, *Theology*, 226. See also Morris, *John*, 128.

What is inexplicable to a degree is that Ladd goes on to say in the next sentence that these sayings do not carry any distinctively universalistic emphasis. What they do merely is to choose mankind as a whole as the object of God's love and saving action in Christ. If universalistic language does not mean universalistic emphasis, what does it mean? Here Ladd follows Prof. Murray in this approach to biblical interpretation, which is most unnatural, therefore, unsatisfactory and unconvincing. Ladd gives no rationale for adopting this particular interpretative practice. Jesus would not have been given the title "Saviour of the world" if He had not come to be the "Saviour of the world."

Jesus died for the world, that is, for the entire human family in all ages. This point is abundantly clear. His sacrifice bought all men's ransom, but all men do not acknowledge the purchase.[502] This understanding supports Baxter's soteriology and is that held by DML-J. Baxter makes an important observation relating to the clarity and frequency with which God declared the true nature of the atonement. He demonstrates from Scripture that Christ died for all (2 *Corinthians* 5:15), and tasted death for every man (*Hebrews* 2:9); that He is the ransom for all (1 *Timothy* 2:6), and the propitiation for the sins of the whole world (1 *John* 2:2). It is, therefore, the responsibility of every believer to explain in what sense it is true that, for example, Christ died for all, than outrightly deny it, as some do.[503] DML-J preaches, "We know why he died. There, on the cross, God was laying on him the iniquity of us all. He is the 'Lamb of God' – as John the Baptist had said – 'which taketh away the sin of the world' Jn.1:29."

What does it mean to say that Christ came to "take away the sin of the world"? Douty is helpful here, saying, this does not mean that when Christ died as the sacrificial Lamb, those for whom He thus suffered and died had, subsequently, no sin to be pardoned.[504] This interpretation is a calumny that those who oppose this viewpoint place on the universal atonement theologians. Rather, Douty explains that Christ, by His death, took the punishment that they were deserving of because of their guilt, a

---

[502] *The Fourfold Gospel* (n.p., n.d.).
[503] Richard Baxter, *Universal Redemption of Mankind*, 7, 8.
[504] Douty, *Death of Christ*, 57.

somewhat different conclusion. So far, they have not received the benefit of salvation because, in line with Calvin, these sinners must acknowledge and forsake their sins, and trust in Christ crucified and risen as their Redeemer.[505] This clarification exposes the fallacy embedded in the notion that Christ's cross saves sinners. Without faith, it is impossible to please God in anything (*Hebrews* 11:6).

Wesley concurs with the above, adding that the sins taken away are the sins of all mankind.[506] Sin and the world are of equal extent, argues Wesley. Even the elect prior to conversion are full of sin, elect unbelievers, thus making sin and the world of equal extent. Elect unbelievers cannot be saved unless and until they come in repentance and trust Christ alone for salvation. For the sinner, any sinner and every sinner to receive the benefits of the redemption purchased by Christ, God requires of him faith in Jesus Christ and repentance that leads to life.[507] "And without faith it is impossible to please Him" (*Hebrews* 11:6).

Gill's exegesis (or is it eisegesis?), reminiscent of Owen's, makes "the world" equal to "the elect," but fails to give his grounds for so doing. It is a purely gratuitous exercise, and dishonest, as Machen would say. By the "sin of the world," is not meant the sin, or sins, of every person in the world, says Gill. So according to his exegesis "the sin of the world" does not mean "the sin of the world" after all. Had John said this in *John* 1:29, he would have avoided confusion in understanding basic English. We would then have known that John the Baptist did not mean "the world" as we understand it.

Indeed, Dr Owen and writer Arthur W. Pink engage in reductionist exegesis (or, is it eisegesis?) when they diminish the meaning of "the world" to refer only to "the elect world." Douty views "the world of the elect" as "an odd expression," and provides the explanation that "we never

---

[505] *Ibid.*

[506] John Wesley's Notes on the NT.

[507] The Westminster Shorter Catechism no. 85 adds to these two requirements the following: "with the diligent use of all the outward means whereby Christ communicateth to us the benefits of redemption."

read of God electing "the world;" He chooses individuals out of it.[508] This wording is not a biblical phrase at all. We concede that, when used of men, it does not always mean everyone. It is undeniable that in its usual usage, it indicates either that or the whole of "mankind contemplated as in an unregenerate condition."[509] According to Westcott, κοσμος is essentially the totality of created being which belongs to the realm of ordered human life, considered apart from and in rebellion against God.[510] It is humanity estranged from God, a reality that belongs to all mankind. By extension, fallen man impresses his character on that order over which he has devolved sovereignty, and of which he is an integral part. Hence, κοσμος comes to denote humanity as it now is, alienated from its Creator, and antagonistic towards Him. So degeneration takes place from an ordered creation (world, κοσμος), to one estranged from God to one opposed to God. The temporal world becomes increasingly hostile to the eternal and divine. According to the Baptist, then, it was the sin of this world that Christ died to take away.

Leon Morris understands the cross in its comprehensiveness.[511] John is referring to the totality of the world's sin, rather than to a number of individual acts. Individual acts are carried out by individuals; therefore, John is not referring to individuals either. His reference is to "the sin of the world" in its totality. Christ's death on the cross is wholly sufficient to meet the needs of all.[512] Despite attempts to question the authenticity of this verse,[513] not one of them was successful. The verse stands intact and teaches us Who Christ is and why He came into the world.

Listen to how Morris catalogues the way Jesus' mission is "dominated" by the world that He came to save. In his commentary on John's Gospel, he

---

[508] Douty, *Death of Christ*, 57.
[509] Goode, as cited in Douty, *Death of Christ*, 58. Douty adds three references from Matthew, one for Mark, and twenty-two from John's Gospel where he claims that Christ used this term in these senses.
[510] Westcott, as cited in Douty, 1972:58.
[511] Morris, *John*, 148.
[512] *Ibid*.
[513] Morris, *John*, 149.

explains that it was the world that God loves, (3:16). When Christ speaks, He shares with the world those things His Father told Him, (8:26). In God's plan, everything He did in Christ in His work of providing atonement is directed towards the world, (1:29). God accomplished atonement in and through the Saviour. That's why He became flesh and entered this world to take away its sin (1:29). The very title the believing Samaritans gave Him, and that He accepted, indicates that He is the Saviour of the world (4:42). The Son of God gives life to the world (6:33), and He does that at considerable cost to Himself – the cost of His life, flesh (6:51). His very purpose in being sent and coming into the world was to save it, no less, not to judge it. The world was already under divine judgement, so what it needed most of all was a Saviour, not a Judge. And God sent a Saviour into the world for that purpose (3:17; 12:47).[514]

Morris is clear about what God's attitude to the world is – He loves it and sent His Son to die for it. What is meant here is not just the world in its "badness" but also the world in its "bigness." Warfield, however, limits the term "the world" to its ethical connotation that he describes as "deep," and not to its breadth. It is that realm where darkness and shame and sin reign.[515] Inadvertently, Warfield is teaching that since shame and sin belong to men as moral beings, the sphere referred to is, therefore, all mankind. Morris presents universal redemption in its most biblical sense. God has within His Being an attitude of gracious and saving complacency towards the rebellious and lost world that He, in Christ, loves and has redeemed. He tells his readers that the Jew was quick to assume that God loved only Israel, and nobody else. He could not cite any passage from any Jewish author who maintained that God has a love for the whole world.[516]

This distinctively Christian idea is acknowledged. God's love is sufficiently wide to embrace the whole world,[517] and proceeds from God's nature as love (1 *John* 4:8, 16). God shows love to the unlovely, unlovable, unloved

---

[514] Morris, *John*, 128. See also Ladd, 1974:226.
[515] B. B. Warfield, *The Person and Work of Christ*. (Philadelphia: Presbyterian and Reformed, 1970), 551.
[516] Morris, *John*, 229.
[517] *Ibid*.

and unloving. So Morris demonstrates that what God has done in Christ has had an incalculable effect on the whole world – He took away its sin. Or, as the Arabic and Ethiopic versions have it in the plural, "the sins of the world."

What then of the issue of "wastage" in regard to the Baptist's statement that "the Lamb of God ... takes away the sin of the world"? Particular redemptionists will argue that if Christ has not saved all men by this "taking away" of sin, then He has failed. It was a wasted effort, carried out for nothing. Well, Ryle, for one, sees no strength in this objection. He argues that we might as well say that because sin came into the world through Adam and marred God's perfect creation, creation was in vain. He argues that because we are dealing with God's works and not man's, there will, of necessity, be much we do not understand. Man's fallen mind cannot fathom the depths of divine knowledge and wisdom, let alone comprehend it. How God can "take away the sin of the world" via His Lamb, and yet that act does not save all men, is a mystery that defies rational thought, and demands humility to accept. The duality entailed in this is noted. Two options are open to interpreters: one is to accept the language of the text as it stands, and the other is to start from a particularistic viewpoint and make the text fit that specific emphasis. It is clear from looking at these two options which one is biblical. We must learn humility in the face of divine mysteries, or mysteries in light, that God has not revealed to us. Man's capacity to reconcile such mysteries is extremely limited and does not reflect the place they have in God's mind.[518] Our tendency towards a scholastic approach must be curbed to prevent diversion into a logic that the Bible nowhere warrants. That there is a sense in which God has accomplished what He says in His Word is accepted, but it is beyond our ability to understand how He did it. Ryle strongly repudiates universal salvation as a dangerous heresy that is utterly contrary to the teaching of Scripture.[519] He believes that the vast majority of mankind will perish in their sins. (How this statement tallies with a verse like *Revelation* 7:9 is difficult to see. Indeed, Ryle provides

---

[518] Robert Letham, *The Work of Christ*. (Leicester: InterVarsity Press, 1993), 245.
[519] Ryle, *John*, 62.

no explanation for his statement). This perishing of the greater part of mankind is not because Christ has done nothing for it, but because it has not trusted Christ alone for salvation, freely offered in the gospel. God provided the remedy and made it available to all, yet many reject it. No one can lay their perdition at Christ's door, but at their own because of their refusal to trust in the God-provided Lamb as their Substitute. Christ accomplished all that had to be done for their salvation – taking their place, bearing their sins away, carrying their transgressions and iniquities, and providing payment that was acceptable to God, the ransom price. "But in the work of Christ in atonement I see no limitation," says Ryle. "The atonement was made for all the world though it is applied to and enjoyed by none but believers."[520] Hypothetically, all can be saved if only they trust in Christ's atonement. No evidence exists that the entire world will enjoy its saving benefits. "But Christ's atonement is a benefit that is offered freely and honestly to all mankind."[521] Ryle is clear; in Christ's atonement there is a general reference to the entire world and a particular reference to believers only. No limitation is needed regarding "the sin of the world," he contends. He sees here "the whole mass of mankind's guilt" converging on the Lamb, something the Bible says Christ took away. He uses the Lombardian sufficiency/efficiency maxim to strengthen his position. When Luther commenced lecturing at Wittenberg in 1509, his subject was Lombard's *Sentences*, and it was from him that he learned the sufficiency/efficiency formula.[522]

Calvin's exposition confirms this position. When John refers to 'the sin of the world,' he is extending this saving favour indiscriminately to mankind, he argues. Why was this done? So that the Jews might not imagine that Christ had been sent to them alone. Since all men are, without exception, *guilty* before God, they too must be reconciled to Him.[523] Calvin equates those under divine wrath with those who need salvation from wrath – all mankind. What one man needs, all need. Our duty is to embrace the benefits of Christ's purchased redemption that is offered to all. Each one

---

[520] *Ibid.*

[521] *Ibid.*

[522] Jones, *Reformation*, 30.

[523] John Calvin as cited in Ryle, *John*, 63. See also his commentary on this passage.

of us in turn, whoever we are, is persuaded that no reason exists why we too cannot come to Him by faith and be reconciled to God.[524]

Calvin's position, contested by the high orthodox, is clear – humanity has had its sin taken away by Christ, and this includes all men without exception. Christ did this in His death, but God has kept the actual mechanics of this within His eternal council. The way the benefits of this "taking away" are received is by trusting Christ, by embracing Christ's offer to all. Faith in Christ is central, not election and predestination. That probably explains why Calvin in his *Institutes* did not deal with predestination until towards the end of his third book.

Milne understands the term, "the sins of the world," as describing the scope of the Lamb's ministry. "Without exception, every kind of sin and evil is covered. There is no sin too heinous, no wickedness too terrible, no habitual failure too often repeated, that it cannot be "taken away" by Christ, our Heavenly Lamb."[525] Milne uses the plural "sins" rather than the singular, "sin." He draws attention primarily to the extensiveness of sin and includes all kinds of sin – all good pastoral teaching. It is important to know and to experience these truths if Christians are to have assurance of their interest in Christ and His interest in them. But to stop there is to stop too far short. Milne does not deal with *those* whose sins are being referred to, therefore sells us short in his exposition of this important soteriological text. So not much help here.

William Hendriksen provides no help either. Instead, he takes us back into ultra-orthodoxy when he avers, "According to the Baptist it is the sin *of the world* (men from every tribe, and people, by nature lost in sin, cf. 11:51, 52) which the Lamb is taking away, not merely the sin of a particular nation (e.g., the Jewish)."[526] This unwarranted exegesis completely misses the point John is making. In any case, Hendriksen, despite his otherwise detailed explanations of contested understandings, does not provide even a hint of his grounds for making this statement on the Baptist's behalf.

---

[524] *Ibid.*
[525] Milne, *The Message of John*. (Leicester: InterVarsity Press, 1993), 54.
[526] Hendriksen, *John*, 99.

It is pure speculation. Where "according to the Baptist" can we find his grounds and warrant for such an interpretation? Exegetically, Hendriksen is stretching his interpretation to breaking-point. He ought not to have "blamed" the Baptist for this spurious interpretation of *John* 1:29. Rather, he ought, with greater integrity, to have pointed to the WCF where Christ is said to have died for the elect (only).[527] For Hendriksen, when explaining this verse, it is more important to be confessionally correct than to be biblically faithful. In order to satisfy confessional requirements, he ignores the universal aspect of the gospel and also of Christ's atoning work. Preachers should listen to Ryle's wise statement. He said, "I have long come to the conclusion that men may be more systematic in their statements than the Bible, and may be led into grave error by idolatrous veneration of a system."[528]

Again, it is clear which interpretation of *John* 1:29 DML-J favours. While he has the greatest respect for commentators like Hendriksen, he does not follow slavishly their exegesis but comes to his own conclusions of what the Scripture text says. The Appendix will repay careful study.

---

[527] WCF, Ch. VIII, sections I, VI, VIII.
[528] Ryle, *John*, 159.

30

John 3:16 – God So Loved The World That He Gave.

Since the atonement proceeds from God's loving heart, we can understand the word, "gave", in two senses. *First*, "God gave the Son by sending Him into the world," but *second*, He "also gave the Son on the cross."[529] It is the Father's love for the world, denoting the race,[530] which the cross displays. The achievement of the cross was not wrung from an unwilling Deity. Morris explains that the Greek construction has the following emphasis: it is not "God loved so as to give," but "God loved so that He gave."[531] The love of God is not a sentimental thing but is a love that acts sacrificially. Denney speaks of God's sin-bearing love. Love mattered much to John[532] because it mattered much to God.

Baxter paraphrases it thus: God, Who is Himself love loved lapsed and lost mankind so much that He gave His Son to take on flesh and to be mankind's Redeemer. He did this by His meritorious life, by His death and resurrection on the third day. He made them this firm offer that whoever truly believes in Him as their Saviour will have his sin forgiven, will never

---

[529] Morris, *John*, 229.
[530] Douty, *Death of Christ*, 59. Guthrie agrees that the reference here is to the universality of God's Love. *The Theology of the New Testament*. (Leicester: InterVarsity Press, 1970), 937.
[531] Morris, *John*, 229. This nuanced point is easily missed because of its subtlety but it is worth making.
[532] *John* 3:16 is John's first use of αγαπαω, a verb he uses some 36 times in this Gospel and 31 times in *First John*.

perish, and enter into everlasting life.[533] For Baxter, God loved a lost mankind and displayed that love in a saving way. Only if "the world" was made to be "the elect" could Owen's interpretation be justified. But it is not made "the elect." The fourth Gospel is clear. God so loved the world.

John goes on to state that it was not a condemner that the world needed – for it was "condemned already." The world needed a Saviour, Someone who would deal with God's wrath problem and man's sin problem. And that Saviour was sent from Heaven for that express purpose – to save the world.

Baxter raises another salient point that if the world is condemned, no one will ever have any cause to lay the blame on Christ when they perish in Hell forever. The reason for this is that Christ did not come into the world to condemn it. His life, teaching, and sufferings demonstrate this truth. Here Baxter aired answers to this objection long before anyone raised it. If Christ died only for the elect and none else, then the non-elect had grounds for blaming the Saviour, and the God Who sent Him, when they found themselves condemned on the last Day. They will never be able to say that there was no Saviour for them. If the world is condemned, it will be condemned because it refused to trust the God-appointed Saviour of mankind. The best evidence exists for its condemnation. God provided a Saviour, and they neglected their souls' salvation when they rejected Him, knowing full well that the Saviour waits to be merciful to them.

Philip Melancthon (1497–1560) believed that the design of universal atonement is clear. Melancthon argues that because sinners must be convinced that the gospel is an undeserved promise made by God, they must also be persuaded that it is a universal promise made by God. This promise is of reconciliation offered to all men. We must hold that this promise is universal, contrary to those dangerous imaginations that some have on predestination so that no one concludes that this promise relates to a few people including ourselves. It was his practice to declare the universality of the gospel promise. We can use certain universal

---

[533] The formatting of the quotation from Baxter is retained, though the spelling has been updated for convenience.

expressions most effectively, such as those used so frequently in the Scriptures to back up this conviction. Melancthon then quotes *John* 3:16 in full, explaining that the reason all those who hear the gospel and do not believe is their wilful opposition to, and refusal to believe in, Christ as He meets them in the gospel.[534]

Davenant agrees with Calvin's comment that God had "put an universal mark, both that he might invite all men promiscuously to the participation of life, and that he might leave the unbelieving without excuse."[535] He endorses Calvin's view that we can understand "the world" in this way. God has shown Himself propitious to "the whole world" so that no sinner could claim that Christ did nothing salvific for him. If they perish eternally, the fault is theirs alone.[536] Bringing in the proper biblical balance, Davenant supports Calvin's position. He writes, quoting Melancthon, "It appears that Christ is set before all, but Christ opens the eyes of the elect alone to seek him in faith."[537]

Not only do Davenant and Calvin agree with this exegesis of this verse, so also does DML-J in his evangelistic preaching.[538] Christ's remedy is applicable for the salvation of every man,[539] the condition of receiving the benefits of the gospel being the same for all men, faith in the Lord Jesus Christ alone. To ensure that preachers preach the gospel evangelistically, Davenant, like DML-J, contends that "that which is given to mankind conditionally, is understood to be given to no one, if the condition is set

---

[534] Philip Melancthon, as cited in Davenant, *Dissertation*, 19.

[535] *Ibid*. Calvin's comment.

[536] The assumption behind this view is that the gospel is faithfully, purely and authoritatively preached in terms that leaves even the most ignorant without excuse, and that also shows the way how a sinner, any sinner, can be reconciled with God. Sadly, this is not being done in every congregation that claims to be evangelical and reformed. Unfaithful preachers, that is preachers who do not passionately preach "Christ and Him crucified" to their people will also bear awesome responsibility on the great Day of Judgement when they will give account of their ministry of the gospel.

[537] Philip Melancthon, as cited in Davenant, *Dissertation*, 19.

[538] See Appendix.

[539] Davenant, *Dissertation*, 25.

aside."[540] No sinner can receive God's salvation without faith in Christ alone. For Davenant, faith is the indispensable condition for receiving salvation. DML-J constantly urged sinners to trust the Saviour if they are to know that God has forgiven their sins. The mere payment of a price does not deliver sinners; what delivers them is their trust in Christ, the Redeemer of the world, to do so.[541] It is, therefore, untrue to say that the cross saves.[542] So the indispensability of faith is hereby asserted, and no one can know God's salvation who does not believe in the Saviour.

Matthew Henry believes that the offer of salvation is a general offer, so that *whoever believes* in him, without exception, might be saved.[543] He adds no restriction to God's intention in sending Christ because it was "the world" that He "so loved." Eaton avers that limited atonement advocates face the challenge of properly exegeting those statements of Scripture that are clearly universalist,[544] and this verse is a case in point. Any exegesis that refuses to accept this is seriously flawed because it is not dealing with the text *qua* text. Reformed scholasticism does serious damage to this most powerful, and best loved, of all biblical texts and makes it say what John never intended it to say. DML-J's soteriology is quite at home in the company of men like Baxter, Davenant, Henry, Wesley and Ryle on this point. He preaches, "His love was so great that he sent his only Son into the world. We read: 'God so loved the world that he gave his only begotten Son, that whosoever believeth in him should not perish but have everlasting life,' *Jn* 3:16."[545] Or again,

> *For the moment humanity comes to see and to believe that, it will realise that its only hope is the hope that is offered in this Gospel. The gospel says, God so loved the world that he gave his only begotten Son, that whosoever believeth in him should not perish but have everlasting life, Jn 3:16.*[546]

---

[540] *Ibid.*, 57, 58.
[541] *Ibid.*, 57, 61.
[542] Davenant, *Dissertation*, 90.
[543] See his commentary on this verse.
[544] Michael A. Eaton, *A Theology of Encouragement*. (Leicester: InterVarsity Press, 1995), 17.
[545] See the Appendix.
[546] See the Appendix..

Wesley says that the world that God so loved refers to all mankind, including even those who despise His love, and will perish finally because of that rejection of God's love and mercy. No restriction is discernible in Wesley's notes on this verse. Notwithstanding his 'alleged' Arminianism, he claimed many times that his theology sits on the very edge of Calvinism or a mere hair's breadth from the reformer's thought.[547] For him, salvation was all of God's free grace; he affirms unregenerate man's inability in anything pertaining to his salvation and excludes all merit from man in his salvation. Using "man" in its generic sense,[548] he recognises no limitation of the atonement to the elect only. Even the Schofield Reference Notes[549] equate "κοσμος" with "mankind," as does A. T. Robertson.[550] He cites the universal aspect of God's love for the κοσμος as appearing in 2 *Corinthians* 5:19 and in *Romans* 5:8. Historically, this view is held by the church and by most Christian theologians – the Reformers, the Puritans, and the Church Fathers from the beginning of the church's life right up until the present time. Included also in this impressive list are virtually all the pre-Reformation writers.[551] Surprisingly, Elwell excludes Augustine of Hippo from this impressive list without justification. Clifford quotes from Augustine's *City of God*, where he writes,

> ...*for all the dead there died the only one person who lived, that is, who had no sin whatever, in order that they who live by the remission of their sins, should live, not to themselves, but to Him who died for all, for our sins, and rose again for our justification...*[552]

---

[547] See Thomas Oden's book, *John Wesley's Scriptural Christianity* (Grand Rapids, MI: Zondervan, 1994), where he quotes from Wesley's "Minutes of 1745." This was where Wesley met regularly with students for specifically theological discussions. He records in answer to Question 23: "Wherein may we come to the very edge of Calvinism? Answer: (1) In ascribing all good to the free grace of God. (2.) In denying all natural free will, and all power antecedent to grace. And (3.) In excluding all merit from man, even for what he has or does by the grace of God." (p. 253).
[548] See Philip, *Confession*, 86.
[549] 1917 edition.
[550] Robertson on *John* 3:16.
[551] Walter A. Elwell as in Elwell (Ed), *Dictionary*, 99.
[552] Alan C. Clifford, *Pregethwr y Bobl John Jones Talsarn – The People's Preacher.* (Norwich: Charenton Reformed Publishing), 292.

In light of this, it is difficult to see how Elwell can conclude that Augustine believed in limited atonement in its Owenite understanding. Many of his statements point in this direction. But the fact that he made this universalist statement (and there are others) indicates that he had room in his theology for a universal aspect that is inherent in the atonement.

P. T. Forsyth asks what is in this great gospel text. He explains that it refers to the world as the primary object of God's love. It was for this world that He gave his own Son that whoever believes in Him should not perish but have eternal life (*John* 3:16). God directed this love to the world in such a way that it ought to have lived in every individual experience. Forsyth focuses on the two words "whoever" and "world." He asks that we dwell on the contrast demanded by these two words. He highlights the point that the world that God "so loved" was not simply certain individuals or group of individuals only. The world that God "so loved" was a world to which He did something special. This love opened the way for anyone in that world, the "whoever," who receives the benefit of His love by believing in Him, to be saved for all eternity. In this way alone can it be possible to make a world of saved individuals possible. Only thus can this result be achieved.

Forsyth takes this idea too far and comes close to advocating universal salvation when he says that God's Son is not understood merely as an Individual because he sees Him as the Representative of mankind. Only Someone larger than the world could save the world. He argues that if Christ was incapable of saving the world, then it follows that He could not have saved any individual. It is universal salvation, not by the sum of all the parts, but in a corporate sense.[553]

Milne is better on this verse than he was on *John* 1:29. He writes, "The all-inclusive *scope* of God's love" is set out in "indiscriminate" terms, adding that it "embrac[es] every man, woman and child."[554] The world is the object of God's love, understood in terms of its "badness." Despite

---

[553] Forsyth, *Work*, 116.
[554] Milne, *John*, 77.

some of his other statements,[555] he is just as clear when it comes to terms of its "bigness."[556] He agrees that this is a fallen world that organises itself in rebellion against God. But he refuses to concede that the term is inclusive of all mankind, thus placing DML-J in disagreement with him. "The world" relates to humanity as it stands under divine judgement but introduces the term "qualitative" to limit its reference. What is it that stands under divine judgement if not the whole world, all mankind! The ἵνα particle points to purpose, indicating that God's purpose in sending Christ into such a world was to save it. It is the world in all its moral and spiritual depravity that God loves and Christ came to save. Perhaps, and to his credit, Dr Milne can handle the "inconsistencies" of Scripture is a way some others cannot, and includes its "bigness" as well as its "badness."

Hendriksen also agrees "the object of this love is the world."[557] The term, he says, "refers to mankind, though sin-laden, exposed to judgement, in need of salvation." This exegesis accurately represents the Bible's overall view of sinful mankind in the world. All mankind is in this eternally dangerous spiritual predicament, yet it was all mankind that is the object of God's love. Comparing this statement with those made by DML-J, one is impressed with the degree of agreement that is evident on this central matter of the faith. He preaches,

> *That is the vital question. 'What think ye of Christ?' Matt.22:42. And the Holy Spirit answers that question throughout that amazing record we call the New Testament. Here it is, in one verse. 'God so loved the world that he gave his only begotten Son, that whosoever believeth in him should not perish but have everlasting life, Jn.3:16.*[558]

Disappointingly but not surprisingly, Hendriksen reverts to his rigid confessionalism when he expounds *John 4:42*, explaining that the world of which Jesus Christ is the Saviour "consists of the elect from every

---

[555] See his comments on *John* 1:29 above.
[556] See Letham, *Work*, 241 on this point. He agrees with Bruce Milne that the focus is on the 'badness' of the world, not its 'bigness.'
[557] Hendriksen, *John*, 140.
[558] DML-J selection, #215.

nation."[559] This interpretation does not reflect the exegesis of a scholar who is "captive to the Word" and its divinely-inspired text. Hendriksen would have, at his ordination, consented to the Scriptures of the Old and New Testaments being the only infallible rule of faith and practice.[560] However, confessionalism carries with it the constant danger of elevating the church's standards above Scripture, and can contribute to a dishonest subscription of these standards. Prof. Dabney is much closer to the truth when he explains that those who see "the world" as "the elect world" have reached the point of "absurdity."[561] The result of such exegesis is "that some of the elect may not believe, and perish."[562] Dabney can accommodate the view that, in some places, "world" means the elect. The Father gave them (from all nations) to Christ as a gift.[563] Moreover, he limits this to those texts that demand such an exegesis. But other texts, such as *John* 3:16, do not fall into this category and demand a wider meaning if they are to make good biblical sense and not end up in "absurdity." Indeed, the relationship between predestination and the death of Christ demands a dual understanding of the divine will, as Davenant so rightly implies.

With Ryle, we discover the same teaching as Calvin's. Ryle states with clarity that the "world" "God so loved" "means the whole race of mankind, both saints and sinners, without any exception."[564] While men like Hutcheson, Lampe and Gill differ in that they see "the world" exclusively in terms of "God's elect out of every nation, whether Jews or Gentiles,..."[565] Ryle maintains that we must take Scripture in its normal meaning. Despite his saying, "By His death He purchased pardon and complete redemption for sinners,"[566] he was not implying any restriction in the design of the

---

[559] Hendriksen, *John*, 176. See his exposition of *John* 4:42 in the next chapter.

[560] This is known as the Protestant Rule of Faith, especially manifest within Presbyterianism.

[561] Dabney, *Systematic*, 525.

[562] *Ibid*. Dabney treats such exegesis of 2 *Corinthians* 5:15 identically, and his exegesis of 1 *John*.2:2 enjoys the same biblically-based criticism.

[563] Dabney, *Systematic*, 524, 525.

[564] Ryle, *John*, 158.

[565] *Ibid*.

[566] Ryle, *John*, 144.

atonement. After all, all men are sinners, and all have sinned and come short of the glory, or praise, of God (*Romans* 3:23). While Ryle knew this, he was not limiting Christ's redemption to particular sinners. It was the world that "God so loved" and for which He purchased redemption at the cost of Christ's precious blood. Nor does Ryle deny that God has a special covenant love for His saints, for he expressly affirms this. Indeed, he finds no weight in the objections levelled against his theory.[567]

John Davenant's exposition of these universal, evangelistic, verses demonstrates that the view of the atonement preached by DML-J was not new or novel. As a commissioner to the Synod of Dordt, Davenant held to universal atonement and defended it vigorously. In his *Dissertation on the Death of Christ*, appended originally to his commentary on *Colossians*,[568] Davenant contended that the promise of the gospel is a universal promise.[569] There is nothing in the world to merit the love of God. However, as Calvin affirms, "[God] shows himself to be propitious to the whole world; since he calls all without exception to believe in Christ." This statement reflects Calvin's soteriological position. Davenant accepts and affirms that God opens the eyes of the elect only, to believe in and receive Christ.

Adhering to the *sola scriptura* principle, Davenant distances himself from all purely human reason by drawing his beliefs from Scripture. He teaches, "that the death of Christ, according to the will of God, is an universal remedy, by the Divine appointment, and the nature of the thing itself, applicable for salvation to all and every individual of mankind."[570] The cross is God's universal remedy for the whole world. When any sinner repents of his sin and trusts Christ alone to save him, he receives this salvation. The "whosoever" of *John* 3:16 demands an openness and availability to all who desire it. He continues, "the intention and offering of Christ in giving himself includes all mankind, in like manner as that

---

[567] Ryle, *John*, 159.
[568] Reprinted by the Banner of Truth Trust in 2005 but *without* the "Dissertation on the Death of Christ."
[569] Davenant, *Dissertation*, 18.
[570] Davenant, *Dissertation*, 24.

of the Father in sending his Son," and refers to this verse.[571] He further affirms, "The death of Christ, and the design of God embracing all mankind promiscuously is excellently expressed," and refers again to *John* 3:16. Davenant adds, maintaining the Bible's theological balance, "But he so loved his sheep, his children, his church, which he determined by his death effectually to derive to them faith and eternal life."[572]

John Owen offers his own idiosyncratic exposition of this verse, denying that we should take "the world" in its natural usage. Instead, he insists that it means "the world" in a limited sense. It refers to miserable, guilty, lost men of all kinds, not just Jews but Gentiles too. It was such that God especially loved. His understanding limits the term "the world" to the elect, and this reductionism is absurd.[573] This wholly unwarranted exegesis is not an isolated statement of Owen's. He contends that this is always the case in the Scriptures – "the world" refers to God's elect only. He sees them in the pre-conversion state as the lost and condemned sinners who are scattered throughout the world, regardless of race, kindred or tongue. He explains "world" in terms of categories or classes of people, and not people *per se*.

So Dr Owen is quite explicit in his exposition of this term. The "world" does not mean the "world" at all, but means "only" the elect of God, and none else. If John intended this, he would surely have said so to avoid confusion. Scripture's clarity is challenged by this approach and virtually dismantles evangelistic preaching. Indeed, the evidence suggests that ministers and churches most firmly attached to Owen's soteriology are the least evangelistic in practice. DML-J, who admired Owen, could not be further from him at this point. What he preaches is much closer to Baxter's soteriology.

Joseph Hall recalls that Calvin's "heirs" have often departed from the balance of the Reformer, thus allowing or even facilitating the severe straining of the nerve of evangelism, if not cut altogether. With Calvin,

---

[571] Davenant, *Dissertation*, 79.

[572] Davenant, *Dissertation*, 169.

[573] Dabney, *Systematic*, 525.

we find an exposition that accords more or less with all the above except Owen and Gill, and to a slightly lesser extent with Milne and Hendriksen. The Reformer believes that in *John* 3:16 taken with *Romans* 8:31, God so loved the world that He did not spare His own Son but delivered Him up for us all. He describes those for whose "sakes" God loved and "did not spare His own Son" in universal terms – "the world."

DML-J writes,

> *And whenever our sins press hard on us, whenever Satan would drive us to despair, we must hold up this shield, that God does not want us to be overwhelmed in everlasting destruction, for He has ordained His Son to be the Saviour of the world.*[574]

Calvin's authentic gospel is therefore clearly expressed. With Baxter, it is now incumbent upon those who deny this clear statement to explain in what sense God did not send His Son to redeem the world than for others to explain what the meaning is.

When we lay DML-J's sermons alongside the expositions of other preachers and theologians, certain clear features will be discovered. For example, when preaching on the Kingdom of God, he affirmed, in keeping with the writings of other theologians,

> *No, the message is this: God 'hath visited and redeemed his people,' Lk.1:68. 'God so loved the world' – this world, this damned, foolish, evil world that you and I live in and of which we are all a part by nature – God so loved it, 'that he gave his only begotten Son, that whosoever believeth should not perish, but have everlasting life,' Jn.3:16.*"[575]

Again,

> *'God so loved the world, that he gave his only begotten Son' Jn.3:16. His concern for this world and its people was so great that 'When the fulness of*

---

[574] Calvin, comm. on *John* 3:16.
[575] Selection #133.

> *the time was come, God sent forth his Son, made of a woman, made under the law...' Gal.4:4. ... and pointing to that cross he says to the whole world, 'Believe on my Son and I will forgive you all your sins'.*[576]

His message was for all people. According to Iain H. Murray, when DML-J preached on Tuesday and Wednesday evenings throughout England and Wales, and at times in Scotland and further afield, his sermons were almost always evangelistic messages. He cared nothing for the scholastic notion of the Saviour dying for the non-elect because he was simply preaching what God has revealed in the gospel. He made no attempt to squeeze it into a confessional Procrustean bed. Not once did anyone call for the compliance officer of high Calvinism to make DML-J's gospel preaching say something the original writer had not intended it to say. His was a "broad" gospel that encompassed the whole world, yet it was a "narrow" gospel that could be received by faith in Christ alone. Why did God send His Son into the world? Let DML-J answer this vitally important question. He states,

> *He sent his only Son into the world, even to the cross to die, his body to be broken, his blood to be shed, so that 'whosoever believeth in him should not perish but have everlasting life,' Jn. 3:16.*[577]

This gospel offers a real and sincere salvation for "whosoever believeth."[578] "Here is the message of the New Testament, this is Christian salvation," he preaches. Implied in this is that whoever limits or restricts in any way the biblical gospel, and does not offer salvation for "whoever will believe," is not preaching the authentic Christian message. Nothing but his sinful unwillingness to come to and trust Christ stands in the way of any sinner being everlastingly saved. All that God requires of him is faith in Christ and repentance that leads to life. Using the outward means of grace that God has provided for His children will enable their growth in grace and also in their knowledge of Christ. There is no hope for the

---

[576] Selection #149.
[577] Selection #154.
[578] Selection #158, 194.

world apart from this message.[579] There is no Christ but the One, Whom the Father gave to redeem the world.[580] Behind all that happened on Golgotha, there was and is a great heart of love, a love that sent God's Son to die for this rebellious, insulting, rejecting and chaotic world of mankind.[581] This thoughtful language reflects DML-J's gospel content, without delimitation, without dilution, or being made to conform to any man-made standard, however good. His gospel was not Arminianism though it shared with Arminianism this feature of redemptive universality, and the condition of faith as the means of receiving the offered salvation. Nor was it high or scholastic Calvinism even though it shared with it the sovereignty of God in salvation. His gospel was biblically balanced and authentically Calvinistic; it was a gospel for the world, in DML-J's view, because the salvation it offered was for the world. It was also the "good news" the world so desperately needed to hear. Again, the discerning eye will see that DML-J was closer to Calvin in his soteriology than he was to Owen or Gill. Further, he was closer to Davenant and Baxter and Ryle and Hall than to those who denied that Christ died for any but the elect.

When we examine DML-J's preaching, we discover an identical emphasis in his evangelistic sermons.[582] The Doctor had no hidden fears or feelings of vulnerability about his soteriological emphasis because he believed, with Wesley, "he had a *prima facia* case in the bare word of God"[583] for what he preached. He did not share the inhibitions of other Reformed preachers of his own or earlier generations and enjoyed the God-given freedom that the gospel gives to those who declare it.

---

[579] Selection #9, 10, 49.
[580] Selection #215.
[581] Selection #218, 272, 310.
[582] See Appendix.
[583] Clifford, *Atonement*, 71, 72.

31

John 4:42 – The Saviour Of The World.

In this verse, we have another universal statement identifying the Person of the Saviour. The context is Jesus' conversation with the woman at Jacob's well in Samaria. The Samaritans who believed in Christ made this statement not just because of the woman's testimony, but because they had heard Him for themselves during one interview with Him. As Jews had no dealings[584] with Samaritans, (*John* 4:9), it is amazing that these "unclean" humans were enabled by God's Spirit to see the truth about Jesus. Many had believed because of the woman's testimony and besought Him to remain with them, and Jesus stayed a further two days in that vicinity (*John* 4:40, 43). The effectiveness and authenticity of her testimony brought these men not only to where Jesus was, but right into a new saving relationship with Him. This spiritual re-awakening amongst the Samaritans indicated that Jesus was not only the Saviour for the Jewish people, but also for the Samaritans. God did not confine His salvation to any one nation or people. He sent it into and for the entire world. Brown is correct when he avers that Christ's two-day stay not only brings many more to the same faith in Him, but raises that faith to a conviction. The Jews never reached that level of conviction about the true identity of our Lord, nor did His disciples attain this level of confession by that time. However, as the Christ, He was *"the Saviour of the world."*[585]

---

[584] The Geneva Bible 1599 translates this word as "meddle." The Geneva Bible notes add, "There is no familiarity nor friendship" between these groupings.
[585] Brown, *Gospels*, 375.

As "Saviour of the world," He was to bring "deliverance ... from serious danger."[586] What more serious danger is there than to be under the divine wrath on account of sin, and from this we need deliverance! This danger implies that Jesus is more than a perfect Example for us to follow. He is the only One Who saves us. The general term "Saviour" is sometimes applied to the Father (*Luke* 1:47; 1 *Timothy* 1:1)[587] and very frequently also to the Son but is found nowhere else in the New Testament. To the word "Saviour," John adds a qualifier, "of the world," which has the impact of enlarging His role and work. Morris explains that this term lifts the title to the level of limitless majesty. The Jews forgot, or perhaps didn't know, that the Lord Jesus Christ does not concern Himself with mere trivial matters. He did not come to be the Saviour of a handful of people when He came into the world. Jesus Christ is none other than the Saviour of the world, and it was to save the world that He was born, lived, suffered and died, and rose again before ascending into Heaven.[588]

Calvin comments that when the Samaritan believers declare that Jesus is the Saviour of the world and the Messiah, where else did they get this knowledge but from His lips. Indeed, Jesus proclaimed that what He brought, namely salvation, was common to all mankind so that these Samaritan Christians should believe more easily that it belonged to them also.[589]

Exclusivity is thereby ruled out by our Lord. The salvation that He brought transcends all geographical and ethnic barriers. It is for all men because all are sinners. God's love is for "the whole world"[590] because the salvation His Son brought is common to all.[591]

---

[586] Morris, *John*, 284. Brown cites the Greek as "the Saviour of the world, the Christ, (p.374). Cf. also Ryle, *John*, 251.

[587] The LXX uses this term for the Father, and secular Greek writers uses it of a multitude of deities.

[588] Morris, *John*, 285.

[589] Comment on *John* 4:42.

[590] Guthrie, *Theology*, 937.

[591] Calvin, *comm.* on *John* 4:42.

Ryle contends that "the singular fullness of the confession" that the Samaritan believers made is significant because it provides "the fullest declaration of Jesus' office as 'the Saviour of the world' that is unequalled in the Gospels."[592] In this view, he was with Calvin and contra Owen and Hendriksen.[593] He raises the point as to whether the Samaritans really understood the significance of the term "Saviour" as applied to Jesus, and Ryle suggests that they did not. However, he affirms that whatever deficiencies existed in their understanding of *that* term, there were none regarding their grasp of the universal scope of what He came to do. To them, He was the world's Saviour, not just the Jews' Saviour. In Ryle's language, He came to be "a Redeemer for all mankind."[594] The religious Jews did not see this truth despite His being with them for upwards of three years. But these people of mixed race and of semi-heathen origin who had only had Jesus with them for two days, grasped the true identity of this Preacher and affirmed His universal and crucial role for mankind.

DML-J preached this same message to his hearers. As he was bringing his sermon on *Acts* 4:1-13 to a conclusion and upbraided the church for her cowardice and unfaithfulness:

> *The church must stop apologising, stop accommodating, stop taking bits out of the Bible. We must face the world and proclaim Jesus of Nazareth, Son of God and Saviour of mankind.*[595]

Already retired from active Christian ministry for almost five years, his universal gospel preaching was still uppermost in his emphasis. In responding to the question as to the reason for the incarnation, he said, "Why does he do that? There is only one answer: He has entered the world

---

[592] Ryle, *John*, 251. He points out that the conversion of these Samaritans can be attributed solely to the grace of God, and that while the Jews were hardened under Christ's preaching, miracles and wonderful works, the Samaritans were softened and believed.

[593] Hendriksen, *John*, 176.

[594] *Ibid.*

[595] See the Appendix.

in order to save it."[596] When explaining why some men hold tenaciously to the truth of the gospel, he said, "Here were men who would sooner die than refrain from preaching the glory of the Son of God as the only Saviour of the world."[597] That Christ was and is the only truly cosmic Saviour there is, was an emphasis in his preaching that none can gainsay. He died as the Saviour of the world, which implies that He died for all men without exception and without distinction. His death was as much for the unbeliever as it was for the believer. When sinners reject the only Saviour of mankind, they are rejecting a Saviour Who suits their case perfectly.[598] Listen to DML-J as he describes those leaders who "[reject] ... the Saviour of the world." "The world ... is rejecting the one whom God has raised up to be the one and only Saviour."[599] Little did they know but the One they were rejecting was "God's only begotten Son, Jesus of Nazareth ... the Saviour of the world."[600] It was He Who died on Calvary, and the only way for sinners to be reconciled to Him is by believing in and surrendering to the Saviour of the world.[601] For DML-J, what Christ accomplished on the cross leaves every sinner who ever lived without excuse. None can ever claim that God in Christ had done nothing salvific for them. He died for them, therefore, had they trusted in Christ alone, they too would have been saved.

Examining these expository comments by the Doctor confirms that he is well-matched to the company of men like Calvin, Amyraut, Baxter, Davenant, Wesley, Ryle, Morris, etc. His expositions do not fit with those of Owen and Hendriksen whose confessionalism determines the meaning of Scripture, rather than the other way round.

---

[596] See the Appendix.
[597] See the Appendix.
[598] It was this teaching that gave rise to the mnemonic JESUS - Jesus Exactly Suits Us Sinners.
[599] See the Appendix.
[600] See the Appendix.
[601] See the Appendix.

32

Hebrews 2:9 – That He Might Taste Death For Every Man

Richard Baxter clarifies this verse that all men's sins had a hand in Christ's death. Christ, therefore, tasted the deepest effects and pangs of death for every man.[602] As the divinely provided Substitute, Christ tasted for each man what each man should have tasted for his sin. Matthew Henry explains that Christ by His sufferings might not only make satisfaction, but go on to taste death for every man. The Saviour underwent and felt in both body and soul the bitter agonies associated with that mode of execution – the cursed death of the cross. By so doing, he placed humanity, not only in His debt eternally, but also brought all before the Judge for trial.

Clearly Henry believed that Christ's sufferings and death were for mankind, having tasted death "for every man." DML-J uses this verse in exactly the same way[603] and cross references it with *Isaiah* 53:6. Simon Kistemaker, otherwise good, is disappointing here and rather sidesteps the issue than deal directly with it. He quotes Calvin as saying that redemption found its mainspring in the infinite love of God for us. It was through this infinite love that He found a way to save us by not sparing His own

---

[602] Davenant, *Dissertation*, 30, concurs. Christ in His death is the procuring cause of salvation to all.

[603] See the Appendix.

Son.[604] His explanation of the Greek used in this verse is less than useful. The only redeeming factor is his clarification of παντος, an adjective in the genitive singular which can be either masculine, meaning *everyone*, or neuter, meaning *everything*. The context, he argues, seems to favour the masculine. So the adjective is personal and refers to people, which gives the rendering "taste death for everyone," for every man (used in its generic sense). F. F. Bruce wrote that because the Son of Man suffered and died, His death avails for all mankind. He adds, further, that because His exaltation then crowned his suffering and death, His death avails for the entire human race.[605] Dr Raymond Brown avoids addressing the meaning of "every man" in this verse.[606]

In His death, God's Son "tasted death for every man" (*Hebrews* 2:9). Hyper-Calvinists such as John Gill state, correctly, that "man" was added by the translators to help to give the sense of the verse. They would suggest that what they should have added is *son*, or *one of the brethren*, not *man*. He gives no reason for this which begs the question, why *son* or *brethren*, and not *man*? Clearly Gill *et. al.* were at pains to preserve the particularist interpretation of this verse, but on what grounds? There are no exegetical grounds for such an inaccurate translation of this verse. Therefore, Christians are not obliged to receive or believe such a purely speculative viewpoint.

Stibbs is crystal clear on this matter. "By a wonderful manifestation *by the grace of God* He became man in order that, for the benefit of mankind as a whole (*i.e. for everyone*), He might thus enter into death."[607] Christ tasted death for the benefit of mankind as man's divinely provided Representative. He tasted for mankind what mankind would have tasted, namely death, had it not been for the rescue provided by the God against whom men had

---

[604] John Calvin as cited in S. J. Kistemaker, *Hebrews*. (Welwyn: Evangelical Press, 1984), 68.
[605] Bruce, *Hebrews*, 39.
[606] Raymond Brown, *Christ Above All – The Message of Hebrews*. (Leicester: InterVarsity Press, 1982).
[607] Alan Stibbs as cited in Guthrie *et. al.* 1970:1197.

sinned. God had provided a Redeemer for mankind, and on condition of faith all who believe will be saved. DML-J shares this conviction.

Calvin (on *Hebrews* 2:9) says that Christ died for us and that he took upon Himself what was our due. Death was our due, and He tasted the bitter pangs of separation from this life, and from His Father's presence, and by so doing He redeemed us from the curse of death. While Calvin does not use universal language in this comment, his frequent use of it demonstrates that this is what he had in mind here.

33

1 John 2:2 – Propitiation ... For The Whole World.

The context here is the denial by some (the Gnostics? Or Jewish Christians? Or, Gentile believers?) that sin shows itself in the conduct of Christian believers. John is at pains to deny such an aberration, and to present the truth to his readers. Allowing that Christians sin, he assures them "we have an Advocate with the Father, Jesus Christ the righteous" (1 *John* 2:1). Who is He? "He Himself is the propitiation for our sins, and not for ours only but also for the whole world." The propitiation for our sins, and for (the sins of) the world,[608] is a Person, Jesus Christ. But John labours to point out that He is more than just the propitiation for the sins committed by believers in general. He writes, "If anyone sins..." Given the Hebrew background to the terms "Advocate" – referring to Israel's High Priest, and "propitiation" – referring to the sacrifice for sins offered on the great Day of Atonement, the New Testament High Priest, Jesus Christ, is also Himself the sacrifice for sin. He is both Priest and Victim.

He is "the propitiation ... also for the whole world," an unmistakable pointer to the atonement. What does that mean? John is teaching that the ἱλασμος had specific reference to both the sins committed by believers, and also for those committed by mankind. It is man's sin that provokes God's wrath, and for reconciliation to take place this divine wrath must necessarily be removed. Its merit extends to the whole world, unbelievers included. Christ the Propitiation atones for the sins of all. According to Haupt, if universal salvation does not occur, the fault does not lie with

---

[608] Douty, *Death of Christ*, 86.

God. It is not that He refuses to forgive sinners. Rather, the fact that they remain unforgiven deliberately offends His Fatherly heart, which moves towards the sinner in compassion.[609] Haupt then distinguishes between redemption accomplished, and redemption applied.[610] Moreover, the Greek lexicons all agree that the term "the whole world" refers to mankind.

Stott indicates that John means that a universal pardon is on offer for (the sins of) the whole world,[611] a pardon that is enjoyed only by those who receive it. Ross agrees that Christ's atonement is for the whole world, adding that the propitiation is as wide as the sin.[612] Since sin embraces the world, so the provided propitiation is co-terminus with it. While the propitiatory work of Christ is a finished work,[613] Ross affirms that the happy result of propitiation follows for everyone who believes in Jesus (*Romans* 3:26), that result being eternal salvation and the richest communion with God. Everyone recognised as a believer in Christ[614] benefits from the propitiation. However, Ross's confessionalism stirs, disappointingly preventing him expounding the phrase "and not for ours only, but also for (the sins of) the whole world." It just remained for him to put flesh on what he had already said by way of explication of the verse.

---

[609] Haupt, as cited in Douty, *Death of Christ*, 87.

[610] Cf. the title of John Murray's book of that name. Murray believes that the redemption has been applied to those for whom it was accomplished. If 'our regeneration and renewal were accomplished (and applied?) by the earthly work of Christ,' as Macleod states in the EQ (page 217), then, on this basis, the elect will be infallibly saved, with or without faith, or repentance, or the new birth. Truly, 'accomplishment and application' are 'part of the one divine plan' but, while the work of each Person in the Trinity is complementary, there is a clear distinction between accomplishment and application in Scripture. Christ's work of redemption was 'finished' on Calvary, but the Spirit still had His regenerating work to do in the elect.

[611] John R. W. Stott, *Epistles of John*. (London: The Tyndale Press, 1964), 84.

[612] A. Ross, *Commentary on the Epistles of James and John*. (London: Marshall, Morgan and Scott, 1954), 151, n.7.

[613] Ross, *James and John*, 153, n.7.

[614] Ross, *James and John*, 152, n.7. Citing Denney (Expositors Greek Testament).

While it is disappointing that he refused to proceed this far, it is gratifying that on this point he was but "a hair's breadth" from the Reformer.

After conceding that it is the normal practice of scholars to conclude that the extent of Christ's death is universal, but the intent is for believers, Kistemaker, refers to the Lombardian formula as authentication.[615] Continuing, he says that the whole world in this text does not relate to every one of God's creatures. If that were, in fact, the case, then the fallen angels would also, by default, share in the redemption purchased by Christ.[616] However, Kistemaker is wrong here because the fallen angels though creatures of God, are not men, and it was for men only that God provided salvation. Quoting Gregory of Nazianzus, McGrath reminds us that what has not been assumed by Christ in the incarnation has not and cannot be redeemed.[617] In the incarnation, Jesus, the Son of God, became a man, not an angel. Therefore, mankind can be redeemed but fallen angels including Satan, who is a fallen angel, cannot. We see evidence of the influence of confessionalism in even the best Reformed exegetes, for if John did not intend to say "the whole world," why did he say it? If God had not wanted to present this idea, in keeping with numerous other New Testament texts, He could have prevented it. Kistemaker imagines he gets around his difficulty by explaining that the term, "world," is a description of the world considered in its totality. It is not necessarily a description of the world considered in its individuality.[618] However, if it means "the world considered in its totality," why cannot it mean the totality of individuals that inhabit that world? When he says "not necessarily," he leaves open the possibility that this could, in fact, be the case; that "individuality" is included in this contested term. It is merely playing with words that leads to and results in semantic confusion. We can all be too pedantic at times, often to the detriment of the gospel.

---

[615] Simon J. Kistemaker, *James and I–III John*. (Welwyn: Evangelical Press, 1986), 253. See the Calvin reference following.
[616] *Ibid.*
[617] A. McGrath, *Historical Theology - An Introduction to the History of Christian Thought*. (Oxford: Blackwell Publishing, 1998), 54. Calvin agrees, *Comm. First John*, 244.
[618] *Ibid.*

Kistemaker denies that there is any universal reference in this verse (1 *John* 2:2). He concludes that Christ died for all those who believe in Him from every part of the world, the standard high Calvinist explanation, which is unconvincing and smacks of special pleading. DML-J places no such restrictions on the meaning of this verse and expounds it as any reasonable preacher would, giving it its full breadth of meaning.[619]

Calvin writes humorously if somewhat sarcastically on this verse when he admits that he simply ignores

> *the dotages of the fanatics, who under this pretense extend salvation to all the reprobate, and therefore to Satan himself. Such a monstrous thing deserves no refutation. They who seek to avoid this absurdity, have said that Christ suffered sufficiently for the whole world, but efficiently only for the elect. This solution has commonly prevailed in the schools. Though then I allow that what has been said is true, yet I deny that it is suitable to this passage; for the design of John was no other than to make this benefit common to the whole Church.*[620]

Henry's exposition of this text is beautiful, giving full biblical emphasis in what he preaches. His characteristic view is, despite his categorisation language used here, that the nature and extent of the atonement are such that it reaches all tribes, nations, and countries. For Henry, what Christ provided in His death is a universal atonement and propitiation that not only extends to all but is intended for all. He limits salvation, of course, to those who are saved and brought into the bosom of God the Father, where they experience His favour and the forgiveness of their sins.[621] There is a particular focus for Christ's death – all tribes, nations, and countries, but there is also the universal focus – Christ is the universal atonement and propitiation for the whole world. Henry's exposition reflects DML-J's soteriology and is the overwhelming understanding of the atonement that still enjoys tremendous support.

---

[619] See the Appendix.

[620] *Comm.* on 1 *John* 2:2.

[621] Matthew Henry comment on 1 *John* 2:2.

SECTION EIGHT

Concluding Comments

34

Drawing The Threads Together

This study's purpose was not to convince readers of the rightness of the authentic Calvinist, or Amyraldian, position. Others are more capable than I of doing this.[622] Rather, it was to demonstrate that the soteriology of DML-J was Amyraldian and not Owenite and that his understanding of the atonement was much closer to that of Calvin and Baxter than it was to Beza and Owen. Bloesch's statement summarises my findings when he affirms that some expressions of the position held by some Calvinists stands in blatant conflict with the witness of the New Testament. These expressions highlight specifically that form of Calvinism that spread through Reformed orthodoxy.[623] This assertion may be to overstate the case because the Amyraldian position is widely acknowledged amongst Reformed theologians to be within the authentic Reformed theological constituency. He further elucidates this point in the endnote for this statement when he cautions us to bear in mind that the position espoused by Calvin and that held by later Calvinism are not identical.[624] DML-J followed Calvin's teaching and eschewed the aberrations of later Calvinism. I think that DML-J's words are sufficient to demonstrate what he believed about and preached concerning the atonement – it was authentically Calvinistic.[625] Clifford demonstrated

---

[622] For example, Brian G. Armstrong, F. P. Van Stam, Curt. Daniel, R. T. Kendall, and Alan C. Clifford.
[623] Bloesch, *Saviour and Lord*, 168.
[624] *Ibid.* See endnote, 1997:282.
[625] Read and study Appendix.

Calvin's authentic Calvinism admirably in his book, *Calvinus*,[626] which readers will find immensely profitable when read alongside the extracted DML-J quotations. This extraction will stand as a great challenge to theologians and preachers alike. It may well provoke outrage from some, initiate a theological re-aligning for others, and will undoubtedly bring great encouragement to preachers who may have preached an all-sufficient Saviour of the world from a bad conscience. I think it will stir up preachers to be more clear and passionate in their preaching of the gospel to a lost, guilty and condemned mankind.

I think that sufficient has been said to indicate that the limited atonement lobby does not have a monopoly on the truth as is often assumed, wrongly, to be the case. There is an abundance of biblical material on which to work to arrive at this conviction. An exposition of these few verses based on disinterested exegesis will demonstrate the same deposit of meanings, all of which clearly endorse DML-J's soteriology. However, the case has been made, and the door left open for further research into this critically important doctrine.[627]

Biblical exegesis of the relevant Scriptural passages tallies with that of the Church Fathers, the Reformers and the Puritans, in general terms. This array of church heavy-weights further confirms the rightness of DML-J's exegesis and gives great confidence that he has the wealth of Christian scholarship and historical theology on his side.

This doctrine is a hotly debated one, and controversy over it shows no sign of abating. Theological scholars and preachers still debate this issue, but it appears from the preceding study that those scholars who tie themselves to a strictly confessional position are no longer on the winning side of this debate. Because of the suffocating stranglehold that confessionalism has on Reformed theologians and preachers, what they write seems to be a regurgitation of the old arguments of centuries ago. Many Reformed

---

[626] Clifford, *Calvinus*.

[627] The work on this book was almost complete when the new Crossway theological tome, *From Heaven He Came And Sought Her*, was published towards the end of 2013, so little opportunity was afforded the author to engage with it.

theologians have broken no new ground, and it becomes rather tiresome to have to wade through what the worthies of the past have said and that has merely been "dressed" up in modern clothes.

However, it is proper to consult past writings. God does not expect us to re-invent the theological wheel, but He does expect us to think for ourselves. However, that is different from saying that we take on board uncritically what history has taught us, an approach that is much more at home within Roman Catholicism than it is within any evangelical Reformed church. There is an urgent need for fresh thinking on issues so central to the Christian gospel. Such thinking will entail challenging those who have departed from the historic Reformed faith. Some of its strongest advocates have followed a theological route that is hostile to the gospel and therefore to the good of the church on earth. Hence the lifelessness that believers experience in many professing evangelical churches. The drive to ensure orthodoxy at all costs seems to be primarily responsible for that spiritual deadness. In addition, the drive for "institutional maintenance" or "corporate protection" above all else is too great a price to pay if, in order to do so, we have to silence the gospel. Add to this the evangelical church's sub-standard and vain attempts at imitating the world in what is called contemporary worship further contributes to the downgrading of true spirituality that is endemic within the churches today. Moreover, were the evangelical churches of today *truly* orthodox in doctrine and practice, as measured by the Bible's infallible and unchanging standard, spiritual deadness would not and could not exist.

This study has demonstrated that the best theological scholars, lexicographers, linguists, etc., whether evangelical or not, have provided the Christian world with numerous tools by which to check the exegesis of theologians and preachers. This approach is to be preferred to merely checking them against the church's confessional standards. This foolproof way ensures that churches demonstrate the supremacy of Scripture in all matters of faith and practice. The church that refuses to change its confessional standards to ensure closer alignment with Scripture is conceding no need for continual re-formation according to God's Word because their confessional standards are already perfect. This stance is as arrogant as it is dangerous ground for any "Reformed" church to take.

The Evangelical and Reformed churches today must acknowledge with deepest sorrow that there has been a "dumbing down" of the authentic gospel within their jurisdictions. They offer cheap grace to those in dire spiritual need without the corresponding call to costly discipleship. They must also acknowledge that they are suffering from the spiritual equivalent of anaemia. This condition has existed for many decades and could prove fatal to churches though not to the Church of Jesus Christ. A careful study of the subsequent history of the seven churches in Asia Minor will reveal this (*Revelation* 2, 3) and the history of other New Testament churches will demonstrate likewise. The concern that Christian church members express about the lack of clear gospel preaching in the churches bears eloquent testimony to the prevalence of this condition. These are the people who are concerned about the health and well-being of the church. But they need to stand firm and take action against this practice. Those who simply 'go with the church crowd' show no interest whatever in the church's health, and do not want to conform the Body of Christ to His likeness. It is arguable that their main motivation is ecclesiastical maintenance, keeping the church show on the road, and not in her wellbeing. Indeed, they show no noticeable concern for the glory of God in the church, despite protestations to the contrary.

Theologians will also have to redraw the theological contours in a way that ensures that we keep this central gospel issue the central gospel issue. In addition, this study has positioned the soteriology of DML-J where some of his "disciples" and admirers will not wish it to be. It is firmly within the authentic Calvinist or Amyraldian and not the Owenite or scholastic theological camp.

Ministers and theologians have a duty to learn what they can, both positively and negatively, from those who went before. Surely the best place to start is with those men who lived and experienced the church in her best times. They can study the works of those men whose theology is at variance with their own so that they can gain a sharpening of their convictions. DML-J studied liberal evangelicals and theologians who were specialists in the area of the atonement but whose doctrine of Scripture he rejected. Like Israel of old, we can go down into Egypt, see what's good and then come up out of Egypt bringing many treasures with us.

We must base any understanding of the cross on God's revealed will in the Holy Scriptures alone. Help from a breadth of studies of earlier and current generations may be consulted with profit, but we must assess their conclusions in the light of Scripture. Effort must be expended to avoid confusing the gospel by the introduction of useless scholasticism, empty philosophy, and control by confessionalism or by the practice of eisegesis. We must take great care we derive our doctrines from the Scriptures, are Bible-based and not the result of the application of cold logic.

The church must return to preaching the cross as the only way of salvation and reconciliation. This urgent demand presses on us because of the chosen defection of large tracks of the church from biblical orthodoxy. Only such a return will reverse the scandalous "lukewarmness" of much of the professing evangelical church (*Revelation* 3:15, 16). The blood of Christ alone cleanses from all sin, and sinners stand in need of hearing this message preached in the power of the Holy Spirit. It is quite pointless of ministers priding themselves on being "Bible teachers" if they fail to preach the cross evangelistically as part of that "teaching." How anyone can teach the Bible without preaching evangelistically is difficult to understand. For many preachers today, the cross is at best relegated to a footnote that the unwary will miss and only the discerning will see. This practice can be an excuse and a justification for not preaching the Word evangelistically. The gospel is being lost to those churches that simply do not have dedicated evangelistic services. DML-J recommended that there should be at least one evangelistic service every week in the churches. Sadly this, too, is seen more in the breach than in the observance.

The writings of DML-J, then, demonstrate that his understanding of the atonement agrees with the plain teaching of the Scriptures and with the expositions of Calvin and Amyraut and Baxter, among others. They also reveal that his soteriology is at variance with some other Reformed preachers and theologians in the twentieth and twenty-first centuries, who adopt high- or ultra-Calvinist positions. In addition, some lesser men have simply followed, uncritically, what their mentors have taught. His soteriology is also at variance with some of the more extreme Reformation confessions. It has, however, much in common with *The Three Forms of Unity* and even the current Confession of Faith held by the Presbyterian Church in Wales. The Doctor cannot be said to have been influenced by what others have taught but subjected every point of view to the clear teaching of the Word of God.

This book has also highlighted the need for academic honesty and intellectual integrity when dealing with the text of Scripture, and also with the views of others, whether admired or not. Also, it is necessary to call the theological positions adopted by preachers by their proper names. If a man is a Calvinist, call him a Calvinist; if he is a Wesleyan, call him a Wesleyan; and if he is an Owenite, call him an Owenite. The church does not need theological confusion by referring to people by names and titles that are inappropriate. It is surely high time for the Church to recognise Owenism as a distinct theological system from that expounded by Calvin, a form of Calvinism somewhat removed from the real thing.

Some have wrongly categorised DML-J as an Owenite or high Calvinist, and we are now beginning to see this travesty for what it is. His published sermons could not be clearer that his soteriology was Calvinist rather than Owenite. His preaching bears the clear stamp of Amyraldianism. DML-J is comfortably settled in the company of men like Calvin, Amyraut, Daillé, Davenant, Baxter, Henry, Chalmers, Edwards, Bellamy, Doddridge, John Jones, Owen Thomas, Calamy, McCheyne, Ryle, Morris, *et. al.* We can only rightly categorise the Doctor with those who oppose medieval scholasticism and barren philosophy in all its forms, including and especially that bankrupt thinking that has been introduced into the Reformed churches. He does not sit well with rigid confessional men or churches though he had many such people as his friends. The fact that he was ordained to the Christian ministry by the Calvinistic Methodist connexion in Wales expounds very clearly that he preached the doctrine of Calvin with the enthusiasm of the Methodists. This is as it should be.

DML-J had a great gospel because he had a great Saviour, a cosmic Saviour, to offer to all. He knew the gospel he preached was the only answer to the needs of mankind. So he offered a full Christ to all who heard him, either in person or through his many books of sermons and audio recordings of his messages.

Theologians and preachers alike require a change of attitude when dealing with matters relating to Calvin. Rather than reading what others say Calvin believed and taught, they would be better served if they read Calvin's writings, not least his sermons. Dr Iain D. Campbell said in his paper on Thomas Shepherd that if you want to get to know the real man, read his sermons.[628] We must also apply this critically important assessment to both Calvin and DML-J. Rather than taking at face value what the bishops and archbishops of Reformed orthodoxy say DML-J believed and taught, a more satisfactory and honest method for Christians to follow is to read his published works. Indeed, it would be a much more truthful way of discovering the Doctor's soteriology, and a way that reduces misrepresentation of his views on the gospel. It would also lead, hopefully, to greater evangelistic endeavour on the part of the churches.

DML-J held the biblical paradoxes in harmonious tension and found no difficulty in emphasising what Scripture clearly stated. I am prepared to go along with J. J. Murray and I. H. Murray and say that DML-J believed in limited atonement. I qualify this by adding that DML-J limits its benefits to all those and only those who trust in Christ alone for salvation. But unlike them I can also go further and say that DML-J believed in universal atonement. He had the rare gift of keeping these antinomies in their proper relations to each other, unlike the Murrays and other high Calvinists. For the Doctor, salvation is limited (to those who trust in Christ alone) but the atonement is universal (God designed it for the salvation of humanity).

This study has shown beyond reasonable doubt that Rev. Dr David Martyn Lloyd-Jones' soteriology is soundly Amyraldian. It stands as an urgent call

---

[628] Dr Iain D. Campbell said this at a Puritan and Reformed Conference held near Belfast in February, 2011.

to all gospel men to preach this universal gospel of grace to all and sundry. They are to be as free as they can be in offering Christ as Saviour and Lord to all men everywhere. To be liberated to tell all men that God loves them and Christ died for them is the greatest message the world can ever hear. To experience His salvation, all that God requires of them is to put their trust in Christ, the Lamb of God and Saviour of the world. May this God-glorifying, Christ-centred and life-transforming message be heralded from every evangelical and Reformed pulpit, not least to honour the name of the subject of this book, Dr D. Martyn Lloyd-Jones.

References and Bibliography

Works By Dr D Martyn Lloyd-Jones (a selection):

The Plight of Man and the Power of God (London: Pickering and Inglis Ltd, 1942).

Maintaining the Evangelical Faith Today (London: InterVarsity Press, 1952, 2nd edit, 1968).

Truth Unchanged Unchanging (London: James Clarke & Co. Ltd, 1952, rpnt 1956).

From Fear to Faith (London: InterVarsity Press, 1953, rpnt 1973).

Studies in the Sermon on the Mount Vol.1, (London: InterVarsity Press, 1959, rpnt. 1970).

Studies in the Sermon on the Mount Vol.2, (London: InterVarsity Press, 1960, rpnt. 1970).

Authority (London: InterVarsity Press, 1958, rpnt 1976).

The Basis of Christian Unity (London: InterVarsity Press, 1962, rpnt 1968).

Spiritual Depression (London: Pickering and Inglis Ltd, 1965, rpnt 1974).

Luther and His Message for Today (London: Evangelical Press, 1968).

God's Way of Reconciliation (London: Evangelical Press, 1972).

The Cross (Eastbourne: Kingsway Publications, 1986/2008).

Spiritual Blessings (Eastbourne: Kingsway Publications, 1999/2008).

God the Father, God the Son (London: Hodder and Stoughton, 1996).

Joy Unspeakable – The Baptism with the Holy Spirit (Eastbourne: Kingsway Publications, 1984).

Prove All Things (Eastbourne: Kingsway Publications, 1985).

Revival, (1986). Marshall Pickering, Basingstoke, England, UK.

The Puritans – their Origins and Successors (Edinburgh: Banner of Truth Trust, 1987).

Healing and Medicine (Eastbourne: Kingsway Publications, 1987, rpnt 1988).

Knowing the Times. (Edinburgh: Banner of Truth Trust, 1989).

What is an Evangelical? (Edinburgh: Banner of Truth Trust, 1992).

D. Martyn Lloyd-Jones – Letters 1919-1981. Ed. Iain H. Murray. (Edinburgh: Banner of Truth Trust, 1994).

Old Testament Evangelistic Sermons. (Edinburgh: Banner of Truth Trust, 1995).

Jesus Christ and Him Crucified (Edinburgh: Banner of Truth Trust, 1999).

Authentic Christianity (6 vols) (Edinburgh: Banner of Truth Trust).

Romans (14 vols) (Edinburgh: Banner of Truth Trust).

Ephesians (8 vols) (Edinburgh: Banner of Truth Trust).

Let Everyone Praise the Lord (1999) Bryntirion Press, Bridgend, Wales, UK.

Life in Christ – Studies in 1 John (2002) Crossway Books, Leicester, England, UK.

Living Waters (2 Vols.). (Eastbourne: David C. Cook, Kingsway Communications, 2008).

True Happiness (Bridgend:Bryntirion Press, 2011).

Out of the Depths (Bridgend:Bryntirion Press, 2011).

Born of God (Edinburgh: Banner of Truth Trust, 2011).

Works On Dr D Martyn Lloyd-Jones:

Murray, Iain H. *D. Martyn Lloyd-Jones – The First Forty Years.* (Edinburgh: Banner of Truth Trust, 1982).

Murray, Iain H. *D. Martyn Lloyd-Jones – The Fight of Faith.* (Edinburgh: Banner of Truth Trust, 1990).

Atherstone, A and Jones, D. C (2011). *Engaging With Martyn Lloyd-Jones – The Life and Legacy of 'the Doctor.'* (Nottingham: Apollos (an imprint of IVF), 2011).

Brencher, J. *Martyn Lloyd-Jones (1899-1981) and Twentieth-Century Evangelicalism.* (Carlisle: Paternoster Press, 2002).

Eaton, M. A (1989). *Baptism with the Spirit – the teaching of Martyn Lloyd-Jones.* InterVarsity Press, Leicester, England, UK.

Murray, I. H (2008). *Lloyd-Jones – Messenger of Grace.* (Edinburgh: Banner of Truth Trust, 2008).

Other Works Consulted:

Adams, J. E. *Competent to Counsel.* (Presbyterian and Reformed Publishing Company, 1970/1975).

Alexander, W. L. *A System of Biblical Theology.* Vol. II. (n.p., 1888).

Armstrong, Brian G. *Calvinism and the Amyraut Heresy – Protestant Scholasticism and Humanism in Seventeenth-Century France.* (Wisconsin: University of Wisconsin Press, 1969).

Barnes, A. *Notes on the Old Testament.* (Grand Rapids: Baker Book House,1950).

_____Notes on *Isaiah.* (Grand Rapids: Baker Book House, 1972 rpnt).

Baxter, Richard (Ed. J. Read) *Universal Redemption of Mankind.* (Shropshire: Quinta Press, 1694/2008).

_____*A Paraphrase of the New Testament.* (London: 1685).

_____*The Scripture Gospel Defended*, (London: 1690).

Beasley-Murray, G R, *Baptism in the New Testament.* (Exeter: Paternoster, Exeter, 1967).

Beeke, Joel R. *The Quest for Full Assurance.* (Edinburgh: Banner of Truth Trust, 1999).

Berkhof, L *The History of Christian Doctrines.* (Edinburgh: Banner of Truth Trust, 1937/1969).

_____*Systematic Theology.* (Edinburgh: Banner of Truth Trust, 1939/1958).

_____ *Principles of Biblical Interpretation*. (London: Evangelical Press, 1973 rpnt).

Blanchard, J. *Dealing with Dawkins*. (Darlington: Evangelical Press, 2010).

Bloesch, Donald G. *Jesus Christ Saviour and Lord*. (Carlisle: Paternoster Press, 1997).

Boettner, Lorraine. *Reformed Doctrine of Predestination*. (Grand Rapids: Presbyterian and Reformed Publishing Company, 1932).

Bonhoeffer, D. *The Cost of Discipleship*. (New York: Touchstone/Simon & Schuster Inc, 1937).

Brown, D. *The Four Gospels*. (Edinburgh: Banner of Truth Trust, 1864/1969).

Brown, R. *Christ Above All – the Message of Hebrews*. (London: InterVarsity Press, 1982).

Bruce, F. F. *The Epistle to the Hebrews*. (London: Marshall, Morgan and Scott, 1964. 5th Imprt, 1977).

Budgen V. *The Charismatics and the Word of God – a biblical and historical perspective on the charismatic movement*. (Welwyn: Evangelical Press, 1985).

Calvin, J (Trans. Leroy Nixon. *Calvin's Sermons – the Deity of Christ*. (Grand Rapids: Eerdmans, 1950).

_____ (Trans. T. H. L. Parker. *Sermons on Isaiah's Prophecy of the Death and Passion of Christ*. (Cambridge:James Clarke & Co, 1956).

_____ (Trans. Arthur Golding). *John Calvin's Sermons on Ephesians*. (Edinburgh: Banner of Truth Trust, 1577, rpnt 1979).

_____ *Institutes of the Christian Religion:*, (Florida: MacDonald edition, n.d.).

_____Commentary on *The Epistles of Paul the Apostle to the Romans and to the Thessalonians*. (Edinburgh: The Saint Andrew Press, n.d.).

_____ Commentary on *Epistle of Paul to the Hebrews and the Epistles of Peter*. ((Edinburgh: The Saint Andrew Press, n.d.).

_____Commentary on *The Gospel of Saint John and the Epistle of First John*. (Edinburgh: The Saint Andrew Press, n.d.).

Carswell, R (2014). *Before You Say "I Don't Believe"* (Leyland: 10 Publishing, 2014).

Clifford, Alan C (1990). *Atonement and Justification: English Evangelical Theology, 1640-1790, An Evaluation* (Oxford: Clarendon Press, 1990).

_____*Calvinus*. (Norwich: Charenton Reformed Publishing, 1996).

_____*The Good Doctor*. (Norwich: Charenton Reformed Publishing, 2002).

_____*Amyraut Affirmed*. (Norwich: Charenton Reformed Publishing, 2004).

_____(Ed.) *John Calvin 500 – a Reformation Affirmation*. (Norwich: Charenton Reformed Publishing, 2011).

_____*Pregethwr y Bobl John Jones Talsarn – The People's Preacher*. (Norwich: Charenton Reformed Publishing, 2013).

Cunningham, W. *The Reformers and the Theology of the Reformation*. (Edinburgh: Banner of Truth Trust, 1862/1967).

_____(1862/1979). 2 Vols. *Historical Theology*. (Edinburgh: Banner of Truth Trust, 1862?1979).

D'Aubigné, J. H. Merle (1960). Trans. H. White. *The Life and Times of Martin Luther.* (Moody Press. No place of publication given).

_____ *The Reformation in England.* Vol.1. (Edinburgh: Banner of Truth Trust, 1971 rpnt).

_____ *The Reformation in England.* Vol.2. (Edinburgh: Banner of Truth Trust, 1972 rpnt).

Dabney, Robert L (1871/1985). *Systematic Theology.* Edinburgh: Banner of Truth Trust, 1971 rpnt).

Dale, A. W. W. *The Life of R. W. Dale of Birmingham.* (London: Hodder and Stoughton, 1898/1902).

Dale, Robert William (1897). *The Atonement.* (London: The Congregational Union of England and Wales, 1897).

Davenant, John. *Dissertation on the Death of Christ.* (Shropshire: Quinta Press, 1832/2006).

Davis, Dale Ralph. *Judges.* (Ross-shire: Christian Focus Publications, 2000).

_____ *1 Kings.* (Ross-shire: Christian Focus Publications, 2002).

_____ *2 Kings.* (Ross-shire: Christian Focus Publications, 2005).

Denney, J. *The Epistle to the Thessalonians.* (London: Hodder and Stoughton, 1892).

_____ *The Death of Christ* (2nd edit). (London: Hodder and Stoughton, 1902).

Douglas, J. D (Ed). *The New International Dictionary of the Christian Church.* (Exeter: Paternoster Press, 1978).

Douty, Norman F. *The Death of Christ*. (Pennsylvania: Reiner Publications, 1972).

Eaton, M. A. *A Theology of Encouragement*. (Carlisle: Paternoster Press, 1995).

Elwell, W. A (Ed) (1985). *Evangelical Dictionary of Theology*. (Basingstoke: Marshall Pickering, 1985).

Ferguson, S. B. *A Heart for God*. (Edinburgh: Banner of Truth Trust, 1987).

Forsyth, Peter Taylor. *The Work of Christ*. (London: Hodder and Stoughton, c.1909).

_____ *The Cruciality of the Cross and The Work of Christ*. (Shropshire: Quinta Press, 1909/2008).

Gay, D. H. J. *The Gospel Offer is Free*. (Biggleswade: Brachus, 2004).

Gammie, A (n.d.). *Preachers I Have Heard*. (London: Pickering and Inglis, n.d.).

Guillebaud, H. E, *Why The Cross?* (London: InterVarsity Press, 1937).

Guthrie, D (1981). *New Testament Theology*. (London: InterVarsity Press, 1981).

Helm, P. *Calvin and the Calvinists*. (Edinburgh: Banner of Truth Trust, 1982).

Hendriksen, W. *John*. New Testament Commentary. (Edinburgh: Banner of Truth Trust, 1954).

Hendriksen, W. *Mark*. New Testament Commentary. (Edinburgh: Banner of Truth Trust, 1975).

Henry, Matthew, *Commentary on the whole BIBLE*. (Marshallton: The National Foundation for Christian Education, 1845 edit).

Hodge, A. A. *Outlines of Theology*. (Edinburgh: Banner of Truth Trust, 1879/1972).

_____ *Evangelical Theology*. (Edinburgh: Banner of Truth Trust, 1890/1976).

Hodge, C (1871/1946). *Systematic Theology*. Vol. II. (Grand Rapids, 1871/1946).

Hulse, E (1973). *The Free Offer*. (Sussex: Carey Publications Ltd and Henry E. Walter Ltd, 1973).

_____ (1986). *The Great Invitation*. (Welwyn: Evangelical Press, 1986).

Jacob, E. *Theology of the Old Testament*. (London: Hodder and Stoughton, 1958, 3rd impr 1964).

Jones, M. *Why Heaven Kissed Earth: The Christology of Thomas Goodwin (1600-1680)*. (Leiden: Doctoral thesis, University of Leiden, 1980).

Jones, R. T. *The Great Reformation*. (Leicester: InterVarsity Press, 1985).

Jones, M. J and Morgan, W. Trans. John Aaron. *The Calvinistic Methodist Fathers of Wales*. 2 Vols. (Edinburgh: Banner of Truth Trust, 2008).

Kendall, R. T. *Calvin and English Calvinism to 1649*. (Oxford: Oxford University Press, 1981 and Carlisle: Paternoster Press 1997).

Kistemaker, S. J. *Hebrews*. (Welwyn: Evangelical Press, 1984).

_____ *James and I-III John*. (Welwyn: Evangelical Press, 1986).

Ladd, G. E. *A Theology of the New Testament*. (London: Lutterworth Press, 1974).

Lane, W. L. *The Gospel According to Mark*. (Grand Rapids: Eerdmans, 1974).

Letham, R. *The Work of Christ*. (Leicester: InterVarsity Press, 1993).

Leupold, H. C (n.d.) *Exposition of Isaiah*. (Vol.1 & 2). (Darlington: Evangelical Press, n.d.).

Luther, M. *The Bondage of the Will*. (London: James Clarke & Co, 1525).

Machen, J. G. *Christianity and Liberalism*. (London: Victory Press, 1923).

_____*The Origin of Paul's Religion*. (Grand Rapids: W. B. Eerdmans, 1925).

_____*God Transcendent*. (Edinburgh: Banner of Truth Trust, 1949/1982).

Macleod, D *A Faith To Live By*. (Ross-shire: Christian Focus Publications, 1998).

_____ *Shared Life*. (Ross-shire: Christian Focus Publications, 2002).

_____ *From Glory to Golgotha*. (Ross-shire: Christian Focus Publications, 2002).

Macleod, J. *Scottish Theology* (2nd edition). (Edinburgh: Banner of Truth Trust, 1946/1974).

Macpherson, J. *Christian Dogmatics*. (Edinburgh, 1898).

Martin, R. P. *Reconciliation*. (London: Marshall, Morgan and Scott, 1981).

Martin, R. P and Waldron, S. E (1989). *A Modern Exposition of the 1689 Baptist Confession of Faith*, (Welwyn: Evangelical Press, 1989).

McGrath, A (Ed) *Modern Christian Thought*. (Oxford: Blackwell Publishing, 1993).

_____*Historical Theology – an Introduction to the History of Christian Thought.* (Oxford: Blackwell Publishing,1998).

_____*Historical Theology – an Introduction to the History of Christian Thought.* (Oxford: Blackwell Publishing, 2001).

Milne, B. *The Message of John.* (Leicester: InterVarsity Press, 1993).

Morgan, E. *John Elias – life and letters.* (Edinburgh: Banner of Truth Trust, 1973).

Morris, L. L. *The Gospel According to John.* (London: Marshall, Morgan and Scott, 1972).

_____*The Apostolic Preaching of the Cross.* (Guildford: Tyndale Press, 1972a).

_____*The Cross in the New Testament.* (Exeter: Paternoster Press, 1976).

Motyer, A. *The Prophecy of Isaiah.* (Leicester: InterVarsity Press, 1993).

Muller, R. A. *Post-Reformation Reformed Dogmatics, Vol.2.* (Grand Rapids: Baker Books, 1993).

Murray, Iain H. *Sermons of the Great Ejection.* (Edinburgh: Banner of Truth Trust, 1962).

_____ *Heroes.* (Edinburgh: Banner of Truth Trust, 2009).

Murray, J. *Redemption Accomplished and Applied.* (Edinburgh: Banner of Truth Trust, 1961).

Needham, N. R. *Thomas Erskine of Linlathen - His Life and Theology 1788-1837.* (Edinburgh: Rutherford House, 1990).

Owen, J. *The Death of Death in the Death of Christ.* (Edinburgh: Banner of Truth Trust, 1959/1983 rpnt).

Packer, J. I. *18 Words.* (Ross-shire: Christian Focus Publications, 1998).

_____ *Under God's Word.* (London: Lakeland, Marshall, Morgan and Scott, 1980).

Parker, T. H. L (Trans. into English, 1956). *Sermons on Isaiah's Prophecy of the Death and Passion of Christ.* (Cambridge: James Clarke & Co., 1956).

Payne, J. B. *A Theology of the Older Testament.* (Grand Rapids: Academie Books, Zondervan Publishing House, 1962).

Peterson, Robert A (Sr). *Calvin and the Atonement.* (Ross-shire: Christian Focus Publications, 1999).

Philip, J. *The Westminster Confession of Faith - Part 1, Chapters 1-8.* (Dundee: Didasko Press (?), c.1966).

Pink, A. W. *The Sovereignty of God.* (London: Banner of Truth Trust, 1961, rpnt 1972).

Piper, J (2004). *The Passion of Jesus Christ.* Crossway Books, Illinois, USA.

Rawlinson, G (1906). Spence and Exell (Eds). *The Pulpit Commentary – Isaiah.* (London: Funk and Wagnell Co, 1906).

Ridderbos, H. *Paul – An Outline of His Theology.* (London: SPCK, 1977).

Ross, A. *Commentary on the Epistles of James and John.* (London: Marshall, Morgan and Scott, Ltd., 1954).

Ryle, J. C. *Expository Thoughts of John.* Vol.1. (Edinburgh: Banner of Truth Trust, 1869/1987).

Schaeffer, Francis A. *Death in the City,* (Leicester: InterVarsity Press, 1969).

Sell, A. P. F. *Defending and Declaring the Faith.* (Exeter: Paternoster Press, 1987).

Smeaton, G. *The Apostles' Doctrine of the Atonement.* (Edinburgh: Banner of Truth Trust, 1870/1991).

_____*Christ's Doctrine of the Atonement.* 2nd Edit. (Edinburgh: Banner of Truth Trust and T & T Clarke,1871/1991).

Stevens, G. B. *The Christian Doctrine of Salvation.* (Edinburgh: T & T Clarke, 1090).

Stewart, J. *A Man in Christ.* (London: Hodder and Stoughton, 1964).

Stott, J. R. W. *Epistles of John.* (London: The Tyndale Press, 1964).

_____ *God's New Society.* (Leicester: InterVarsity Press, 1979).

_____ *The Cross of Christ.* (Leicester: InterVarsity Press, 1986).

Thomas, O. *The Atonement Controversy.* Transl. John Aaron. (Edinburgh: Banner of Truth Trust, 1874 in Welsh, 2002 in English).

Tozer, A. W. *Worship - the Missing Jewel* (n.p., n.d.).

Van Stam, Frans Pieter. *The Controversy over the Theology of Saumur, 1635–1650* (Amsterdam: Holland University Press, 1988).

Von Rad, G. Trans. J. E. Steely. *Biblical Interpretations in Preaching.* (Nashville: Abingdon Press, 1973, rpnt 1978).

Vos, G (1948/1975). *Biblical Theology - Old and New Testaments.* (Edinburgh: Banner of Truth Trust, 1948/1975).

Warfield, B. B (1970). *The Person and Work of Christ.* (Ed. S. G. Craig). (Philadelphia: Presbyterian and Reformed Publishing Company, 1970).

Wendel, François. *Calvin*. Transl. Philip Mairet. (London: Collins, The Fontana Library, 1963).

White, R. E. O. *A Guide To Pastoral Care*. (London: Pickering & Inglis, 1976).

Wiersbe, W. *Walking with the Giants,* (Grand Rapids: Baker Book House, 1976).

Williamson, G. I. *The Westminster Confession of Faith*. (Philadelphia: Presbyterian and Reformed Publishing Company, 1964).

Zodhiates, S (1992). *The Complete Word Study Dictionary – New Testament*. (Chattanooga: AMG Publishers, 1992).

Academic Journals.

Reformed Theological Journal. Eds E. Donnelly, C. K. Hyndman, F. S. Leahy, No.8, November. Pp.54-64. (Belfast).

Evangelical Quarterly. Ed. I. H. Marshall. Vol.81:3. (Exeter: Paternoster Press, 2009).

Boersma, Hans. *Evangelical Quarterly*. EQ64.4 (1992), 333-355. "Calvin and the Extent of the Atonement."

Scottish Journal of Theology, (1972). Eds Iain Torrance and Bryan Spinks. Vol.25, No.3. Cambridge University Press, England, UK.

_____ (2005). Eds Iain Torrance and Bryan Spinks. Vol. 58, No. 3. Cambridge University Press, England, UK. Pp.333-352.

Evangel (1985). Eds N. M. de S. Cameron, G. Bray, D. F. Kelly, J. G. McConville, R. E. H. Uprichard. Vol.3:3, Winter. Pp.2, 3.

_____(1985). Eds N. M. de S. Cameron, G. Bray, D. F. Kelly, J. G. McConville, R. E. H. Uprichard. Vol.3:4, Spring. Pp.2.

Appendix

DML-J's understanding of the atonement *in his own words*.

I give the location where and the year in which DML-J preached these sermons, after the book title. For example, Sandfields, 1927–1938, indicates that he preached the sermons at Sandfields between the years given. WCL, 1955 indicates sermons that he preached in Westminster Chapel, London, in 1955. The page number follows at the end of the quotation.

EVANGELISTIC SERMONS, 1983. Sandfields, 1927–1938.

1. "This to me is the whole of Christianity. The ablest and the best man in the world cannot save himself, but God, who can do everything, can save all – even the most ignorant and the worst and vilest." (9).

2. "…it is the belief of the Christian, who believes in the unity of the human race and who regards all men and women as being equal, it is his belief that what has happened once can always happen again, that if one man has been saved, all men can be saved." (17).

3. "…there's enough gospel in that fact alone to save the whole world." (18).

4. "…they immediately saw that He could save all people. 'We know that this is indeed the Christ, the Saviour of the world'!" (21).

5. "'He who has saved me can save anyone, can save the whole world,' says the Christian." (21).

6. "...and know that this is indeed the Christ, the Saviour of the world." (22).

7. It is the voice of God calling us from sin unto salvation. It is our heavenly Father sending us a message of pardon and forgiveness and calling us back to our home." (26, 27).

8. "The breadth of scope, the all-inclusiveness of the gospel, becomes very apparent when we compare it with every other teaching which has ever been held before mortal man." (40).

9. "His message was that 'God so loved *the world* that He gave His only begotten Son that *whosoever* believeth in him should not perish, but have everlasting life.' Nothing could be wider or more inclusive. Those were his constant words – 'the world', 'whosoever'!" He seemed to see a hope for everyone and everybody!" (40, 41).

10. "But here in this passage with which we propose to deal this evening, we find a strange limitation. Here we find this Person – whose ministry was characterised above all else by the wideness of its scope and the hope He held out for all – here we find Him stating quite definitely that for a certain class of persons, there is no hope whatsoever!" (41).

11. "...but remember, if you believe that Christ had to die on the cross to save you, it means of necessity that you were in such a dreadful condition and plight that nothing but that death could possibly save you." (56).

12. "Well, what was that gospel? Just this, that Jesus Christ, is the Son of God, that in dying He fulfilled the Law and destroyed the power of death, and that by so doing He cancelled the power of sin and wiped out the sinful debt of humanity and that by the power of His Spirit a man can be created anew and start upon a new life which is an eternal life." (63).

13. "Some appear as if they had never done any wrong, as if they had no need to repent and had no need for Christ to die for them on Calvary." (85).

14. "But look at *His death* for a moment and consider it as an expiation for the sin of the whole world." (87).

15. "Well, those sufferings were enough, according to John, for all. Listen! 'He is the propitiation for our sins; but not for ours only, but also for the sins of the whole world' 1 Jn.2:2. The whole world!" (88).

16. "But listen to the words of our Lord Himself as He calls from the cross, 'It is finished'. The sins of the whole world He had borne upon Himself …" (88).

17. "The sacrifice was completed. It was indeed finished, once and for all, world without end!" (88).

18. "We cannot see why God insists upon our believing that Christ died for us and that that is the only way to His heart." (97).

19. "He gave His Son to death and the cross for our sake. Oh! What a gift! What amazing love! What mercy and generosity!" (100).

20. "…once Paul saw Him and realized who He was and what He had done for him and for the whole world, he just cried out in effect, 'O Lord, what can I do for you? …'" (113).

21. "All must come through this. Our Lord makes it plain and clear here that the Pharisees and the chief priests and elders were expected to repent quite as much as the publicans and harlots whom He also mentions." (119).

22. "That is what God wants us to do – to believe that He forgives us all because Christ died for us, to believe that He of His love sent Christ specifically for that end and, believing that, to give up our life of sin, trusting to Him to keep and sustain us." (128, 129).

23. "He asks you to become a little child and say, 'I believe Jesus Christ died for me, I believe God forgives me for that reason only, and because of that I turn my back on sin and evil from tonight, trusting Jesus Christ to keep me and protect me.'" (129).

24. "Heaven, without money and without price, but simply on the condition that I acknowledge my sin and confess my need of Him. Everything, simply on the condition that I confess and realize my nothingness! Mercy and forgiveness for my every sin on the simple condition that I see my need of it!" (130).

25. "...even the Pharisees and the chief priests might have been forgiven and might have entered the kingdom at this same price, if only they had repented." (131).

26. "...when they are told that Jesus Christ came to die for sinners and therefore, for them, they say that they accept and believe it as a fact." (138).

27. "Do you sincerely believe that Jesus Christ the Son of God came to rescue and ransom you from your sin, and to reconcile you to God?" (140).

28. "The gospel is not only a great offer of salvation, it is not merely a glorious invitation from God Himself, it is a test and a discipline also." (141).

29. "Justification is by faith only. But let us also remember that it is equally true that 'Faith without works is dead', and that true faith always shows itself by certain definite actions." (141).

30. "Accepting His offer of salvation ..." (144).

31. "He has called us to be pure. He sent His only begotten Son to suffer and die in order to bring this about." (145).

32. "There is the offer, the free offer of pardon and forgiveness to all who believe in, and trust to, Jesus Christ as their Saviour and Redeemer from sin and from hell." (146).

33. "The first [general proposition] is that the gospel calls for a decision, and asks us definitely to make up our minds and take a definite stand with regard to certain matters." (148, 149).

34. "...during every period of power and strength, the preaching of the church has driven people to decision. ...the preaching tries to move them to a definite decision. ...the gospel calls for a decision. ...nothing short of a definite decision is of the slightest value." (150).

35. "But here comes the gospel offer which tells me that Christ having died for me, God is willing and ready to pardon and forgive me, and give me a new life, and that he calls upon me to leave my sin and give myself definitely to Him." (157, 158).

36. "Refusing God and His offer of eternal salvation in His Son, ... Oh, the madness of it all!" (159).

37. "...unless we definitely decide for Christ. Not to decide for Him is to be against Him. ...Jesus Christ, the Son of God, came from heaven and lived and died and rose again in order to save you, but if you do not believe in Him and accept Him, He will become your damnation." (160).

38. "Such will be yours, but infinitely worse and more terrible, if you do not decide for Jesus Christ." (161).

39. "Do they live as realizing that the end must soon come, that soon they will have to go, and that in the meantime they are deciding and determining their *eternal* future?" (163).

40. "...what is the value of a Saviour unless He can save and rescue you when you need Him most of all?" (170).

41. "No! The first thing you have to realize is that there are conditions in these matters, and that the conditions are always to be laid down by Him." (171).

42. "It means believing that He is the only Son of God who came on earth to save us." (172).

43. "'I *know* whom I have believed,' says Paul, 'and am persuaded that He is able to keep that which I've committed unto Him against that day.' That certainty is possible for all. The conditions are still the same." (173).

44. "...it is also exceedingly dangerous from the deeper and more spiritual standpoint, for it always tends to mean that the true position is hardly ever occupied. For the true position is never at one extreme or the other, but always in the middle." (175).

45. "What is it about this great salvation which is offered to all that leads always invariably to 'wonder, love and praise.'?" (194).

46. "…a God whose love is actually so great that He not only forgives but also persuades us to be forgiven." (196).

47. "Yes! God so loved the world that he gave his only begotten Son, John 3:16.'" (198).

48. "...this great salvation which is offered to us by God is to the natural man something which is inherently incredible." (201).

49. "...in view of the fact that salvation is of God and therefore supernatural, although we cannot understand it, it holds out a hope for all. ...It is God's work, and because it is His work, it is possible for all and can be offered to all. ...There is literally hope for all." (203).

50. "The gospel just asks you to allow God to forgive you, to pardon you, to cleanse you, to fill you with a new life by believing that he

sent His only begotten Son into the world, to live and die and rise again in order to make all that possible." (204).

51. "...there He was in the house of Simon, full of power, yea more, full of a love to mankind which made Him long to exercise and use that power for their welfare." (206).

52. "Or do you recognize in Him the Son of God come down to earth, the Saviour of your soul?" (212).

53. "Listen to Him as He tells you that He has died for you, that He has reconciled you to God, that your past can be blotted out, and that your eternal future is safe." (221).

54. "The great point, surely, is that there is hope for all, that God's love extends even to the publicans and sinners." (227).

55. "What new hope for mankind appeared in Him!" (228).

56. "There was not, and there never had been, any hope for the hopeless in the world before Jesus Christ came. He alone taught the possibility of a new start and a new beginning." (229).

57. "...the gospel is not something vague and general like the world's message, *but something to which definite conditions are attached.*" [Italics his]. (232).

58. "The love of God does not merely talk about a new beginning, it makes a new beginning. 'God so loved the world that He *gave.*'" (237).

59. "...realize that this is the very Son of God come on earth to deliver us." (250).

60. "They follow Christ solely to serve their own ends, and not because He is the Son of God, and the Saviour of the world." (264).

61. "I am like that farmer: I am sowing the seed of the Word of God which leads to eternal life. Ultimately men will be judged by their reaction to that seed sown in their lives." (272).

62. "It is there [in the Christ of the cross] that the whole of humanity is focused. He is the representative of the whole of humankind. He died for all." (278).

63. "But after all what shows how utterly blind this worldly type of life is is the way in which it *ignores God and His gracious warnings and offers of deliverance.*" [Italics his]. (292).

64. "But by that very death He was preaching pardon and forgiveness for all who believe in Him. ...He Himself has given the warning. But He Himself also has provided the way of escape, the way of salvation. He offers free pardon, however deep and great our sin, a new beginning and a new life." (293, 294).

LET EVERYBODY PRAISE THE LORD – Exposition of Ps.107.
WCL, 1955

65. "The children of Israel have been brought into being by God, and he has used them as an illustration and an example to the whole world of his way of dealing with mankind." (10).

66. "Here is an invitation to all and sundry, as it were, to come together to sing this universal anthem." (17).

67. "He invites them 'from the east and from the west, from the north and from the south.' He says that all these divisions and distinctions are completely irrelevant. They make no difference at all. He is calling men and women who come from entirely different backgrounds to join in the same praise." (17).

68. "Still the invitation goes out to all to come together and to unite in the same words and in the same anthem of praise." (18).

69. "...though you may have been guilty of every sin known to man ... he will not refuse you. He will listen to you. He will receive you now, and he will tell you that he sent his Son into the world to die for you and your sins;..." (45).

70. "So the only hope for the world, says the writer, is in God, and it is only those who realise their utter hopelessness and helplessness, and who cry out unto the Lord in their trouble, who are delivered and set free." (66).

71. "...he died that you and I might be forgiven. He died that we might be reconciled to God." (80).

72. "Do not plead anything, but admit it all, and then believe him when he tells you that he sent his Son to die for you and for your sins, and that he will give you life anew." (82).

73. "Why did God not abandon the world to itself? ... Why has he ever looked upon it? But he does. 'For God so loved the world ...' (Jn.3:16)." (96).

74. "That was God's way of doing it [salvation]. He has done it in this person, and he has even gone to the extent of 'laying upon him the iniquity of us all' (Isaiah 53:6). He has put your sins and mine and our guilt upon the person of his only begotten Son." (131).

75. "God has 'made him to be sin for us'. He has 'laid upon him the iniquity of us all.' 'With his stripes we are healed' (Isaiah 53:5, 6). And the Son was taking our sins upon himself in his own body on the tree." (132).

TRUE HAPPINESS – Exposition of Ps.1. WCL.

76. "If any of us ever arrives in hell we will have nobody to blame but ourselves." (24).

77. "'No,' says the Bible, 'but God so loved the world, that he gave his only begotten Son, that whosoever believeth in him should not perish, but have everlasting life' (John 3:16). 'The Son of man came to seek and to save that which was lost' (Luke 19:10). Listen to this instruction, this Law of the Lord, and it will tell you, Repent and believe the gospel. Acknowledge your sin; acknowledge your failure; believe that Jesus of Nazareth is the Son of God and that He came into this world and died on the cross to bear the punishment of your sin, to set you free, to reconcile you to God, to give you new life, and to make you an heir of eternal bliss." (33).

78. "...our destiny ... is determined by our life and our attitude in this world." (92).

ATONEMENT AND JUSTIFICATION – ROMANS SERIES, 1970. WCL, 1957.

79. "[God's] way of salvation ... has been made possible and available through the redeeming work of the Lord Jesus Christ." (30).

80. "He is the God of the whole world, so the righteousness that He has provided is in the same way open to the whole world." (30, 31).

AUTHORITY, Ontario, Canada. 1958. (Banner of Truth edition 1984).

81. "In the early days of the Church the apostles went everywhere preaching the resurrection, Jesus as the Saviour of the world, and Jesus as Lord." (30).

82. "They preached Jesus as the Son of God and Saviour of the world in the context of the message of the Old Testament Scriptures." (30).

83. "...he presents Jesus of Nazareth as the Son of God and the Saviour of the world... (30, 31).

OLD TESTAMENT EVANGELISTIC SERMONS, 1995. Sandfields and WCL, 1927 – 1960.

84. "He had met the God who was offering him pardon for his failure, who assured him that he would place his hand upon him, who gave him there a vision of his own future as the father of a nation, the father ultimately of the Lord Jesus Christ who was to be the Saviour of the world." (31).

85. "…God in his infinite love had actually sent his only-begotten Son into the world to live and die and rise again in order to make a way of salvation and in order that God might reconcile the world to himself." (47).

86. "He came to die for our sins and to open the door of heaven for us." (83).

87. "We shall not die because he has died for us and accomplished a perfect atonement in our behalf." (84).

88. "The Saviour of the world was not born in Jerusalem, he was born in Bethlehem." (124).

89. "They did not know it but the Saviour of the world was about to come into their very midst." (124).

90. "…go to Jesus of Nazareth, the Son of God and you will be cured. He can remove your guilt because he has already taken it away…" (127).

91. "Go to him, that is all you have to do, he is the *all*-sufficient Saviour, he is 'the power of God unto salvation to everyone that believeth'." (127).

92. "'What', said the Greeks, 'our great philosophers asked to believe that a carpenter in Nazareth dying on a cross is the Saviour of the

world, and that we have got nothing to do but believe in him and to surrender to him?'" (139).

93. "This is God's way, this is God's only begotten Son, Jesus of Nazareth, he is the Saviour of the world." (139).

94. "God has sent his only Son, his only begotten Son into the world for us men and our salvation and the only way in which even he could do it was to die for us." (140).

95. "Though mankind had turned away from him, God in his love did not turn away from us. He sent his Son after us to save us, and yielding ourselves to him the profit we desire is pardon from our sin, peace with God; power to live life worthy of the name; the removal of the fear of death; sonship of God and heirship of eternal bliss. That is offered to all now. It is the only offer and the last offer. The consequences of your choice you will experience to all eternity. Surely nne can hesitate." (180).

96. "What God offered to do for Israel under the old dispensation he now offers to all in Christ Jesus our Lord." 196).

97. "It [the gospel] does not ask us to do the impossible but tells us that Christ has done it for us all and that all we have to do is to accept what he has done and then show our gratitude by yielding ourselves to him and living only to please him." (206).

98. "…the New Testament does not limit the offer to certain people only. It offers it to all. It draws no distinctions between one type and another, and assures us all that 'the same God over all \is good unto all.'" (263).

LIFE IN THE SPIRIT – IN MARRIAGE, HOME AND WORK. (1974). WCL, 1959/60.

99. "It is the same sort of love wherewith Christ loved the church; indeed, wherewith God has loved the world." (142).

100. "Christ loved the church and gave Himself for her – yes, but also 'for me', for every one of us as individuals." (145).

THE CROSS. Gal.6:14. WCL, 1963

101. "The whole of the human race is in this condition." (72).

102. "Do you know why Paul gloried in it [the cross]? It is because he had come to see that God had got a plan for this miserable, wretched, failing sinful world." (73).

103. "The cross, you see, is the centre of God's plan. It is the heart of God's way of saving the world." (74).

104. "God has made his own Son to be sin for us, though he knew no sin, in order that he might be able to forgive us …" (83).

105. "Paul who in Romans 8:32 describes why he glories so much in the cross: 'He [God] that spared not his own Son, but delivered him up for us all.' Now that is a wonderful description of what happened on the cross. God, in his great love to us, delivered up for us his only begotten, dearly beloved Son, who had never disobeyed him and had never done any harm to anybody, to the death of the cross." (83).

106. "…we have seen how the cross is a revelation of the character of the eternal God, … God's eternal wisdom; God's plan for this world and the whole cosmos; God's justice, righteousness, holiness." (89).

107. "The whole world is going to be judged, and going to be destroyed. … On that cross, the Lord Jesus Christ took upon himself the punishment that is coming to all who belong to the world. … there is only one way whereby you can be separated from the punishment of that world, that is by believing that Christ has borne the punishment for you, that he bore your sins in his own body on the tree, and that he has received your punishment…" (106).

108. "He delivers me from the world. He died that, 'Whosoever believeth in him should not perish but have everlasting life.'" (107).

109. "And if you believe in him and in his message, if you believe that that person dying on that cross on Calvary's hill was the Lord of glory, and that he was dying in order to save you and to separate you from the world..." (108).

110. "And I, if I be lifted up, will draw all men unto me." (123).

111. "He came to do good. He came to teach. He came to deliver mankind." (124).

112. "Christ died, and he became the Saviour of the world. He draws all men, men of all nations, and of kindreds and of climes unto himself." (129).

113. "You both look up together into the face of the one and only Saviour, the Saviour of the world, the Lamb of God that taketh away the sin of the world. He is not only the Saviour of the western world, he is also the Saviour of the people the other side of the Iron Curtain..." (150).

114. "He has come to save souls, the Saviour of the world, 'the Lamb of God which taketh away the sin of the world'. ... Here is the only one who can encompass the whole world, the whole universe, and all in utter helplessness can look to him. ... It is his going to that cross, and submitting himself as the Lamb of God, and having our sins put upon him by his Father, and bearing the stroke, the punishment, for us, that is what saves us." (151).

115. "Here is the hope in this world today and there is none other." (152).

116. "...he came to save the soul. 'The Son of man is come to seek and to save that which was lost,' and what is lost is man's soul." (159).

117. "God has always said that sin is to be punished. ... On the cross he is doing it publicly. There he is, once and for all, at the central point of history, pouring out his wrath upon the sins of man in the body of his own Son." (165, 166).

118. "That is what has happened. God and sinners reconciled." (166).

119. "'God was in Christ reconciling the world unto himself....' It was God who 'laid on him the iniquity of us all'." (185).

120. "...God loves us with an everlasting love." (186).

I AM NOT ASHAMED – Advice to Timothy, 1994. *WCL, 1964.*

121. "This is not a hope merely for certain kinds of people; it is offered as a hope to any and to all. 'Whosoever!' 'Whosoever comes' he can have this." (33).

122. "I am simply recommending in that sense because of this great gift which the gospel holds out to all men everywhere." (52).

123. "That God so loved the world that he sent into it – 'He gave' – and even to the death of the cross, 'his only begotten son, that whosoever believeth in him should not perish but have everlasting life.' 'God was in [and through] Christ, reconciling the world unto himself.' (69).

FROM FEAR TO FAITH, 1953. *WCL.*

124. "There are those who have been praying about someone who is dear to them for many years, and God does not seem to answer. They reason within themselves like this: 'Sq2urely it is the will of God that a man should become a Christian? Well, I have been praying for him all these years and nothing seems to happen. Why? Why is God thus silent?" (16).

LIFE IN CHRIST, 2002, Sermons, WCL, 1948/9.

125. "...the death of Christ upon the cross is the propitiation for my sins—indeed, for the sins of the whole world—and that all my sins have been dealt with and are covered, are removed and banished there in Him." (134).

126. "'Ah, yes,' says someone, 'but you do not know how terribly I have sinned ...' My dear friend, 'He is the propitiation for ... the sins of the whole world,' and you and all your sins are included." (158).

127. "We can say with John that he is enough, sufficient to cover the sins of the whole world." (179).

THE KINGDOM OF GOD, 1992. WCL, 1963.

128. "God had a plan and a purpose for this world and it is a plan to deliver men and women such as ourselves out of the morass into which we have fallen." (14).

129. "No, the message is this: God 'hath visited and redeemed his people,' Lk.1:68. 'God so loved the world'—this world, this damned, foolish, evil world that you and I live in and of which we are all a part by nature—God so loved it, 'that he gave his only begotten Son, that whosoever believeth should not perish, but have everlasting life' Jn.3:16." (23).

130. "How, then, can I enter? He is the answer. This is the Good News, that He bore our sins 'in his own body on the tree, that we being dead to sins, should live unto righteousness,' (1 Pet 2:24). Here is the message: 'God was in Christ, reconciling the world unto himself, ...' 2 Cor 5:19. And thereby by dying on the Cross, He has opened the gateway into the kingdom and He says, 'Today is the day of salvation, enter in.'–'Come unto me all ye that are weary and heavy laden and I will give you rest' (Mt 11:28." (24).

131. "And this is the answer: 'The time is fulfilled, the Kingdom has come'; the King is the Lord Jesus Christ and He loved you so much that he died for you and your sins, and all He says to you is, 'Repent, think again, believe my message.'" (24).

132. "I bore your punishment in my body on Calvary's Cross. Your sins are forgiven, your righteousness is abolished, it is washed away and vanquished in my blood. Come let Me clothe you with the robe of my own righteousness." (44).

133. "We must realise that He brings us into His Kingdom by dying for us; by bearing our sins in His own body, by being made the Lamb of God for us; that He bears our punishment and that it is our only way of deliverance and salvation." (66).

134. "Christians, awake! salute the happy morn, Whereon the Saviour of mankind was born." (99).

135. "If he had only realised his need and his lost estate and his condition and that this was the Son of God who was sent to save the world–..." (169).

136. "To leave Christ is always a spiritual suicide. You are turning away from your Saviour, away from life which is life indeed, away from the Son of God who came to die for you and to save you..." (170).

137. "He came into the world because the Law of God condemns us all. ... We are therefore all lost, but 'the Son of man has come to seek and to save that which is lost!'" (187).

138. "... our Lord says that this [the new birth] must happen to 'all' men. This is most important." (195).

139. "God is holding out an offer to the human race!" (216).

140. "...God sent Him into this world to bear your sins in His own body on the tree." (217).

141. "Believe that Jesus is the Son of God and that He came to be the mediator of a new covenant, that He came to die to save you and to offer you free pardon and forgiveness,..." (222).

A NATION UNDER WRATH, 1997. WCL, 1964.

142. "The nation of Israel is but a kind of specimen, a type, which God set forth in order that through her he might speak to the whole of mankind. ...the whole world belonged to God then, as it does now. ... But the whole world belongs to God. ... we are seeing at the same time what God has to say to everyone. ... It is a book that speaks to every age and generation because mankind remains the same in all its essential qualities, and God remains the same." (11).

143. "So the message is put to us in many different ways in order that we may all come to an understanding of the truth. ... the great message of the Bible with respect to the whole human race." (13).

144. "He raised up this nation of Israel; through them he has spoken to the whole world and look at his patience with them!" (24).

145. "'God so loved the world, that he gave his only begotten Son' (Jn 3:16). His concern for this world and its people was so great that 'When the fulness of the time was come, God sent forth his Son, made of a woman, made under the law...' (Gal 4:4). ... and pointing to that cross he says to the whole world, 'Believe on my Son and I will forgive you all your sins.'" (25).

146. "an example which God set before the whole human race in order to convey his great message ..." (29).

147. "The message of the gospel is for everybody; it does not recognise any divisions or distinctions." (51).

148. "This is the Christian gospel. This is the manifestation of the love of God – that God has sent his Son into the world to save us from the wrath of God upon sin." (186).

149. "...God so loved you that he has put your sins and mine on his only begotten, dearly beloved Son, and the Son took them willingly upon himself." (187).

150. "So you will never know anything about the love of God until you realise God's way of saving us and saving us from perishing, from bearing the punishment that our sin so richly deserves." (188, 189).

151. "If you have seen this truth, acknowledge it to God and enter in through that gate. God will be waiting and willing to pardon all your sins, to apply the blood of Christ to you, ..." (190).

AUTHENTIC CHRISTIANITY, Vol. 1. 1999. Sermons, WCL, 1965

152. "He [Jesus] said that he had come into the world because it was the only way by which anybody could be saved." (10).

153. "Everyone needs to be saved, however great, however illustrious. We are all sinners. We are all born in sin..." (30).

154. "He sent his only Son into the world, even to the cross to die, his body to be broken, his blood to be shed, so that 'whosoever believeth in him should not perish but have everlasting life'" *John* 3:16. (30).

155. "...Christianity is a message for all people: 'Whosoever shall call on the name of the Lord shall be saved'" (*Acts* 2:21). (31).

156. "We are all under the condemnation of the law until we believe, but the moment we believe, we are no longer under condemnation..." (73).

157. "'...And I, if I be lifted up from the earth, will draw all men unto me' (*John* 12:23, 27, 32)." (118, 119).

158. "Why did he come into the world? ... 'that whosoever believeth in him should not perish but have eternal life' (*J"ohn*.3:16)." (122).

159. "How can I be reconciled with God? There is only one answer: 'God was in Christ, reconciling the world unto himself, not imputing their trespasses unto them... He hath made him to be sin for us, who knew no sin; that we might be made the righteousness of God in him' (2 *Cor.* 5:19, 21). This is the only hope, this gospel, this apostolic teaching, this preaching that Christ, the Son of God, was crucified for our sins, was buried, rose the third day, ascended to heaven, and is seated at the right hand of God, sending down the Holy Spirit." (139).

160. "...there is only one message of hope,... It is this: 'God so loved the world, that he gave his only begotten Son...' (*John* 3:16). Here is the message of the New Testament, this is Christian salvation." (161).

161. "Listen to John: '...Jesus Christ the righteous: and he is the propitiation for our sins: and not for ours only, but also for the sins of the whole world.' (1 *John* 2:1–2). All this means that God has laid our sins on his Son, and has smitten him." (164).

162. "I know that God so loved me that he sent his only Son into this world to bear the punishment of my sins..." (168).

163. "But under this preaching, they were brought low and saw what fools they had been. How blind! How ignorant! How dull! Pitting their little minds against God, crucifying the very Son of God himself, and the Saviour of the world." (177).

164. "They had crucified their own Saviour and Redeemer!" (183).

165. "[The world] had said, 'Is it possible that the Saviour of the world can be just a carpenter, especially one who comes out of a place called Nazareth?' ...The one despised is the Lord of glory and the Saviour of the world. ... He is filled with pity joined with power, and is looking down upon you. He knows all about your paralysis. That is why he is come into the world..." (235).

166. "He is the Saviour of the world (*John* 4:42)." (258).

167. "'Behold the Lamb of God, which taketh away the sin of the world' (*John* 1:29). Here is God's lamb, the lamb that will really do that." (266).

168. "Do you realize that you killed the Prince of life, the Son of God, the Saviour of the world? Do you realize that you denied and rejected the only one who can save you?" (267, 268).

169. "The world ... denies him—denies him as the Son of God, denies him as the Lamb of God, denies him as the Saviour who shed his blood that the world might be forgiven." (268).

170. "Men delivered him up to death, but the message of the gospel is that God delivered him up to death, for us all. ... He came to give his life a ransom for you. God delivered him up for you, whatever you may have been, whatever you may have thought of him until this moment. ... So repent and believe on the Lord Jesus Christ and you shall be saved." (269).

171. "...we want to know what the Christian Church has to say to us and to the whole world in which we live." (270).

172. "As you look at the world, as you look at your own life, as you look at history, as you read this word, are you still ignorant – of God, of your immortal soul, and, in between, of God's own Son, Jesus of Nazareth, the Saviour of the world." (299).

173. afresh, you will not be refused. He said, 'Him that cometh unto me I will in no wise cast out' (*John* 6:37). (324).

174. "Christ Jesus came into the world to save sinners..." (1 *Tim*.1:15). (325).

175. "...that your sins may be blotted out. I proclaim this to you in the name of Jesus Christ of Nazareth who has died, been buried and has risen, to make it possible for you." (328).

AUTHENTIC CHRISTIANITY, Vol 2, 2001. WCL, 1965.

176. "It is God who sent his Son into the world, it is God who sent him to the cross, it is God who 'laid on him the iniquities of us all,' (*Isa.* 53:6). It is God who has taken your sins and put them on him and punished them in him and is offering you a free pardon; it is God who has done it." (14).

177. "They geered at the idea that someone dying on a cross could be the Saviour of the world. ... But if you tell them that God 'laid on him the iniquity of us all' (*Isa.* 53:6), they will rise in fury and say that it is insulting and immoral." (41).

178. "Here was God incarnate, sent to save the world…" (47).

179. "He, in and of himself, and alone, is the Saviour of the world." (55).

180. "Here is 'the Lamb of God, which taketh away the sin of the world' (*John* 1:29). Here is one who has never sinned; here is one who is spotless; here is one who has never broken a commandment, never defied his Father. He has pleased his Father in all things and in all ways. And, 'God has laid on him the iniquity of us all' (*Isa.* 53:6)." (62, 63).

181. "Say, 'Yes, he is the only one, he is the Saviour of the world, and he is *my* Saviour.'" (65).

182. "He came into this world to save it." (73).

183. "Listen to the apostle Paul writing to the Romans: 'I am not ashamed of the gospel of Christ' – why not? – 'for it is the power of God unto salvation to every one that believeth' (*Rom.* 1:16). (75).

184. "…this Jesus whom they had been following and with whom they had been working was none other than the only begotten Son of God who had come into the world to save them." (78).

185. "Why had he ever come into the world? He had told them why: 'the Son of man is come to seek and to save that which was lost' (*Luke* 19:10). He came into this world because we have all gone astray, we are all lost, and we cannot save ourselves. …there is only one who can save us – Jesus, the Son of God." (93).

186. "We know why he died. There, on the cross, God was laying on him the iniquity of us all. He is the 'Lamb of God' – as John the Baptist had said – 'which taketh away the sin of the world' (*John* 1:29.'" (93, 94).

187. "The Christian message … is the message of facts; of 'things seen and heard' about the Lord Jesus Christ, and then the interpretation of them, their meaning, their relevance to everyone of us." (95).

188. "Because our whole contention is that this gospel is 'the power of God unto salvation to every one that believeth' (*Rom.* 1:16),…" (96).

189. "These men exulted in the gospel; they gloried in it. They said with the apostle Paul, 'God forbid that I should glory, save in the cross of our Lord Jesus Christ' (*Gal.* 6:14); and, 'I am not ashamed of the gospel of Christ: for it is the power of God unto salvation to every one that believeth' (*Rom.* 1:16). (103).

190. "His love was so great that he sent his only Son into the world. We read: 'God so loved the world that he gave his only begotten Son, that whosoever believeth in him should not perish, but have everlasting life,' (*John* 3:16)." (120).

191. "God told his Son to start a new human race, to rescue and deliver them. … So what is your objection to the love of God, that love which is 'so amazing, so divine', that love that 'spared not his own Son, but delivered him up for us all' (*Rom.* 1:16) – come, be reasonable, what is your objection to it?" (121).

192. "The God who so loved the world that he sent his only Son into it, and put our sins upon him and smote him for us, he will be the judge." (126).

193. "…Christ is his Son, who came into the world to save them." (143).

194. "…God's gracious message is still: 'God so loved the world' – God so loved this world as it is! …God anointed his Son to be our Saviour and our Deliverer,…" (158).

195. "In your bewilderment, …simply believe that Jesus of Nazareth is the eternal Son of God and that he came into the world to save you." (161).

196. "It is this message of reconciliation, that 'God was in Christ, reconciling the world unto himself, not imputing their trespasses unto them' (2 *Cor.* 5:19), that is the great central message of the Christian faith." (164).

197. "*The* Lamb, God's own Lamb, the Lamb that God himself has provided, not the lamb provided by the priests in the tabernacle and in the temple. Here is God's own lamb that will take away the sin of the world." (170).

198. "Jesus Christ the Son of God was born in Bethlehem in order that he might taste death for everyone." (172).

199. "He sent his only Son into this world 'for the suffering of death … that he by the grace of God should taste death for every man' (*Heb.* 2:9). God's Son took our sins upon himself: 'He hath laid on him the iniquity of us all' (*Isa.* 53:6).'" (173).

200. "I proclaim to you that Jesus of Nazareth is the Son of God and the Saviour of the world." (183).

201. "He loved the world, remember – the world that had rebelled against him and ridiculed him, spat into his face and thought it knew better

than he did. ... Paul makes a magnificent statement of this in his letter to Titus: 'For the grace of God that bringeth salvation hath appeared to all men,' (*Titus* 2:11).' The grace of God!" (243).

202. "The end will come, and God will judge all those who have rejected the knowledge of him, all who have remained dupes of Satan, and have refused God's offer in Christ, his only begotten Son, whom he sent into this world that 'whosoever believeth in him should not perish but have everlasting life' (*John* 3:16).'" (267).

203. "For the moment humanity comes to see and to believe that, it will realize that its only hope is the hope that is offered in this Gospel. The gospel says, 'God so loved the world, that he gave his only begotten Son, that whosoever believeth in him should not perish but have everlasting life, (*John* 3:16).'" (280).

204. "The thing that modern people reject most of all is the thing that they need most of all. It is, I repeat, because they have never seen the need that they are not open to receiving this good news of salvation that 'God was in Christ reconciling the world unto himself (2 *Cor.* 5:19).' ... Whatever your past may have been, to everyone that believeth the gospel is the power of God unto salvation (*Rom.* 1:16)." (295).

205. "That is the vital question. 'What think ye of Christ?' (*Matt.* 22:42). And the Holy Spirit answers that question throughout that amazing record we call the New Testament. Here it is, in one verse. 'God so loved the world, that he gave his only begotten Son, that whosoever believeth in him should not perish, but have everlasting life (*John* 3:16).'" (308).

206. "On the cross he bore the punishment of my sins. He took my guilt upon him – that is why he came. He came to 'taste death for every man,' (*Heb.* 2:9)." (309).

207. "No, no; the gospel message tells of a supernatural, godlike deliverance. Paul puts it like this: 'I am not ashamed of the gospel

of Christ' – why not? – 'for it is the power of God unto salvation, (*Rom.* 1:16).'" (310).

208. "He had taught them that they were all sinners, that they were all lost and damned but that he had come into the world to save them. He had told them that he was dying that their sins might be forgiven, that he had borne their punishment in his own body on the tree, that he had risen again to justify them, and that he had gone to heaven to prepare a place for them. ...You will know that he loved you and died for you and your sins." (325, 326).

209. "They knew that there was a heart of love behind all that happened, that righteousness and peace had embraced each other, and that God almighty had sent his Son into the world 'that whosoever believeth in him should not perish but have everlasting life, Jn.3:16.'" (328).

210. "They were not horrified by the deaths of Ananias and Sapphira or by the shaking of the building. They knew it was the power of God but they knew now that the gospel 'is the power of God unto salvation to every one that believeth (*Rom.* 1:16).'" (328).

AUTHENTIC CHRISTIANITY, Vol. 3. WCL, 1966

211. "Men and women reject the message that the great God who made this world and made us all, the God who is over all and is our Judge eternal, the one against whom we have sinned and whom we have reviled and spat upon, is nevertheless a God who so loved us that he planned a way to set us free – the way of salvation." (14).

212. "In his sermon, he reminded them of the tragic fact that they had rejected the Lord Jesus Christ, and all that he had come to do for the human race. Indeed, it is this tragedy that accounts for all the others because here humanity is rejecting its one and only way of salvation." (39).

213. "And this is the great message of the Bible: it is God's way of saving the human race. ... He is the fulfilment of all that God had planned for the salvation of humanity." (42).

214. "Here is God acting for the salvation of humanity. ... The authorities slew the one who had come to save them,..." (44).

215. That is the tragedy, and that is why the world is as it is. But why does it reject its Saviour?" (45).

216. "So the first reason for the world's rejection of its Saviour is that it does not know its real need." (46).

217. "The world ... is rejecting the one whom God has raised up to be the one and only Saviour." (48).

218. "...who are the leaders in the rejection of the Saviour of the world." (50).

219. "That is how God reconciled humanity to himself." (65).

220. "It is this Saviour and his great salvation that men and women are rejecting." (82).

221. "If you believe this message that you are a vile, damned sinner, that Christ the Son of God has borne your sins and your punishment and has died for you and risen again, if you believe that, then God pronounces you righteous." (89).

222. "Here were men who would sooner die than refrain from preaching the glory of the Son of God as the only Saviour of the world." (123).

223. "Because the sins of the human race were upon him." (129).

224. "This Jesus, whom the Jews had rejected and slain upon a tree, is God's Prince, the Prince of the universe, the Saviour of the world." (135).

225. "God is saving the world and he is doing it through his only begotten Son." (137).

226. "We see God laying on him the iniquity of us all and punishing him that we might be forgiven." (160).

227. "The gospel, therefore, is also a command. It is just as much a command from God as the Ten Commandments. Does that come to you as a surprise? It should not. God commands men to go out and preach it and he commands men and women to believe it. So believe the gospel. I say again – it is his commandment." (171).

228. "...God commands us to believe the gospel." (173).

229. "God is holding this gospel before you, and he commands you to believe." (177).

230. "What was happening there was that God was laying upon him the iniquity of us all." (208).

231. "The gospel ... calls for our obedience to God who sent his only Son to be our Saviour." (208).

232. "The 'Name' that God has set before humanity..." (215).

233. "God appointed his Son as a Saviour. That is why he ever came into the world." (218).

234. "The Son of God becomes Son of man, the Redeemer of the world." (252).

235. "There is no second chance. You decide is this life what your eternal existence is going to be." (258).

236. "Be careful! Honest men, good men, have sometimes tended to add to it – that is the besetting sins of theologians. We press forward our

logic, not stopping when the Scriptures stop, so that we sometimes add to the Scriptures." (276).

237. "Believe that God so loved you that he sent his only Son into this world for you, to bear your sins,..." (281).

238. "The whole biblical record is the record of God coming to save humanity,..." (287).

239. "'A great company of the priests were obedient to the faith', the operative word is 'obedient.'" (313).

240. "You start with the mind, and the mind influences the heart and the heart moves the will. ... It involves the whole person. The mind is engaged, the heart is engaged, and the will is engaged." (316).

241. "God has so loved us that he sent his only Son into this world and laid on him the iniquity of us all. ... You are to believe that when you cry out to the Lord for mercy and compassion, he will say, 'I have given it to you. I have already done it. I have laid your sins on him.' He has taken your punishment. You are free. You are pardoned. I put upon you the righteousness of my only begotten Son." (323).

242. "As we have seen, the mind, the heart, and the will are all involved." (324).

243. "God's Son died to redeem us, to redeem the world and the universe." (340).

AUTHENTIC CHRISTIANITY, Vol. 3, 2004 WCL, 1966/7.

244. "This is the most wonderful and the most amazing good news that has ever come to the human race." (3).

245. "Then ... they completely failed to see the glory of the Lord Jesus Christ; to see the meaning of his message; to see the truth concerning

him; and to se that he was the Son of God and the Saviour of the world." (12).

246. "We are all sinners and he died for our sins." (36).

247. "God has appeared, he has come down and knocked on our door, the door of the world, the door of humanity. God is paying a visit, he has visited and redeemed his people." (50).

248. "Even as things are in the world today, if you, you as an individual, believe this message, and believe that God so loved you that he sent his only begotten Son to bear the punishment of your sins and to die on the cross for you, and rise again to justify you, then you will be forgiven and you will be given new life and you will become a new person..." (51/2).

249. "...that same God of glory not only visited man and appeared to him, he also told him what he was going to do about him and about the world, and about the whole need of the human race and of the universe." (61).

250. "He must send his only Son into the world because this is the only way whereby the world can be saved." (69).

251. "He laid your sins upon him." (84).

252. "Now we have been considering this call that comes to all of us. It is a universal call, by which I mean that it is a call to everybody who has ever heard the Gospel. The gospel invitation is given to all who are ready to listen. But it is very clear, is it not, that all do not respond to it, all do not accept it or believe it, all are not saved, all are not Christians." (101).

253. "There is only one way to become a Christian, and that is to see your utter hopelessness and helplessness, and to trust yourself, just as you are, to Jesus of Nazareth, the Son of God, who died on the cross to bear the punishment of your sins." (115).

254. "This is what is offered to the world by this Christian message: to be for ever 'safe,' for ever 'blest' – taken out of our misery and wretchedness and given a life that is worthy of the name." (130).

255. "We claim that he is the Saviour of the world, and that he came into the world to save it,..." (133).

256. "It is a wonderful picture - ... and this is the message of Christmas. 'God so loved the world' – the world that has rebelled against him and rejected him and spat upon his laws, and turned his paradise into chaos – 'God so loved the world, that he gave his only begotten Son, that whosoever believeth in him' – however vile a rebel, however foul the heart, whatever may have been done – 'whosoever believeth in him should not perish, but have everlasting life' (*John* 3:16). '... when we were enemies, we were reconciled to God by the death of his Son (*Rom.* 5:10)." (141).

257. "...if you but acknowledge your blindness and the blackness of your evil heart and your sin and your hopelessness, and cast yourself upon God's mercy, he will receive you and tell you that he has 'loved you with an everlasting love.'" (141, 142).

258. "Why did the Father avert his face? It was because our Lord was bearing your sins and mine. God was punishing them in him." (156).

259. "The first great principle is that the Lord Jesus Christ has been appointed by God and empowered by him to be the Governor and the Saviour of the universe." (159).

260. "The world is the Son's, so he is now made responsible for its salvation. ...before time, a great Council was held between the Father and the Son and the Holy Spirit about this question of the world and its salvation." (161).

261. "And it is an essential part of the message of salvation in Christ to say that all the world has derived benefit from his coming." (168).

262. "When and how do we receive this great salvation that has been provided for us by the Son of God?" (169).

263. "He works in a way that ridicules the world. Son of God, Saviour of the world – helpless babe in a manger." (185).

264. "God's great plan and purpose of redemption for the human race." (196).

265. "The most important thing that has ever happened is the redemption that God has made possible for us." (199).

266. "...the Sanhedrin ... charged Stephen with blasphemy because he was preaching Jesus of Nazareth as the Son of God and the Saviour of the world." (205).

267. "The only hope for an individual and for the world is the intervention of God – God's salvation!" (218).

268. "God, by sending his own Son to the cross on Calvary, and laying your sins upon him and punishing you in him and raising him again from the dead by his almighty power, has opened for you and for me a way of salvation." (220).

269. "Stephen said, in effect, 'I am on trial because I am preaching this Jesus. I say he is the Son of God and the Saviour of the world and you are ready to put me to death because I am saying this." (259).

270. "...to give you what God has promised you as a member of the human race." (267).

271. "The call of God comes to everyone of us in some way or another. The call to follow Christ is universal." (276).

272. "...and especially of the crowning action of the world in rejecting and crucifying God's own offered Saviour and Redeemer." (288).

273. "But then here is the terrible thing – all this made the children of Israel blind to the identity of their Saviour." (297).

274. "Those who are not Christians hate above everything else the doctrine of rebirth through faith in Christ who died for them. ...The very Son of God came into this world ... in order to save it." (310).

275. "If you do not see that Jesus Christ is the Son of God, that he died, gave his life for your salvation, if you do not see that that alone saves, without any addition, you are guilty of the same thing – 'thou art the man!' May God have mercy upon all who have not submitted to our Lord as their only-sufficient Saviour and Redeemer.'" (313).

AUTHENTIC CHRISTIANITY, Vol. 5, (2006). WCL, 1967.

276. "In doing that, he is above all teaching them of God's great purpose of salvation, of God's ways with respect to the human race." (3).

277. "But – and this is what I want to leave with you – this is not only the only hope, this is a hope *for all, for anybody.*" (17).

278. "It offers us a new start, a new beginning; it offers us a new power, which is 'the power of God [himself] unto salvation' (*Rom.* 1:16). It offers us power to live the rest of our lives in this world, and at the end it promises us a like conquest over death, a glorious resurrection, and an eternity in the presence of God." (30).

279. "He will tell you that he has loved you with an everlasting love, that he so loved you that he sent his only begotten Son into the world to die for you, that you should not perish but have everlasting life." (35).

280. "..the world is still rejecting the Saviour of the world." (36).

281. "Its [the world's] failure to understand its need and its problems accounts for its unawareness of what God in his infinite grace has done about us and about our salvation." (39).

282. "First of all, God has not forgotten or abandoned this world. ...My message is that God himself announces that he has not abandoned the world." (40).

283. "It is because the great God who made this world ... is still concerned about it, and has pledged himself to redeem the whole cosmos. ...But God has a purpose and a plan for the redemption and salvation of the universe; that is the message of the Bible.'" (41).

284. "It [the Gospel] is our only hope. God has promised this redemption in spite of us, in spite of the worst that is true of the worst person in this congregation." (43).

285. "This is but a picture of what God has done for you and for me in the person of his only begotten Son. ... This is God's way of salvation. He sent his Son into this world to bear your sins in his own body on the tree.'" (49).

286. "God had sent him to provide deliverance, salvation, redemption for all who believe in him." (50).

287. "...you believe the message that he has sent his Son into the world and to the death of the cross in order that you might be forgiven and reconciled to him." (51).

288. "In the same way, though the world has rejected the Son of God, he is still the Saviour of the world." (56).

289. "My friend, your eternal destiny depends on your reaction to this Word." (97).

290. "'God so loved the world' – this world that has been exposed under his law, he loved that – 'that he gave his only begotten Son, that whosoever believeth in him should not perish, but have everlasting life' (*John* 3:16). ... Believe this Word that tells you that when his Son died on the cross, God laid your sins upon him and punished him there, and is offering you free pardon." (115).

291. "He is the Lord of the universe, God the Father gave it as a gift to his Son. That is why he is interested in it. And that is why he came into it to save it." (145).

292. "The world is his inheritance, and he came into it to save it, to punish all his enemies,..." (146).

293. "...he has a plan for the salvation of humanity,..." (149).

294. "He sent his only Son into the world, and has put my sins on him, and has punished him for me, and offers me free pardon and forgiveness – that is the message." (161).

295. "Stephen ... is preaching that Jesus of Nazareth is the Son of God and the Saviour of the world." (163).

296. "What is it [the death and resurrection of Christ] all about? Why did he do this? And the astounding answer is that he did it for us, he did it for you, he did it for me." (178).

297. "He calls himself 'the Son of man'! The Man! The Saviour of the world!" (188).

298. "... the only way even he could save anybody was by giving his life a ransom for us, by dying for us, to 'bare our sins in his own body on the tree' (1 *Pet.* 2:24)." (189, 190).

299. "... believe that this Person is the Son of God and that he has borne your punishment and died for your sins, then your sins from this moment are completely pardoned and forgiven, and God looks at you as if you had never sinned at all. That is called 'justification by faith'. He offers you that. This blessed Person offers you free pardon, full pardon, complete pardon of all your sins." (190, 191).

300. "He has come to give us a new birth, to make a new birth possible." (191).

301. "God, at the cost of the death of his own Son, has made it possible for you and for me to be forgiven, ..." (226).

302. "I have already punished them in the Person of my only begotten, dearly beloved Son." (229).

303. "Oh, the blessings that God has promised to the human race!" (235).

304. "...God, in his great kindness – it is what we call 'common grace' – puts limits and restraints upon sin." (236, 237).

305. "God is trying to awaken the human race. ... But 'God so loved the world' that he is engaged in opening its eyes to the inferno that it is creating." (241).

306. "Because the Son has made himself responsible for sinners and for the sin of humanity." (243).

307. "Believe the Word of God concerning Jesus Christ, the Saviour of the world." (244).

308. "They cannot see that God was only using their history as a temporary plan, a method and expedient, to produce a great blessing for the whole world." (284).

309. "What does this mean? Well, Stephen sees a human form, the representative of humanity." (294).

310. "Have you seen him as the Lamb of God, taking away your sins?" (298).

AUTHENTIC CHRISTIANITY, Vol. 6. 2006. WCL, 1967/8.

311. "He came for the whole world of men and women; he is the Saviour of the world." (9).

312. "He said: I have come to help you. I have come to redeem you. I have come to tell you about God. I have come to put you into relationship with God." (13).

313. "...has so loved us that he has not only taken his place by our side, but has assumed human nature because we are human." (38).

314. "[The gospel] is a message that tells you about something that God has done for you and about you and that can put you right to all eternity." (47).

315. "The only hope for you individually, the only hope for the cosmos, lies in the Son of God, the Saviour of the world." (86).

316. "'Listen,' said Philip, 'I am talking about the Son of God, "Who loved me and gave himself for me"' (*Gal.* 2:20). And he has done that for you" ... The Son of God, Jesus of Nazareth, came into the world in order to die for you, in order that your sins might be remitted. He has borne your punishment, he has taken your guilt upon him and received the punishment it deserves. He died for you, in your stead, in your place." (103).

317. "...he has so loved you that he sent his only Son into this world for you. He sent him to the cross to bear your sins, to receive your punishment. He so loved you that he has done that for you! Can he withhold any lesser thing? Of course not. He is pledged to you, he set his heart upon you, he loves you 'with an everlasting love,' and nothing can happen to you apart from God." (122).

318. "Having brought us to realise that we have souls and that we are guilty before God, and that we are lost, the Spirit reveals to us the truth about the Lord Jesus Christ as the Son of God, as one who has taken our sins upon himself and has borne our punishment so that in him we can be forgiven." (135).

319. "Why does he do that? There is only one answer: he has come into the world to save the world." (150).

320. "...God had laid on his own Son the iniquity of us all, that he had smitten him and stricken him, and that it is because of that that we are pardoned and forgiven and saved and reconciled to God." (155).

321. "Our eternal destiny is determined in this world and in this life, and it is all dependent upon our relationship to this person [the Lord Jesus Christ] ... Even to a man like Simon the sorcerer the apostles still say: pray to God. Repent. Cast yourself upon his mercy. It is not too late." (164).

322. "If the Bible is right in saying that nothing less than the coming of the Son of God into the world can save humanity, then the problem of human sin must be profound." (169).

323. "Very well; look to this Christ. Here is the message for you: he died for you. He has borne your punishment. He has taken your guilt upon himself. ...It is the message that God so loved the world that he has given his only begotten Son, that whosoever – whatever he has been, whatever he has done – believes in him should not perish but have everlasting life." (182).

324. "Here he is, the Deliverer, the Saviour of the world." (186).

325. "And even when he set out on his public ministry, when he took up the task of being the Saviour of the world, he did it in a way that the world regards as being almost ridiculous." (187).

326. "Thank God for a gospel that holds out a hope for any of us, for all of us, and an equal hope for all of us. ... Because the gospel is altogether of God, there is hope for all. ...it is to believe that Jesus of Nazareth is the Son of God, that he came to die for your sins, to reconcile you to God, and to give you new life and an everlasting hope of glory." (199).

327. "It is a gospel for 'whosoever believeth':..." (200).

328. "My only hope at this moment is that God, the everlasting and eternal God, has not turned his back on this world of ours, but that, on the contrary, he is very concerned about it, and has a plan for its redemption, for its deliverance, for its restoration to the condition in which he originally made it. ...God's plan for this world is a redemptive plan." (210).

329. "...God's concern for each of us individually." (213).

330. "He was saying: 'O my Father, if it be possible that I can save the human race in any other way but this, oh, let me do it, show it to me." (283).

331. "If you will recognize it, and believe that God has so loved you that he has given his only begotten Son to that death for you, has punished him for you, you will immediately receive remission of sins. Your sins will be forgiven, God will blot them out as a thick cloud, ... Just say, ... He is the Lamb of God. He died for me:..." (285).

332. "It was this awful problem of sin, it was this awful problem of the human race that he had come to deal with." (297).

333. "He was tasting death for every man (*Heb.* 2:9). He was dealing with this problem of man in sin ... all human sin was on him. His Father had 'laid it all' on him." (298).

334. "But why did the Son of God suffer like this? It was because this was the only way whereby you can be forgiven. ...He suffered all this so that you might not suffer, that you might be reconciled to God. ...The Son of God so loves you that he did that for you. ... your whole eternal future depends upon your understanding and knowledge od this message that the Son of God has loved you, and given himself for you." (299).

335. "God would never have allowed it if the salvation of humanity could have been procured or effected in any other way." (301).

336. "Son of God, Saviour of the world." (311).

PROVE ALL THINGS (1985). Sermons, WCL.

337. "...this is the business of the church, to tell the world as it is that of this great and glorious salvation which is in Christ Jesus. He is the only hope of the world. ... The church is to preach Christ, and him crucified, as the only hope, the only Saviour of the world; ..." (16).

338. "...what happened on the day of Pentecost ... is the indication of the universality of the Gospel." (147).

LEEDS SERMON (1973).

339. "The church must stop apologising, stop accommodating, stop taking bits out of the Bible. We must face the world and proclaim Jesus of Nazareth, Son of God and Saviour of mankind." *Tuesday, 20th February, 1973, Oxford Place Methodist Chapel, Leeds, at which I was present.*

BORN OF GOD, WCL, 1962.

340. "...to realize the truth concerning our Lord and what he has made possible for us by his work on our behalf." (34).

341. "This is the nation through which God is going to redeem the world, and out of which, eventually, his Son will be born as Saviour of the world." (59).

342. "The greatest trouble with all of us, indeed, with the whole world, is our failure to realize what God has done for us in and through his dear Son, our Lord and Saviour Jesus Christ." (75).

343. "...here is the Lamb of God who really does take away the sin of the world." (158).

344. "Or, as John puts it here in his Prologue, '[He] was the true Light, which lighteth every man that cometh into the world.'" (161).

345. "The essence of Christianity is that God has not abandoned this world in spite of what is true of it. ... God has not abandoned the world. ... God's concern about the world... God has a plan and a purpose for the world." (193).

346. "...he might address the whole world ... God is concerned about the world... we see yet more clearly God's great concern for this world. ... And this, I say again, indicates one big thing - God's concern for, and interest in, this world." (194).

347. "...indicative of his concern about the world. ...This is all because it does not know that God is concerned about it [the world]." (195).

348. "It was God who 'laid on him the iniquity of us all' (*Isa.* 53:6). ... It was God who was 'in Christ, reconciling the world unto himself, not imputing their trespasses unto them' (2 *Cor.* 5:19). My friend, it was God who did all these things - for you!" (199).

349. "...we are told of John standing and saying, 'Behold the Lamb of God, which taketh away the sin of the world' (*John* 1:29)." (212).

350. "Now that is personal. Paul does not say, 'I subscribe to the doctrine of the atonement: I believe that Christ died for the sins of the world' - that is not what he says. That is not enough. It is right, we must believe that." (387).

GENERAL INDEX

A

All men xiii, xv, 5, 33, 44, 166, 263, 276, 277, 281, 287
Amyraldian vii, xiv, 5, 8, 9, 34, 128, 146, 151, 167, 241, 247
Amyraldianism xiii, 12, 34, 128, 146, 147, 175, 199, 246
Amyraut, M vii, xiii, 12, 15, 18, 19, 29, 30, 32, 33, 34, 129, 146, 165
Arminian 50, 170
Arminianism 16, 31, 51, 55, 73, 147, 217
Arminius, J 15, 16, 30, 120
Armstrong, B. G 31, 33, 34
Assurance 5, 12, 177, 211
Atonement 3, 4, 5, 8, 9, 11, 12, 17, 18, 21, 23, 55, 56
Atonement, centrality of 81
Atonement, design of 56, 100, 135, 145, 152, 156, 171, 214, 220, 222
Atonement, extent of 7, 15, 56
Atonement, limited 113, 114, 115, 127, 128, 135, 137, 142, 143, 145, 155, 156, 159, 167, 168, 173, 175, 176, 179, 184, 186, 193, 196, 216, 217, 242, 247
Atonement, universal 17, 51, 77, 100, 137, 155, 156, 157, 159, 168, 169, 171, 174, 192, 198, 205, 214, 218, 237, 238, 247
Atonement, value of 7
Authentic Calvinism xiii, 146, 147, 148, 149, 151, 175, 246

Authentic Calvinist 46, 129, 146, 148, 241, 244
Authentic Christianity 42, 129
Authority 40, 84, 107, 109, 110

B

Banner of Truth Trust xii
Bare sufficiency 135, 136
Bare universalism 175
Barnes, A 192
Barren orthodoxy 80
Baxter, R 8, 69, 120, 137, 146, 151, 165, 166, 182, 201, 203, 205, 213, 216, 222, 225, 230, 231, 241, 245
Belgic Confession 16
Bellamy, J 246
Beza, T xiii, 12, 15, 19, 29, 30, 120, 128, 138, 241
Biblical Gospel 18
Biblical religion 3
Biblical text xii, 33
Blanchard, J 22
Bloesch, D. G 241
Blood of Christ 80, 81, 95, 245, 281
Body of Christ 85, 86
Brown, D 203, 227, 253
Bunyan, J 169, 171

C

Calamy, E 246
Calvary 28, 265, 276, 279, 294
Calvinism 120, 129, 146

Calvinistic xii, xiii, 8, 9, 59, 225
Calvinistic doctrine 59
Calvinistic Methodist Connexion 39
Calvinistic Theology 3
Calvin, J vii, xii, xiii, 3, 8, 11, 15, 18, 19, 24, 26, 28, 29, 30, 32, 33, 34, 74, 82, 91, 97, 102, 105, 109, 113, 115, 116, 119, 128, 137, 138, 146, 151, 165, 177, 189, 194, 197, 198, 203, 206, 210, 220, 222, 225, 228, 230, 231, 233, 238, 241, 245, 247
Calvins theology 15
Cameron 33, 262
Cameron, J 33
Campbell, I. D 247
Canons of Dordt 17, 33, 151, 157
Carroll, L 156
Catherwood, C 8
Chalmers, T 131, 138, 246
Christian faith 8, 286
Christian Gospel 3, 64
Christian preaching 26
Christian Theology 11
Christology 21, 23
Church xii, xiii, 3, 11, 12, 267, 272, 274, 275, 283
Church member 38
Clifford, A. C xiv, 29, 30, 34, 97, 141, 167, 186, 195, 217, 241
Commercial theory 167, 184
Confessional correctness 28, 101, 130
Confessionalism 13, 49, 80, 219, 230, 236, 237, 242, 245
Confessional standards 220, 243
Confessions 49, 82, 157, 246
Conservative evangelical 4
Conservative evangelicalism 59
Conversion 39, 54, 86, 100, 117, 138, 139, 206, 222
Conversions 39, 100
Covenant theology xiv

D

Dabney, R. L 8, 191, 220

Daillé, J 146, 246
Dale, R. W 45, 71, 73, 89, 91, 123
Davenant, J 8, 120, 136, 137, 195, 214, 216, 220, 225, 230, 246
Dawkins, R 22, 23
Death of Christ 25, 83, 92, 203, 238, 278
Decrees 32, 116
Denney, J 55, 59, 71, 91
Denominations 43, 64, 149
Denominations, compromised 43
Design 3, 5
Developed Calvinism 15
Divine holiness 83
Divine love 75, 86
Divine sovereignty 4, 51
Divine will 29, 94, 116, 220
Divine wrath 51, 75
Doctrinal controversy 102
Doctrine 3, 8, 11, 24, 25, 27, 32, 196, 295
Doddridge, P 246
Dogma-driven 147, 184
Double payment 166, 168
Douty, N 135, 138, 196, 205, 206
Dualism 106, 139, 140, 142, 209
Dualistic 29

E

Eaton, M. A 8, 9, 216
Ecumenical 42
Ecumenical council 16
Edwards, J 8, 246
Eisegesis 25, 206, 245
Elect 4, 5, 17, 25, 44, 138, 144, 206
Election xiv, 4, 26, 29, 30, 32, 46, 99, 100, 116, 211
Elect unbelievers 159
Elias, J 98
Error 212
Evangelical 4, 8, 11
Evangelism xiv, 19, 40, 49, 95, 99, 100, 119, 148, 149, 222, 224
Evangelist 4, 12, 28, 64, 113, 148
Evangelistic xii, 4, 12, 27, 122

Evangelistic ministry 12, 39
Evangelistic preaching 12, 71, 87, 105, 111, 215, 222
Evangelistic sermons xiii, 77, 225
Evangelistic theology 138
Exclusivity 183
Exegesis xii, xiii, 25, 30, 33, 120, 155, 165, 191, 196, 199, 206, 212, 215, 216, 220, 242, 243
Expiate 17
Expository preaching xi, 41, 62, 116
Extreme Calvinism 49

F

Fairbairn, A. M 48, 49
Faith xiii, 3, 4, 30, 33, 87, 291, 295
Fall 159
Final judgement 81
Five Points of Calvinism 16
Forensic theory 167, 168, 184
Forgiven 266, 268, 271, 279, 283, 288, 290, 292, 296, 297, 298, 299, 300, 301
Forgiveness 22, 51, 64, 73, 75, 76, 81, 85, 96, 141, 177, 213, 264, 266, 267, 270, 280, 297
Forsyth, P. T 53, 71, 79, 89, 218
Free offer 267
Freudians 160

G

Gammie, A 256
Gill, J 190, 206
Glorification 81
Gods judgement 84
Gods love xiv, 39, 40, 55, 83, 93, 95, 130, 146, 148, 175, 181, 183, 205, 208, 213, 214, 217, 218, 219, 221, 228, 231, 269
Gods secrets 109, 110
Gospel xv, 3, 4, 5, 11, 12, 18, 24, 26, 28, 29, 266, 274, 282, 287, 290, 292, 296
Gospel-centred 105

Gospel, everlasting 101
Gospel-focused 105
Gospel offer 137

H

Hall, J 222
Heidelberg Catechism 16
Hell 47, 70, 101, 150, 166, 267, 271
Helm, P 157, 256
Hendriksen, W 197, 198, 211, 219, 223, 229, 230
Henry, M 120, 191, 194, 203, 216, 231, 238, 246
Hidden will 32, 106
High Calvinism 23, 147, 224
High Calvinists 22, 32, 118, 119, 130, 173, 176, 178
High orthodox 9, 11, 15, 17, 19, 24, 33, 99, 155, 211
Hodge, A. A 21
Holy grace 80, 84
Holy judgement 80
Holy Spirit xiii, 21, 38, 41, 62, 88, 121, 150, 151, 155, 167, 282, 287, 293
Hopelessness 271, 292, 293
Huguenot University 18
Humanist 31
Humanity 5, 32, 145, 264, 270, 287, 288, 289, 290, 291, 292, 298, 300
Human race 5, 17, 25, 64, 263, 275, 279, 280, 285, 288, 289, 291, 292, 294, 295, 298, 301
Human reason 51, 73, 107
Human redemption 75
Human responsibility 27, 89
Hutton, J. A 38
Hyper-Calvinism 120, 149, 151
Hyper-Calvinist 70
Hyper-Calvinists 232
Hypothetical universal 170
Hypothetical universalism 12, 18, 32, 33, 152, 175

I

Immoral 284
Inconsistency 111
Iniquity 28, 271, 277, 284, 285, 286, 290, 291, 300, 303
Institutional maintenance 161
Interpretation 25, 87, 111, 119, 138, 177, 191, 192, 196, 197, 285

J

Jesus Christ 12, 22, 24, 27, 38, 228, 264, 266, 267, 269, 272, 273, 275, 279, 282, 283, 285, 286, 288, 291, 293, 295, 298, 299, 300
Jesus of Nazareth 23, 272, 273, 274, 283, 286, 292, 294, 297, 299, 300
Jones, J 71, 97, 246
Justification 70, 81, 121, 176
Justification by faith 70, 297

K

Kendall, R. T 34, 113, 114, 176
Kingdom of God 75, 110, 223
Kistemaker, S. J 231, 237
Κοσμος 204

L

Ladd, G. E 204, 205
Lamb of God 24, 92, 111, 150, 194, 201, 202, 203, 204, 205, 209, 248, 276, 279, 283, 284, 285, 298, 301, 302, 303
Latimer, H 27
Liberal theologians 23
Limited Atonement 4, 15, 24, 114, 166
Lostness 28, 84, 101, 159, 202
Love of God 129, 269, 280, 281, 285

M

MacArthur, J 183
Machen, J. G 23, 206, 258
Macleod, D 8, 145
Magisterium 26

Mankind xii, xiv, 4, 25, 50, 51, 269, 270, 274, 276, 280
Mans inability 100
McCheyne, R. M 8, 43, 246
McGrath, A 21, 237
Melancthon, P 214
Methodology 11, 48
Milne, B 211, 218, 223
Ministry xi, xii, xiii, xv, 4, 18, 24, 28, 264, 300
Moral ability 83
Morgan, G. C 40
Morris, L. L 63, 207, 208, 213, 228, 230
Mortification 81
Motyer, J. A 193
Muller, R 34
Murray, I. H 8, 70, 71, 173, 181, 184, 224, 247
Murray, I. M 69
Murray, J 17, 155, 170, 205
Murray, J. J 173, 181, 184, 186, 247

N

Natural ability 32, 83
New Testament 5, 23, 256, 274, 282, 287
Non-elect 116, 224

O

Once for all 56, 265
Original sin 32
Orthodox vii, xiv
Owenite vii, xiii, 8, 9, 23, 129, 143, 146, 241
Owenite Soteriology 5
Owen, J vii, xii, xiv, 12, 15, 19, 25, 29, 34, 69, 114, 128, 136, 138, 206, 225, 229, 230, 241

P

Particular Atonement 17
Particularism 12, 143, 171, 181
Particularity 141, 183
Particular redemption 9

Particular redemptionists 136
Paul 265, 275, 284, 285, 287
Person of Christ 21
Philip, J 299
Philosophical formulations 80
Philosophy 11, 45, 60, 106, 107, 108, 110, 116, 177, 245, 246
Pink, A. W 142, 143, 206
Preach 24, 65, 290
Preachable theology 62
Preaching ministry 63
Predestination xiv, 4, 26, 32, 106, 116, 121, 169, 186, 211, 214, 220
Presbyterian xii, 38, 57, 64, 145, 148
Presbyterian Church in Wales 41, 57
Profession of faith 38
Professors of religion 85
Propitiation 73, 75, 80, 86, 93, 94, 95, 96, 138, 139, 149, 155, 205, 235, 236, 238, 265, 278, 282
Protestantism 11
Protestant liberalism 53
Protestant magisterium 156
Protestant Reformation vii
Published sermons 18, 44
Puritans 42
Puritan theology 50

R

Rationalism 120, 122, 125
Reconciled the world 88
Reconciliation 5, 51, 55, 63, 64, 65, 73, 81, 83, 87, 88, 89, 92, 94, 214, 235, 245, 286
Reconciling judgement 84
Reconciling the world 92, 277
Redeemer 94, 193, 213, 267, 282, 290, 294, 295
Redeemer for all mankind 229
Redeemer for mankind 233
Redeemer of the World 12, 29, 85, 128, 216
Redeeming grace 85, 167
Redeeming love 51, 74, 204

Redemption 75, 81, 83, 86, 141, 152, 170, 177, 192, 210, 231, 294, 296, 301
Redemption, universal 208
Reductionism 23
Reductionist 23
Reformed 3, 4, 8, 11, 12, 16, 23, 26, 34, 151
Reformed faith 16
Reformed orthodoxy 4
Reformed preachers 115, 116, 130, 147, 149, 153, 225, 242, 245
Reformed preaching xiv
Reformed scholasticism 122
Reformed scholastics 124
Reformed theologians 18, 44
Reformed theology 34, 147
Remonstrants 15, 16
Repentance 48, 56, 83, 84, 85, 87, 96, 116, 121, 131, 170, 206
Revealed will 32, 77, 106, 110, 116, 119, 139, 140, 151, 245
Robertson, A. T 204, 217
Roman Catholicism 125, 156, 243
Roman Church 22
Rule of faith xii, 220
R. W. Dale 45, 46
Ryle, J. C 8, 201, 209, 210, 212, 220, 225, 229, 230, 246

S

Sacrificial death 4, 75
Salvation xiii, xiv, 3, 4, 5, 21, 25, 26, 28, 29, 30, 99, 150, 264, 266, 267, 268, 271, 272, 273, 274, 278, 279, 282, 284, 285, 287, 288, 289, 293, 294, 295, 296
Salvation of humanity 297
Sanctification 81
Sandfields 263, 273
Satanic 24
Saumur 32, 34
Saumur Academy 18, 31, 32
Saviour xiii, xv, 4, 5, 12, 21, 32, 33, 38, 263, 267, 269, 272, 273, 279,

282, 283, 286, 289, 290, 294, 295, 297
Saviour of mankind 214, 229, 279, 302
Saviour of the universe 293
Saviour of the World 7, 22, 24, 27, 29, 32, 39, 76, 116, 119, 128, 130, 203, 205, 208, 223, 227, 228, 229, 230, 242, 248, 264, 269, 272, 273, 274, 276, 282, 283, 284, 286, 289, 292, 293, 294, 295, 296, 297, 298, 299, 300, 302
Schaeffer, F 28
Scholarship xiv, 42, 107, 242
Scholastic Calvinists 123, 131
Scholasticism xiv, 50, 107, 114, 123, 125, 245, 246
Scholastic philosophy 12
Scholastic theology 125
Scriptural data 18, 29, 178
Scripture alone 26
Semi-Pelagian 170
Seriousness of sin 51, 73
Sermons xii, xiii, 4, 12, 24, 27, 28, 38, 247
Sin-bearing death 76
Sin-bearing love 65, 213
Sin-expiating love 95
Sin of the World 24, 76, 92, 93, 94, 111, 128, 138, 150, 169, 178, 189, 190, 194, 201, 203, 205, 207, 209, 210, 211, 276, 286, 303
Sins of the world 87
Sola Scriptura 221
Soteriological xiii, 12, 18, 24, 26, 34
Soteriology xiii, xiv, 4, 8, 9, 11, 18, 23, 24, 33
Sovereignty of God 50, 116, 117, 142, 225
Speculation 212
Spiritual deadness 101, 117, 243
Spurgeon, C. H 61
Stott, J. R. W 43, 63, 236
Sub-orthodoxy 120
Sufficiency 18, 32, 135
Sufficient 5, 12, 17, 273, 278, 295

Supreme authority 26, 155
Supreme standard xii
Synod of Dordt 16, 221

T

Tension 9
The Cross 8, 24, 27, 33, 275, 278, 279
The Doctor vii, xiii, 4, 8
Theological liberalism 41, 61, 63, 83
Theology xii, 4, 9, 11, 12, 33
The Three Forms of Unity 246
Thomas, O 71, 246
Trinity 150
Trueman, C. R 34
Truth 16, 17, 24, 280, 281, 291, 299
Turretin, F 15, 19, 34

U

Ultra-orthodoxy 120, 211
Ultra-reformed 138
Unbelievers 177
Universal 8, 33, 129, 143, 215, 270, 292, 294
Universal Atonement 17, 29, 32, 44, 166, 175, 203
Universalism 141, 185
Universalistic texts 17, 111, 152, 179
Universality 32, 33
Universal language xii, xiii, 17, 156, 190, 192, 233
Universal offer 32
Universal redemption 9
Universal salvation 175, 176, 177, 202, 209, 218, 235

V

Van Stam, F. P 34

W

Warfield, B. B 69, 208
Wastage 209
Welsh Calvinistic Methodist Fathers 43, 69, 71, 120

Welsh Calvinistic Methodists 96
Wenkel, D 170, 171
Wesleyan 246
Wesley, J 69, 95, 117, 192, 194, 206, 216, 225, 230
Westminster Chapel 24
Westminster Confession 260
Westminster Confession of Faith xii, 146
Whitefield, G 64, 69, 70
Whoever 121
Whole world 3, 17, 263, 265, 270, 272, 275, 276, 278, 280, 282, 283, 298
Whosoever 28, 87, 202, 216, 219, 221, 223, 224, 264, 272, 277, 278, 281, 285, 287, 288, 293, 296, 300

Wiersbe, W. W 46, 49
Work of Christ 21
World xii, xiii, 3, 5, 22, 23, 25, 28, 143, 263, 264, 265, 268, 269, 271, 272, 274, 275, 276, 277, 278, 279, 280, 281, 282, 283, 284, 285, 286, 287, 288, 289, 290, 291, 292, 293, 294, 295, 296, 297, 298, 299, 300, 301
Wrath of God 165, 169, 195, 228, 280

Z

Zodhiates, S 197, 204